Spend Shift

How the Post-Crisis
Values Revolution Is Changing the
Way We Buy, Sell, and Live

John Gerzema
Michael D'Antonio

Foreword by Philip Kotler

JOSSEY-BASS
A Wiley Imprint
www.josseybass.com

Published by Jossey-Bass
A Wiley Imprint
989 Market Street, San Francisco, CA 94103–1741—www.josseybass.com

Readers should be aware that Internet Web sites offered as citations and/or sources for further information may have changed or disappeared between the time this was written and when it is read.

Jossey-Bass books and products are available through most bookstores. To contact Jossey-Bass directly call our Customer Care Department within the U.S. at 800–956–7739, outside the U.S. at 317–572–3986, or fax 317–572–4002.

Jossey-Bass also publishes its books in a variety of electronic formats. Some content that appears in print may not be available in electronic books.

Library of Congress Cataloging-in-Publication Data
Gerzema, John, 1961–
     Spend shift : how the post-crisis values revolution is changing the way we buy, sell, and live / John Gerzema, Michael D'Antonio.—1st ed.
          p. cm.
     Includes bibliographical references and index.
     ISBN 978-0-470-87443-1 (hardback)
     1. Consumption (Economics)—Social aspects—United States.   2. Consumers—United States—Psychology.   3. Cost and standard of living—United States.
     4. Recessions—Social aspects—United States.   5. United States—Economic conditions—2009–   I. D'Antonio, Michael.   II. Title.
     HC110.C6G475 2010
     306.30973—dc22
                              2010026648

Printed in the United States of America
FIRST EDITION
HB Printing   10   9   8   7   6   5   4   3   2

Contents

Foreword

In my book *Chaotics*, I explain a new world where businesses must adapt to a new Economic Age. We have entered an era when increased turbulence is a fact of business life. Today's managers must operate within an environment of endless volatility. The new reality is a world of continuous and at times crushing change.

The lessons for marketers are sobering. Brand equity changes in compressed periods of time. Competitive disruption happens without warning. And consumers are increasingly powerful and unpredictable. For those prone to celebrating a leadership position or a competitive market advantage, commoditization lies just around the hairpin corner.

In a post-crisis world, with the specter of a jobless recovery and more limited purchasing power, consumers themselves have experienced chaotics. Yet there is new, hopeful data to suggest that people are redefining their lives and reviving core values, things like hard work, thrift, fairness, and honesty. They are separating want from need and discriminating more carefully both in product and brand choice. Consumers are buying into brands with meaning—brands with integrity, social responsibility, and sustainability at their core.

This values-led consumerism is not a small, isolated target market. Over half the U.S. population is now embracing these values shifts. They are seeking *better* instead of *more*, *virtue* instead of *hype*, and *experiences* over *promises*. The post-crisis consumer, already highly marketing-savvy and armed with the leveling powers of social connection and critique, is now an even more potent and unpredictable force in the marketplace. People are looking for value *and* values.

I came upon these ideas when John Gerzema, Guy Kawasaki, and I were speaking at a marketing conference in Las Vegas in the fall of 2009. Over breakfast we talked about the implications for consumer behavior in the economic recovery. John's research, based upon the world's largest database, BrandAsset® Valuator, gave credible evidence that consumers were shifting their values and their spending accordingly, and many prescient businesses had already adjusted to the new consumer mentality.

But Gerzema wasn't predicting a wholesale era of endless frugality and "a consumer in retreat." Rather, his data demonstrated that brands—in a world devoid of trust—were increasingly *more* important. And companies could find new forms of competitive advantage by understanding and sharing in the values that were becoming more important to consumers, such as ethics, community, empathy, and accountability.

The lessons in this book are useful to anyone examining their business strategy after the crisis. They explain the new psyche and values shifts that are influencing the spending habits of the American consumer. Along with his partner, Michael D'Antonio—a Pulitzer Prize–winning writer and reporter—Gerzema details exemplary strategies of multinationals and small businesses alike. He shares the methods of adaptation among large Fortune 500 companies, while exposing us to new start-ups who are capitalizing on the values shifts in this new market landscape.

While the data is extensive and thorough, perhaps even more compelling are the stories the authors have gleaned from their travels across America. Through these accounts Gerzema and D'Antonio help us understand the lasting impact of the crisis on middle-class families, small business owners, entrepreneurs, and CEOs. They also help us understand the strategies people are already using to move forward. As voting patterns define the societal mood, consumption patterns do the same. How we spend our money and our time as well as our energy and efforts reveals how a values shift is, indeed, reshaping capitalism.

Spend Shift offers insights into how our lives are changing after the Great Recession. It explains a new consumer movement that you should understand regardless of whom you define as your target market. And it carries forward my lessons from *Chaotics*, offering managers, marketers, and entrepreneurs insights into how to understand and cater to the consumer of the post-crisis world.

Philip Kotler
S. C. Johnson Distinguished Professor
of International Marketing
Kellogg School of Management
Northwestern University

Introduction

NUMBERS AND
THEIR MEANING:
KANSAS CITY, MISSOURI

The typical evening seminar crowd at the Nelson-Atkins Museum in Kansas City, Missouri, could hardly be described as ragingly radical. The city lies smack in the middle of the conservative heartland and the museum is a traditional limestone landmark that draws heavy support from old-money families. Few institutions would seem more connected to the forces of stability and propriety. Until a few years ago it was still the site of the annual Jewel Ball, where debutantes paraded for high society.

About a month before our appearance, the Atkins had hosted Edgar Bronfman, one of the richest businessmen in the world. A few weeks later would come a former president of the World Bank, James Wolfensohn. Sandwiched between these pillars of the corporate establishment, we worried about how *our* message—that America was undergoing a radical but ultimately positive shift in consumer values—would play in a state where the official motto, "Show me," promises a cold welcome to know-it-all outsiders.

As it turned out, a few factors had prepared the crowd to hear us. First and foremost was the condition of the economy in the summer of 2009. With unemployment racing toward double digits and business activity declining, America was approaching the low point of the worst business crisis since the 1930s. Dubbed the Great Recession, this downturn had shattered public confidence in the usual sources of wisdom, including financiers, economists, and politicians. To be sure, the crisis had made lots of people angry and resentful, but the shared suffering had broken down some of the barriers that can separate us and made many people more eager to hear fresh ideas, especially if they were based on solid information.

The analysis we brought to K.C. was built on the world's largest reservoir of data about consumer attitudes, preferences, and values. Based on seventeen years of quarterly data involving more than 1.2 million people, this wealth of information has been gathered by the international marketing and communications company Young & Rubicam, where it is overseen by John Gerzema. One of the two authors of this book, John manages this ongoing study, which is called BrandAsset® Valuator, as Young & Rubicam's chief insights officer. Young & Rubicam has invested over $130 million in the data, which goes back to 1993. In all he has spent twenty-five years studying and analyzing how people behave in the marketplace. His coauthor, Michael D'Antonio, is a writer with long experience in addressing social and economic trends.

BrandAsset Valuator holds data on more than forty thousand brands in more than fifty countries, and every quarter it is supplemented with new results—on purchasing and social attitudes—from seventeen thousand respondents in America alone. This information helps us understand what people prize in a material sense and how that changes over time. More important, as people reveal their preferences about products and companies, BrandAsset Valuator opens a window on their inner drives, motivations, and values in ways that other models cannot.

BrandAsset Valuator reflects the way people shop in the real world, meaning we can assess a given company or brand against thousands of others in the marketplace on more than eighty metrics, which include everything from awareness and relevance to social reputation, quality of service, or level of trust. We can quantify which brands people think are different, authentic, more innovative, or more responsible. And because BrandAsset Valuator is tied to financial metrics, we can detail correlations to pricing power, consumer loyalty, usage, and preference, and trace the linkage between brand performance, financial earnings, and stock price. The BrandAsset Valuator consumer panel also allows us to peer into their lives to understand everything from their political affiliations to their values, attitudes, and behaviors. Most important, it gives us leading indicators of marketplace change, often far before the complete picture emerges in data such as market share and consumer sales.

The challenge for the folks in Kansas City (or at least the challenge we expected) would be in the interpretation of the numbers. However, we felt the evidence was incontrovertible. The numbers said that the consumerism we have known for nearly thirty years, the main force behind the American economy, is finally died. Say good-bye to all the easy signs of wealth we knew from the recent past—McMansions, SUVs, and recreational shopping. Say hello to a lifestyle more focused on community, connection, quality, and creativity.

In the long run all this change will yield a wonderful renaissance of hope and purpose in our lives as individuals and in the life of our country. But in the short term, the process is going to challenge us all to be brave, resourceful, and energetic. Knowing that no amount of sugarcoating would influence our audience, John decided on a "first the bad news" approach. After being introduced, he walked out onto the stage, waited for the polite applause, and began by saying:

"Thirteen trillion dollars worth of wealth has *evaporated* over the last two years."

It's a shocking number, equal to almost 15 percent of America's net worth, and roughly the same as an entire year's gross domestic product.[1] For individuals, the losses associated with the Great Recession, which started at the close of 2007, had been much less abstract. Millions of people were laid off from their jobs, saw their investment and retirement funds disappear, and lost nearly a third of the equity in their homes.[2] The most unfortunate suffered multiple hits, including bankruptcy and foreclosure. On the day we were in Kansas City, the foreclosure rate was at a sixty-five-year high. At the same time, one-quarter of all mortgaged homes were "underwater," which meant that the owners owed more to their lenders than their houses were actually worth.[3]

With the number thirteen trillion still hanging in the air, John then turned to a slide that appeared on a giant screen. Titled "The New Fear Economy," it showed that unemployment had risen, the real estate and stock markets had crashed, interest rates were a great big question mark, and prices for commodities—like Missouri rice and soybeans—were wandering around like a drunk walking home from a tavern. Oil had been a wild roller-coaster ride, from $51 per barrel at the start of 2007 to $145 in the summer of 2008 and then down to almost $30 at the start of 2009.[4] No one, from the homeowners trying to heat their houses to the fuel buyers for major airlines, had any idea how to plan their fuel expenses or protect themselves from sudden price shocks.

Although no one needed to be told that we were in the worst economic crisis since the Great Depression, John couldn't get to the "good news" part of his talk without a more detailed review of recent events. As he reminded the audience, consumer spending, the driver of America's economy—had contracted in the fourth quarter of 2008 to its second-lowest level on record.[5] This kind of decline is far more important today than it would have been in the past because our economy has become much more dependent on the consumer. Except for a blip when soldiers returned from World War II, between 1940 and 1982 consumer spending never accounted for more than 63 percent of the economy. Then it began to rise to the point where it now represents 73 percent. In raw dollars, this means we've spent an extra $1 trillion that we didn't earn, *every year*.

Why did consumer spending take over more of the economy? It happened in large measure because foreign competitors began eating into the business of our manufacturing industries and we became a net importer of goods rather than an exporter. (The Chinese accelerated this process by keeping their currency grossly undervalued, which made their goods even cheaper.) America became the main consumer of the world's output, whether it was Middle Eastern oil, Korean electronics, or Chilean fruit. The transition from a production economy to a consumer economy was evident in the shuttering of factories and the rise of shopping centers. In every community of any size big retail chains built new outlets, and they were followed by restaurants, movie theaters, tanning salons, and countless other businesses that arose along the highway to help us spend our cash.

For a time all this retail activity preserved the sense that we had a rich and vibrant economy. Rising equity and property prices, coupled with falling interest rates and financial deregulation, led to a myriad of mystical new ways to borrow money. And as lenders steadily weakened their own credit standards to sell more debt, individuals, families, and the government kept spending at an impressive pace. The result is that from 1951 to today, total corporate and consumer debt has more than doubled as a percentage of GDP.[6]

When we finally ran out of savings and credit to support the binge, the Great Recession struck. Real estate values plummeted, foreclosures skyrocketed, and millions of people were thrown out of work. The spectacle of busted banks riveted the business press, but thanks to federal supports no depositors lost any money and government bailouts saved the financial system. Individuals and families weren't so fortunate. Homes were abandoned, retirement accounts were ruined, and businesses struggled as more than seven million jobs disappeared.

We all understand that real pain—psychological, financial, even the physical pain of hunger—lies behind the numbers. (Dr. Sam Cohen, a psychotherapist who consults with business, told us that millions of people have been genuinely traumatized by the Great Recession. Although most will eventually come out of the crisis with a renewed sense of purpose, in the short run "they are being forced to acknowledge they are powerless over certain things.

It's like a cancer diagnosis that snaps people to attention and makes them reconsider what's really important in life.")

At the Nelson-Atkins Museum the data on lost jobs, foreclosures, and busted investments cast a pall over the auditorium. For a bit of comic relief John noted that the recession had a few bright spots. A dentist in Manhattan had seen a 25 percent increase among patients with problems from grinding their teeth.[7] The surgeon-in-chief at the Cornell Institute for Reproductive Medicine reported a 48 percent jump in vasectomies because couples found it cheaper than paying for contraception or new babies.[8] And the University of Florida reported a 32 percent decline in shark attacks in 2009, because fewer would-be swimmers could afford to vacation at the beach.[9]

The dentists, surgeons, and sharks, who have blood and pain in common, won a bit of nervous laughter from the audience. And when John said that in light of the Great Recession people had begun to question the very future of the capitalist system and the government's basic competence, a murmur of assent swept through the hall.

Apparently more than a few in this crowd had been sufficiently shaken by recent events to start openly challenging the leaders who had gotten us into this mess and the mind-set that had allowed us to follow them. This kind of feeling was common across the political spectrum and fueled both the anti-government "tea party" rallies in Washington and the anti-bailout protests on Wall Street.

When the histories of our Great Recession are written, politicians, regulators, bankers, and speculators will take the greatest share of the blame, because they caused the most damage. The level of excess at the top of the power pyramid was breathtaking, as leaders of every stripe grew intoxicated with a kind of magical thinking about ever-expanding wealth. (One of the few sober analysts in this period, Bill Gross of PIMCO Investments, estimated that assets were overvalued by $15 trillion during this time.[10] Much of this illusory value was posted as collateral so people could borrow against it.) Whether through ignorance, incompetence, inattention, or greed, our leaders failed so spectacularly that you might expect the population to revolt. But Americans generally resisted the urge to grab torches and pitchforks and go looking for the bad guys. Perhaps this is because we were aware, on some level, of the way almost every one of us had played a role in the debacle and could accept a measure of responsibility.

Unless you were a novice with the Sisters of Charity, you almost couldn't avoid participating in the culture of acquisition that blossomed in the last three decades. In this time Americans bought so much stuff that an entire industry—self-storage rental units—emerged just so we would have some place to put it all. Once isolated to a few operators with garagelike premises, self-storage now counts fifty-three thousand facilities nationwide with 1.8 billion square feet of space, most of it built in the past decade and filled with goods Americans acquired during a time when we spent more than we earned.[11] In part this spending was encouraged by plummeting prices. But we were hardly bargain shoppers. As *Newsweek*'s Dana Thomas reported in her 2007 book *Deluxe*, between 1985 and 2005 luxury became so mainstream Chanel sold one bottle of its No. 5 perfume every thirty seconds.

Whether it came from the luxe category or the shelves at Sam's Club, almost everything we bought, from Cokes at McDonald's to TV sets for our living rooms, was bigger. The average size of the American home grew from 983 square feet in 1950 to 2,349 square feet in 2006, increasing 20 percent each decade.[12] Our cars increased steadily in horsepower, interior room, and what manufacturers call curb weight, which is the weight of a car when it's delivered to a customer. (In 1990, the average American car weighed less than 2,900 pounds. In 2005 it weighed more than 4,000.) Our beds got bigger, as thicker mattresses and king sizes became more popular, and we bought so many clothes that the market for closet renovations grew 25 percent per year between 1996 and 2006.[13]

At first, we got the money to pay for all this excess by cutting back on savings. In something we call the *fifty/twenty paradox*,

Americans had spent fifty years developing a savings habit that saw us put away more than 10 percent of our income up until the mid-1980s. At that point, as the consumer culture heated up, our savings rate cooled off. It took us just twenty years to reach a negative savings rate. In 2007 the national savings rate hit a seventy-three year low.[14] Not surprisingly, at that moment, the press also reported that thanks to inflated real estate and stock market values, aggregate net worth exceeded $63 trillion dollars, or roughly $500,000 per household.[15]

When we no longer had money in the bank, many of us felt we had plenty in our homes. To keep on buying, we pledged our future incomes and net worth to run up credit by using housing as an ATM. In 2007, the Kennedy-Greenspan estimates of mortgage equity withdrawal (when people refinance with cash out or draw down their home equity lines of credit) was accounting for nearly 9 percent of Americans' disposable income.[16] In the early 1980s, when the era of consumption began, household debt equaled just 44 percent of gross domestic product (a measure of the nation's total economic activity). After a twenty-year climb, it exceeded 100 percent in 2007.[17] No one forced us to abandon the saving habit or forged our signatures on the mortgage papers that consumed the equity that once rested comfortably in our homes. We did it all, willingly, which means, as John told the crowd in Kansas City, "As consumers all of us, in our daily lives, contributed a large part to the problem."

"And yet," John then said, "there is the upside to the downside": in this moment of crisis, we can see the beginning of an era of social change, influenced not by government, Wall Street, or big business, but by of all things, consumerism.

Even as people find themselves less rich, they are deploying their dollars in a more calculated and strategic way to influence institutions like corporations and government. They realize that how they spend their money is a form of power, and they are using it to communicate their values and reward those companies that truly reflect them whether they are pro-environment, anti-bailout, or concerned about some other issue. In this way, each dollar resembles a vote and every day is Election Day for companies that provide goods and services.

The proof of this values revolution emerges in the BrandAsset Valuator data, which we had been crunching with the help of John's partner Ed Lebar (CEO of BrandAsset Consulting) and some independent experts, including professors Philip Kotler at Northwestern, Kevin Keller at Dartmouth, and Natalie Mizik at Columbia Business School. Together we had seen that despite declining economic strength, the American consumer was actually wielding greater power in the marketplace. By restraining their demand (through more thoughtful spending), people were pushing businesses to deliver higher quality and more responsible behavior. In other words, they were using their ever-more-precious dollars to buy a better experience, a better community, even a better world.

As Professor Mizik noted, this move toward more values-based spending reflects an "adaptation to a 'life event' that has been shared across society. When a great number of people experience a crisis of this magnitude, needs replace wants and consumerism become not just thrifty but strategic." Looking at the global economy, and the lingering effects of the recession, Mizik wondered if the crisis was "really over." Her uncertainty, which was widely felt, suggested that the "spend shift" we had observed would only intensify.

Expressed by people at every point in the political spectrum and in every part of the country, the values we saw emerging even before the official start of the recession could be grouped in five categories:

- *Indestructible spirit:* Optimistic and resilient people are leveraging hardship into opportunity.

- *Retooling:* Fiercely self-reliant, we retain our faith in our core traditions and actively seek to better our communities and ourselves.

- *Liquid life:* We are adopting a more nimble, adaptable, and thrifty approach to life.

- *Cooperative consumerism:* Crisis has prompted people to collaborate to solve problems and create new options.

- *From materialism to the material:* Old status symbols no longer appeal as purpose, character, authenticity, and creativity become pathways to the new good life.

The surge in positive values actually began to appear in our data almost twenty years ago. In the early 1990s BrandAsset Valuator showed that people were becoming much savvier about the advertising techniques used to sell them things, and they began to feel a healthy skepticism about the value of marketing claims. Some even began developing arguments to counter the rampant consumerism that swept the country. In Seattle, public television station KCTS and filmmaker John De Graaf produced a rather disturbing documentary—*Affluenza*—that warned of the economic, social, and psychological effects of overheated consumerism. In Tennessee a devout Christian named Dave Ramsey challenged the popular "prosperity gospel" offered by preachers who equated wealth with God's grace. At churches and then over the radio airwaves Ramsey advocated Christian thrift and responsibility. Ramsey's first book, *Financial Peace,* taught readers how to find contentment by curbing debt and living simply. At his public appearances he made a big impression by welcoming members of the audience to share their stories and then invited them to cut up their credit cards on the spot. (Many did.) He called this procedure a "plastectomy."

While a few thinkers and commentators rallied people to resist material excess, millions of people turned to the Internet to become more intelligent economic agents. Through sites like Yelp,

Tripadvisor, and Zillow, they studied product ratings and scoured the marketplace for the best deals. For the first time in history people around the world were empowered to trade information on products and services instantaneously. One of the clearest examples of this phenomenon is the way fans texted instant reviews that panned the movie *Bruno* the weekend it was released. The movie moguls had a new term for it, the "death by Twitter" effect.

The intelligence and assertiveness we saw developing prior to the Great Recession meant that consumers could shop for lasting quality and seek out goods and services from suppliers who match their sense of ethics. They could and did move from mind*less* consumption to mind*ful* consumption, taking care to purchase goods and services only from sellers who met their standards. They could also use the Internet to create groups of consumers who could exercise even greater power.

This desire to use money to express values stands out in our BrandAsset Valuator data, and was expressed by many of the people who participated in a series of Digital Town Halls we conducted to gain insight into the mind-set and motivations of post-crisis consumer behavior. Together, they reveal that a majority of Americans already say they have changed their lifestyles and the way they behave in the marketplace. This great shift in how people spend their time, energy, and money is a societal response to the Great Recession. Awakened by the economic crisis, people are returning to old-fashioned values—optimism, self-reliance, practicality, hard work, thrift, community, honesty, kindness—and they are applying these ideals in their relationships and their careers, and in their consumption habits as well.

Who are the spend shifters? Well, they aren't "radical frugalists," Christian ascetics, or extreme New Age anti-materialists. They are merely people who, in adapting to crisis, have subtly adjusted their lives to seek greater balance and a more fulfilling existence. According to our data, 55 percent of all Americans are fully part of this

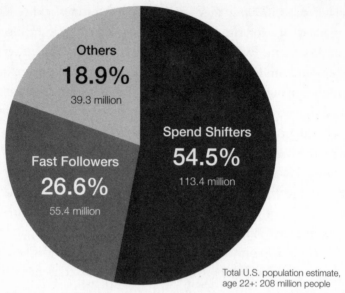

Figure I.I.   The Spend Shift Movement Among the U.S. Population
Source: U.S. Census Bureau.
Source of values data: Young & Rubicam proprietary survey conducted in
July 2009 among a nationally representative sample of 2,300 adults.

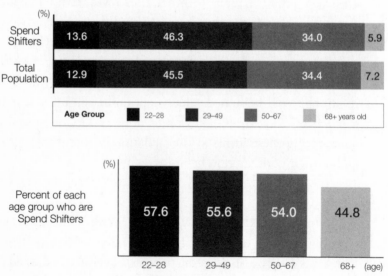

Figure I.2.   Values Shifts by Age Group

undeclared movement. In addition, about one-quarter of the U.S. adult population expresses many of the same attitudes and characteristics (call them "Fast Followers," as in Figure I.1 and Figure I.2).

The spend shift encompasses people from all walks of life, as outlined in Figure I.3. It is blind to age, education, income,

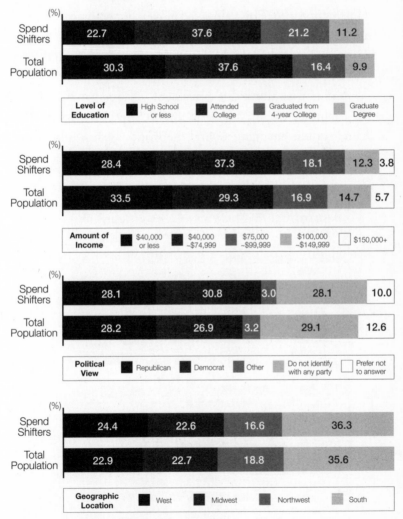

Figure I.3.   Values Shifts by Demographics
Source: Young & Rubicam proprietary survey conducted in July 2009 among a nationally representative sample of 2,400 adults.

political affiliation, and geography. Millennials (the generation born between 1980 and 1998) lead the movement, yet nearly half of all senior citizens belong, too. They are both highly educated and not, with 21 percent college educated and 23 percent having a high school degree or less. They are rich and poor and equally represent Republicans, Democrats, and independents (28, 31, and 41 percent each). This values-led movement embraces people from all across the nation as well—17 percent are from the Northeast, 23 percent are from the Midwest, 36 percent are from the South, and 24 percent are from the West.

And lest we think this movement is purely an American one, we examined country data in BrandAsset Valuator and found spend shifters emerging around the world, as shown in Figure I.4.

Country	Spend Shifters	Fast Followers
France	53%	31%
Canada	51%	36%
Switzerland	49%	30%
Greece	48%	30%
Netherlands	46%	34%
Austria	46%	34%
Belgium	46%	36%
Portugal	46%	37%
Germany	45%	36%
Italy	45%	37%
Australia	45%	35%
Singapore	44%	41%
Turkey	44%	38%
U.K.	44%	37%
Hungary	42%	41%
Brazil	41%	42%
Poland	41%	40%
Chile	39%	41%
Russia	38%	41%
Spain	38%	33%
India	34%	53%
Mexico	34%	47%
Czech Republic	34%	42%
Japan	26%	40%
China	21%	41%

Figure I.4.   The Spreading Spend Shift
Source: BrandAsset Valuator Data by Country.

(This was a global crisis, after all.) Interestingly, there are fewer spend shifters in fast-growing economies like China and India and the Czech Republic, where consumerism is still emerging.

What unites the shifters is a common sense of optimism and newfound purpose, as illustrated in Figure I.5. They are living with less and yet feeling greater happiness and satisfaction. Seventy-eight percent report they are happier with a more down-to-basics lifestyle. Eighty-eight percent report they buy less expensive brands than they used to, and nearly the same number report that possessions do not have much to do with how happy they are.

The irony of people feeling happier even though they are less wealthy and more constrained by the economy is easier to explain than you might expect. When we looked back at the data, we saw that a great many people never were all that comfortable with the overheated consumer economy. "Keeping up with the Joneses" can be a physically and spiritually draining pursuit, and many who participated felt a nagging sense of unhappiness, as if with every trip to a big box store they were betraying some higher value.

We heard many expressions of this concern about higher values and consumer behavior in the digital town halls we conducted to talk about these ideas. Sweetmom (the online user name of a forty-five-year-old woman from Seattle) said, "I believe and hope that today's economic crisis will have taught all of us a lesson. I was raised that you didn't buy something unless you had the money for it. Credit cards were OK if you paid them off monthly. That seems to be 'old school' thinking—but it was the right thinking."

Another digital town hall participant called Dancingdiva, who was twenty-eight and from Salt Lake City, said, "The recession has been a true eye-opener for me. I have had to say 'no' to things that I ended up not missing after all. The recession has helped me to really distinguish between needs and wants."

Like Dancingdiva, 78 percent of all the people we surveyed find it off-putting when people show off expensive purchases, but this

They are driven by down-to-earth value; they view money differently

	Total Population	Spend Shifters
"I find the more I have the more I want"	**63.0**%disagree	**63.7**%disagree
"Money is the best measure of success"	**77.9**%disagree	**87.5**%disagree

They are more self-reliant and resourceful

	Total Population	Spend Shifters
"These days, I feel more in control when I do things myself instead of relying on others to do them for me"	**84.1**%agree	**92.5**%agree
"Since the recession, I am interested in learning new skills, so I can do more myself and rely less on others"	**64.7**%agree	**80.3**%agree

They are adaptive, flexible, and focused

	Total Population	Spend Shifters
"Since the recession, I realize I am happier with a simpler, more down-to-basics lifestyle"	**64.8**%agree	**77.4**%agree
"Since the recession, I realize that how many possessions I have does not have much to do with how happy I am"	**76.1**%agree	**86.4**%agree

They believe in the power of community and accountability

	Total Population	Spend Shifters
"I believe my friends and I can change corporate behavior by supporting companies that do the right thing"	**65.5**%agree	**69.0**%agree
"I make it a point to buy brands from companies whose values are similar to my own"	**70.9**%agree	**75.0**%agree

Figure I.5.   How Our Values Are Changing

sentiment is even stronger among people who earn $100,000 a year or more. Similarly, people aged fifty to sixty-four and the generation that is between eighteen and twenty-four share the same aversion to status brands and the same interest in doing things for themselves.

Young adults are more comfortable than all the others when it comes to reordering priorities and adapting. Fully 77 percent of them, compared with 66 percent overall, said they realize they are actually happier with a simpler, more down-to-basics lifestyle. They identify strongly with their grandparents, members of what's called the Greatest Generation—the ones who survived the Great Depression and won World War II—who were, of necessity, experts in self-sufficiency and sustainability. (They didn't use those terms, of course. Instead they just went about growing their own food, reducing their consumption of expensive energy, and making everything they owned last longer through upkeep and repair.)

Like the Greatest Generation, Millennials want to learn more skills, take responsibility for their own well-being, and tackle problems and projects on their own. They pursue life with the feeling that they lost little by way of financial and material wealth in the recession, so this leaves them free to take risks. Were you laid off in Cleveland? Go buy a $500 building in downtown Detroit and start a business. Did your manufacturing job get shipped overseas? Go back to school and become a nurse.

When you have a flexible, nimble approach to life, you refuse to be defeated by temporary setbacks and you willingly take risks in order to take advantage of new opportunities. In fact, 88 percent of young adults state they believe that their own imagination is the key to the future.

The data also shows that across society, people don't just feel empowered as individuals, they feel inspired about their ability to band together to influence big institutions like corporations, and to improve their communities. On Main Street, where people don't get bonuses and bailouts, values-based consumerism offers not only economic but democratic clout. Overlyanalyticalsusie, a twenty-six-year-old from Philadelphia, put it this way: "I think the power of the penny is one of the greatest powers there is. I think that if more people realized how much their dollars affected companies and policies, they would: 1. Act with more urgency to change things, 2. Feel more powerful and 3. Be more responsible about how they spend their money."

Nearly two-thirds of all the people who responded to the BrandAsset Valuator feel they can affect corporate behavior through their purchasing habits, with the same amount avoiding companies whose values contradict their own. Three-quarters of these "conscious consumers" are aligning their spending with their values to support responsible companies. For example, MamaBear (a thirty-five-year-old from Iowa City), said, "I know that if they have similar values to mine, then I would be more apt to purchase products from them." And January (a twenty-three-year-old from Seattle) said, "There are MANY other areas in a budget where Americans can cut back, but conscious consumerism should not be one of them."

As John told the crowd in Kansas City, "Now, by restricting their demand, consumers can actually align their values with their spending and force capitalism and business to not be just about *more* but about *better*."

With those last words, about how people would push business to be better in every sense of the word, the audience started to applaud. It was that kind of spontaneous reaction that comes when you have connected with something people know is true but haven't been able to articulate themselves. We took it as yet another signal that at the grass roots, people are well ahead of the pundits, corporations, and political leaders. In fact, they—really "we"—began to make adjustments *long before* anyone had even begun to talk about meltdowns, bailouts, and foreclosure rescue schemes. We compare this to the widely observed phenomenon of animals racing for safety well before human beings even notice that an earthquake or tidal wave is about to hit. Something deep inside of us knew we were on the wrong path and we didn't need to be told to seek a better direction.

Some of the most important numbers supporting this trend come from the U.S. Bureau of Economic Analysis reports on personal savings. The reports show that soon after savings rates bottomed out in 2005, something told us to start squirreling away a bit more money, and most of us listened. Ordinary Americans began raising their deposits in saving accounts and other secure investments *a full two years before the start of the recession*. Even as unemployment surged past 10 percent and almost matched the worst levels since World War II (10.8 percent in December 1982), we socked away more money every month. By the middle of 2009, as the press brought us gloomy stories of layoffs and foreclosures, we were saving about 7 percent of our disposable income, a figure that hadn't been seen since 1995.

The big federal data banks also tell us that people cut back on spending, in all areas, many months before the recession began. In fact, we reduced our consumption so sharply that in the middle of 2008 it dropped below our disposable income and just kept falling.[18] This discipline wasn't a short-lived fad. As the months passed we maintained a positive balance of income and spending throughout all of 2009. For many months the net surplus, when you compared disposable income with what we actually spent, was greater than we had seen in twenty years. Without being scolded, lectured, or led from above, Americans had quietly shifted their behavior.

We detect early signals of a values renaissance in our data as far back as the early 1990s. It appears when we study, for lack of a better term, the materialistic desires of the typical American. In response to questions about how they preferred to spend their money, people expressed steadily declining interest in objects of desire—fancy cars, flashy jewelry, trendy clothes—and a stronger attachment to products and services that meet their needs reliably, day in and day out. Drawn on a graph of 900,000 consumers, it's clear that people were editing *want* from *need* well before the recession began (Figure I.6).

Perhaps on some level, people were becoming truly uncomfortable with their own excess. The Pew Center too reported that in 2009, the majority of Americans no longer considered TVs, dishwashers, dryers, and air-conditioning to be necessities.[19] In the report *What Americans Need*, it found that these items had become luxuries, according to more people in its national survey.

Along with provocative data related to how people vote with their dollars, our BrandAsset Valuator surveys also give us a revealing portrait of the human qualities people prefer to meet as they explore the marketplace. People still participated in the economy, and they even gave themselves treats like travel and restaurant meals. Christmas presents and Valentine's Day chocolates never went out of style. But between 2005 and 2009 we saw some remarkable shifts as people rejected snobbishness and exclusivity and

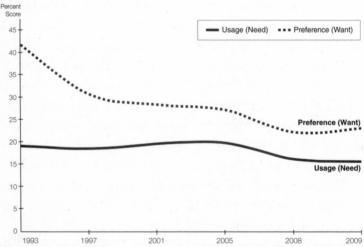

Figure I.6. Shifting Concepts of Necessity: The Need-Want Gap Began to Close
Source: BrandAsset Valuator 1993, 1997, 2001, 2005, 2008, 2009—top 20 percent desirable brands.

embraced attributes that bring people closer together or suggest a commitment to making our world a better place. Among the once-prized attributes that declined in this period were

- *Exclusive*—down 60 percent

- *Arrogant*—down 41 percent

- *Sensuous*—down 30 percent

- *Daring*—down 20 percent

- *Trendy*—down 13 percent

On the opposite side of the scale, the attributes Americans found more important as they began to sense the impending recession and then suffered through the crisis were

- *Kindness and Empathy*—up 391 percent

- *Friendly*—up 148 percent

- *High-quality*—up 124 percent

- *Socially responsible*—up 63 percent

- *Leader*—up 40 percent

The increase reported for "Kindness" is not a typo. Between 2005 and 2009 American consumers expressed a nearly fourfold increase in their preference for companies that show kindness in both their operations and their encounters with customers. This desire for companies to be more empathetic in how they treat customers is the biggest shift in any attitude that we have ever seen during the seventeen-year life of the BrandAsset Valuator survey.

———————

Altogether, the numbers we draw from Young & Rubicam's ongoing BrandAsset Valuator survey and from the more generally available economic data that flows from government, academic, and business sources paint a surprisingly bright picture of both the present and the future. Yes, the Great Recession has destroyed millions of jobs and trillions of dollars in wealth, and it has been a huge financial setback for countless Americans. But when you look beneath the surface, you see that everyday Americans are resilient, sensible, and sturdy. A few social commentators have seen evidence of these strengths in declining crime rates, rising interest in public libraries (68 percent of Americans have library cards, the highest ever), and a recent burst of volunteerism led, remarkably, by people who have lost their jobs.[20]

The Great Recession's "hidden virtues," as writer Michael Gerson called them, mirror the nation's experience during the Great Depression, when families and communities watched out for each other and many indicators of social well-being, including crime rates, voter turnout, and participation in social groups like bowling leagues, scouting, and 4-H all improved. "Many Americans who struggled through the Depression adopted a set of moral and economic habits such as thrift, family commitment, savings and modest consumption that lasted through their lifetimes—and that have decayed in our own," wrote Gerson. "The Depression Generation controlled the things it could control—including its own consumption and character."[21]

The same thing seems to be happening now, as the shock of our economic loss wears off and people try to redefine what it means to be successful and happy. In early 2010 the *New York Times* reported on polls that showed people are spending more time doing things with friends and family and enjoying hobbies like gardening and baking. Our interest in low-cost shared experiences—museum visits, picnics, and movies—seems to be rising as our interest in shopping declines. According to the Bureau of Labor Statistics, we are also putting more time into community service and religious and spiritual activities.

We see obvious implications for businesses in the numbers that John shared with the audience in Kansas City. Americans are demanding more of the people they trade with, and this includes using their dollars to influence them to do good as they are doing well. "You can't fight and control this," said John. "Companies will need to find different ways to offer an exchange of value with consumers." Then he flashed another slide on the screen. It was a quote from Andy Grove, one of the founders of Intel. It read: "Bad companies are destroyed by crises. Good companies survive them. Great companies are improved by them."

"The crisis that exists today is real," allowed John, "but it is also a tremendous opportunity for those who can see where the economy is headed. I'm convinced we're entering an era where values now define consumerism. The demand that built the largest consumer economy in the world will now prefer 'better' instead of 'more.' With a clearer understanding of their necessities, consumers can reconstruct capitalism to be creative rather than destructive. To bring greater value to the world we live in and offer us the opportunity to connect with companies that share our beliefs. We see a very hopeful picture for the future of America."

It wasn't a highly dramatic ending. We didn't post an image of Old Glory on the screen and cue a Sousa march. Nevertheless, the crowd burst into applause. Afterward, we were met by a long line of people who shared their own stories of shifting values, and the satisfaction that comes with surviving a crisis. The most poignant one came from a middle-aged woman who lived in a comfortable suburb where many of the men, in their forties and fifties, have been laid off by companies that aren't likely to ever ask them to come back. After a bit of grieving, these men have come together to support each other in the struggle with unemployment. To keep their spirits up they began organizing block parties—something they had never done before—and found a wealth of friendship to replace the material wealth they had lost.

Others in Kansas City said that they had tired of the consumer juggernaut many years ago and welcomed the prospect of living in a world where character and values mattered more than the size of your car or house. They were actually excited about changes that, until this moment, had made them more anxious than optimistic, more fearful than hopeful. However, they wanted to know if we had deep, firsthand experience with the type of consumers we were describing—earnest, demanding, humane—and contact with companies that were adapting and prepared to succeed in the post-crisis economy of less frenzied buying and selling.

Standing with those "show me" people from Missouri, we realized that while we believed in the research, and in the inevitability of the change that was under way, we didn't have enough on-the-ground evidence to have the whole story. In that moment we realized that something very exciting was going on "out there" and decided to devote as much time as was required to find and document it.

In the months that followed we traveled to dozens of communities in eight states (both Red and Blue) to study the spend shift and discover how people intend to live in the post-recession age. We talked with people across kitchen counters, in restaurants, on street corners, in factories, and in boardrooms. We shopped with people in supermarkets and big box stores. We watched people network at job fairs. We walked the floors of start-up companies. We interrogated small business owners. And we observed how Fortune 500 CEOs were adjusting their business models. What we learned both affirmed and amplified the trends suggested by the data. A values revolution is reshaping the consumer marketplace. American companies, regardless of their size or their target market, must understand the significance of this social trend. Those who grasp it and adapt will find extraordinary opportunities. Those who ignore it will do so at their peril.

Chapter One

THE NEW
AMERICAN FRONTIER:
DETROIT, MICHIGAN

At sunrise on the first Friday in December, a film crew from a
European television network blocks the oak-paneled entry
hall at the Inn on Ferry Street in Detroit with a pile of black
equipment bags that hold tripods, lights, and boom microphones.
While somewhat annoyed fellow guests squeeze around them to
reach their morning coffee, which waits in the parlor of the ele-
gantly restored Victorian house, the TV folks talk excitedly about
the great images they shot and the powerful interviews they
conducted.

After a week in pursuit of "America in decline," as one of the
crew describes their mission, they had captured the "shocking"
story of Detroit circa 2010 and were heading home like big game
hunters with their trophies. (Were there actually antelope heads
in those bags?) "No one would believe this was the story of
the Motor City," he says, "but it's a disaster and we have the
pictures."

Outside, a horn announces the arrival of the van that will take
the crew, just the latest of many who have come to chronicle the
city's demise, to the airport. As one of the technicians struggles
to get the bulky equipment bags outside, he complains about
the chill—a cold front had swept through overnight—but smiles
to signal that he was happy to be leaving with his mission
accomplished.

The story that the film crew bagged was the easiest "economy in crisis" piece any journalist could pursue in 2009. Long in economic retreat, Detroit had been further savaged by the Great Recession that started at the end of 2007. The median home price had dropped from an already low $60,000 in August 2005 to below $8,000.[1] Commercial real estate had seen an even more precipitous decline, as evidenced by the recent sale of the 80,000-seat Silverdome stadium in nearby Pontiac for $583,000—roughly the equivalent of a studio apartment in Manhattan.[2] Local unemployment, thanks mainly to the troubles of the automakers, was estimated at 28.9 percent (not counting those who had given up looking) compared with 10.2 percent nationwide.[3] Desperate for work, many Detroiters had fled; the city's population, which had peaked at 1.8 million in 1950, was estimated to be less than 900,000.[4]

Far more compelling than the statistics was the city's landscape: abandoned factories, vacant commercial buildings, and neighborhoods where three-quarters of the homes have been boarded, burned, or bulldozed. In the most desolate residential areas you could drive for blocks and see few signs of life except for stray dogs and, occasionally, a coyote. Some of the houses had been abandoned for so long that small trees and vines have grown to cover entire walls.

Detroit's poignant decay has become a favorite subject of photographers who always seem to make special note of decrepit landmarks: the Michigan Theater building, where cars now park beneath the ornate lobby arches, and the hollowed-out Michigan Central Railroad Depot. Once one of the great railroad stations in the country, the eighteen-story story building is now gutted and barricaded behind a security fence that couldn't keep thieves from tearing the copper wire, pipes, and anything else of value out of the building. It looms over the west side like some science fiction monster.

Given the apocalyptic panorama, any first-time visitor who landed in Detroit in late 2009 and drove around the city for the first time would half expect to see marauding Mad Max figures come roaring down the street on handmade battlewagons powered by Allison diesel engines. The decay and loss were writ large across the city, and you didn't need a TV cameraman's eye to see it. But if you looked more closely, you could find something that most outsiders miss: a Detroit that is vibrant, creative, and optimistic.

On the same morning when the foreign journalists were departing from the Inn on Ferry Street (more about the inn later), a bunch of regulars were crowding into a café that serves as a little oasis of comfort just a few miles away, in the heart of the crumbling city. This is the part of the Detroit story most visiting journalists never see—or acknowledge. It is a thriving business in a place that others consider a wasteland, and it represents an indestructible human spirit that arose in the very depths of the Great Recession in the place that was hit hardest of all. It was also the first stop in a remarkable adventure that revealed that a hard-luck city could also be a modern frontier of opportunity.

Le Petit Zinc occupies a small lot on the corner of Trumbull and Howard Streets in a downtown neighborhood dominated by machine shops, a drug rehabilitation center, halfway houses, and riverfront warehouses. The building itself is a nondescript, single-story rectangle faced in the kind of dusty yellow brick that was used to build countless elementary schools in the 1950s. In fact, it was last used as a preschool and day-care center, and proprietor Charles Sorel has made good use of the chain link fence that once surrounded the playground. He has created a secure parking lot, which is great for business in a place where the center city has emptied out and walking is no longer practical. In the sheltered yard near the door he installed an herb and vegetable garden complete with a bubbling fountain and outdoor seating. An artist as well as an entrepreneur, Sorel painted the sign out front, which features the jaunty rooster that is a symbol of the French spirit. He also designed the café's interior, which welcomes customers with warm yellows and bright blues that echo the Cote d'Azur.

On this windswept Friday, Sorel arose before five o'clock so he could enjoy a shower and a cup of tea before getting to his shop at six. There he was joined by a cook named Molly Motor (her real name) and server named Rachel Harkai. Within minutes the hot stove and coffee machines filled the place with the aromas of breakfast and coated the cold windows with condensation. Sorel's first patron was a local judge who enjoys the quiet and the quality of the croissants, baguettes, and espresso. By eight o'clock Le Petit Zinc (French slang for "the local bar") bustles with a crowd of regulars and a handful of first-timers. Thanks to word-of-mouth and a few good reviews, the bistro now draws travelers and explorers from the suburbs.

After the morning rush, forty-eight-year-old Sorel takes a break at one of his handmade tables. Born in Martinique but raised in France, he's a lanky fellow who traces his ancestors to both Europe and Africa, and he speaks somewhat fractured English in a lilting accent. His curly black hair is flecked with silver and not completely tamed. The wild style gives him the look of an excited, energetic man on the move, which is exactly what he is. Resourceful, unflagging, and relentlessly optimistic, he is the kind of immigrant who has always helped fuel the American economy with energy and a zest for life.

The death of Sorel's father-in-law (his wife Karima is from Detroit) brought him to the city where, like most newcomers, he was taken aback by the conditions. But he had succeeded once with a café in Brooklyn (his first home when he came to America in 1989) and decided to stay and try again. "We have to live," he said in a puzzled reply to a question about why he might open a French bistro in a neighborhood where it's hard to find even a good hamburger. "I have to feed my family, and I had no other qualifications here."

In fact a welcoming little eatery—something like a family kitchen where the coffeepot is always on—makes for the perfect start-up business in any community, especially one that is short of comforts. The ultimate social animals, human beings naturally seek each other, and from farm communities in the west to big-city neighborhoods, cafés serve as gathering spots. Sorel recalled the places in Paris that made him feel good and set about creating one. He started by focusing on the food. Detroit didn't have a nice French-style bistro with real Parisian coffee and authentic cuisine, he says, adding, "People like quality." Then he mentions the staff. In a depressed employment market he was able to hire what may be the most motivated, educated, and experienced café staff anywhere. Every person on the team is devoted to making both the cuisine they serve and their service "so professional."

Unsatisfied with his own answers, Sorel pauses and looks around at the crowded tables. He cocks his ear to hear the warm din of conversation punctuated by the clatter of dishes and silverware. A smile comes over his face as he realizes that the secret of his success is even more basic than good food and service. To succeed, he says, "You need to cheer people up."

Good cheer—"We have optimism all the time"—is at the emotional heart of Sorel's business, but it is not the only inspirational element of his business plan. From the moment he began to plan the café he set down some operating principles that would communicate certain values to his staff and his customers. First, the books would be completely open to everyone who works at the bistro, so they could see how the business was doing, month-to-month. Second, work would not be rigidly assigned. At any moment you might wait tables, wash dishes, or prepare food or drinks, which meant work was never boring. Third, all the workers, including the founder, would draw the same pay. This policy means that everyone had good reason to provide the highest quality at the lowest price in order to build the business. It also means that they must find some satisfaction in rewards beyond cash.

Passing behind the boss (not a term actually employed at Le Petit Zinc), server Rachel Harkai balances a tray loaded with coffee, croissants, and *salade de fruit frais* and tosses off a comment on the way to a table. "Obviously we're not here to make money," she quips.

After delivering the order, Harkai, who is tall with curly blonde hair, stands for a moment to explain that "here" refers not only to the café but also to the city she adopted after graduating from the honors program at the University of Michigan in 2007.

"I'm twenty-four, and I'm coming of age at a time when the economic boom is over and we were faced with hardship, but that changed what we valued." Trained in creative writing, Harkai had imagined herself as an independent writer and teacher, and in Detroit she didn't have the wait to reach her goal. For $440 per month, including utilities, she was able to rent a huge space with an office, an art studio, and a vegetable garden in the empty lot next door. Soon she was doing readings at the Detroit Artists Market, a gallery that was founded during the Great Depression and is now one of the most prestigious art venues in the Midwest. A local literacy program made her a writer-in-residence in the Detroit schools and she began contributing to *Model D*, a local online culture magazine. Work at the café supplemented the income she made from writing and teaching. It also connected her to the local community.

For a young person starting life, adds Harkai, Detroit was a low-cost alternative to Chicago or cities on the coast where it's easy to get lost in the crowd of people trying to make it. Here, whether it's business, art, or education, the cost of taking a chance is extremely low; almost anyone is welcome to try; and failure just brings another opportunity. Of course, few Detroiters spend much time contemplating what Harkai called the macro-level economic factors that have made the city a kind of urban frontier. They are too busy with the struggle. "Sometimes I feel like it can be hard to live here," she adds. "But sometimes I feel like we're the smartest people in America to be living here."

If Harkai and her peers are smart, it's a kind of smart that is focused on making life about more than earning and spending money. Like other employees at the café she has made a commitment to the community by promising to live in the city proper and not move to the suburbs. The idea is for people to earn and spend their money locally and to stand against the fear that has been driving others away. This is not so much a tactic as an attitude, an expression of hope that in the long run, individuals who choose to remain in the central city may one day see its revival.

This impulse is consistent with a trend that began before the Great Recession and then accelerated—deglobalization. Marked by declining exports—they dropped 12 percent in 2009—and sharp reductions in currency trading, this process is driven by the realization that many local economies, if not entire countries, have suffered in the face of international competition and need time to rebuild.[5] Without knowing it, Detroiters are much like the people in poor countries around the globe who are more concerned about their neighbors and fellow citizens than winning at the game of foreign trade. They want to create businesses that serve local citizens and make neighborhoods bustle with life.

"My dream," says Charles Sorel, "is to bump into someone on the street in Detroit."

By this he means that he hopes for a day when sidewalks and parks are crowded and the business district pulses with life. For the time being, however, Sorel tries to give the city a pulse by opening the café to community events. The most successful so far were 2008 "Debate Nights," when he kept the café open late so that viewers could watch the Republicans and Democrats who sought the White House square off on the issues.

Politics matters deeply to Sorel, as it does to every other person who has staked a claim to Detroit's future. In his case, the idea of

America as a place of opportunity looms large in his sense of what the country should be. Here he has found that despite his broken English and inexperience, people have been willing to support him because of his work ethic and enthusiasm. He loves the culture of acceptance, and this love makes him worry about preserving it.

"We have optimism, all the time," adds Charles Sorel. "But we also have anger." His main concern is the school system, which needs to be repaired so that young people can be prepared to build Detroit's future. "That is America, a place where everyone, the middle class and everyone, gets a chance." Ideally, elected officials would lead the way to better schools and a renaissance of Detroit, but Sorel says the spectacle of the city's broken local government makes him fear the politicians are all liars. Unwilling to wait, he and pioneers on the Detroit frontier are determined to make the community better all by themselves.

Doing his part, Sorel has created a business that supports five employees and their dependents. By Sorel's hiring policy, those five employees also must live in Detroit and thereby support the city with their dollars and their presence. In recent months he has seen that others appreciate the energy and opportunity in a place that is still the eleventh-largest city in the country (bigger than Boston, Seattle, or Denver). One group of investors came and bought twenty houses. Another group purchased thirty buildings and lots. These people are betting on the long-term future of Detroit. Even more inspiring are the young entrepreneurs who believe so strongly in the place that they are willing to pour their lives into it.

"It inspires me," says Sorel, "to see that I am not the only one."

Today's Detroit seems to Sorel like an urban frontier of opportunity. Like other frontier regions it is a challenging environment that lacks many of the supports you might find in places with more stable infrastructure and institutions. Here, city services like fire, police, public works, and education are minimal, and the supports a business might hope to find from investors or banks just don't exist. On the other hand, real estate is so cheap and labor is so plentiful that almost anyone with energy and an idea can get a start. And when it comes to community spirit, there may be no better spot in America for a hardy entrepreneur.

"Because there is so much hunger for hope, everyone here wants you to succeed," says Sorel, "even the people who are supposed to be your competition."

Indeed, when Sorel began renovating the space for his café, he attracted other restaurateurs who actually wanted to help him get established. The owners of Slow's, a famous local barbeque spot, advised Sorel on the city permit process and donated their time and energy to build tables for Le Petit Zinc. The proprietor of a cross-town coffee shop helped him find a source for high-quality beans, and Dave Mancini of Supino Pizza got him a supply of paper slips for his credit card machine. Most remarkable of all was the aid that came from Torya Blanchard, who owned a tiny crepe stand—Good Girls Go to Paris—that was Sorel's only direct competition in the city. Instead of getting defensive, she visited Sorel and helped him refine his crepe recipe. It was an act of generosity consistent with the mind-set of her generation and the spirit of her city.

"Detroit needs all of us," explains Blanchard during a brief break in her workday at her shop. A thirty-one-year-old African American woman, she wears fashionably clunky eyeglasses and proudly dons a hairnet whenever she's in the kitchen. She says her parents taught her by example to work hard and seek challenges. "The people who have stayed here when so many others moved out are committed," she says. "They love the city—I mean I love the city—and there are still enough of us around that there is enough business for everyone who wants to try something. In fact there's a little bit of a captive audience because while there are thousands of people who still work downtown every day, there aren't many places for them to eat, or shop."

In many ways Blanchard is more typical of Detroit's new-spirited entrepreneurs than Sorel. She's a Detroit native, she's young, and unlike Sorel she had absolutely no previous experience in business. Her first passion is not the bottom line but all things French, from the language to the history to the delicate, wafer-thin pancakes dusted with powdered sugar that she devoured on her first trip to Paris at age sixteen. That trip inspired her to spend a year working in France as an au pair and then become a French teacher in the Detroit city school system, which was the job she left to go into business. It also gave her the name for the little take-away shop she opened in a space once occupied by a hot dog stand. "Only good girls go to Paris," was the admonition she heard from her mother when she got caught shoplifting on the eve of a planned trip to France.

"I was a total kleptomaniac," laughs Blanchard, recalling her youthful indiscretion. "My mother came to get me at the police station and made sure I understood what was expected of me." Fortunately for Blanchard—and for Detroiters who love French-style fast food—she was basically a good girl, and her parents let her take the trip. Fifteen years later, when she was a little bored and felt she had nothing to lose, Blanchard cashed in her retirement fund, called the landlord who owned a downtown space that had been occupied by the Motor City Pit Stop hot dog stand, and got to work on renovations.

"That was my *Fight Club* moment," says Blanchard, recalling a movie that inspired her to give her all to the demanding challenge of opening a business in Detroit. She refurbished the kitchen, installed a neon sign above the window that said simply "Crepes," and opened for business in the summer of 2008, as the Great Recession raged. Within a few weeks she could count on a line forming on the sidewalk at lunchtime every day.

"The space was forty-six square feet, which gives you some idea of how low my overhead was," adds Blanchard. In fact, expenses were so low at the Good Girls store that she was able to support herself on the income almost immediately. Like Charles Sorel, she stressed quality food at a low price and began to draw customers from beyond town. Soon customers were suggesting she either expand or open a second shop where they could get table service. In the summer of 2009 she opened Good Girls Go to Paris in the Park Shelton building in the city's Midtown district.

Opened in 1926 as a hotel and apartment block, the Park Shelton is a historic landmark where Diego Rivera lived while he painted his world-famous mural Detroit Industry—an ode to the automobile era—at the nearby Detroit Institute of Arts. The fifth-largest fine arts museum in the country, the DIA is one of several institutions (including Wayne State University and the Detroit Medical Center) that bring tens of thousands of workers and visitors to Midtown every day. This traffic is so good for business that Good Girls Go to Paris grew to a staff of twelve. That's a dozen jobs Detroit needed.

Although Blanchard is too modest to declare herself a success, she will admit that she's discovered some of the ingredients that go into making a business work in hard times. She followed her passion, avoided debt, delivered high quality, and poured huge amounts of time and energy into her enterprise. She also credits her youth and the edgy atmosphere in the city, which seems to encourage risk taking and innovation. "I guess there is something about my age and this place," she says. "I'm just not afraid to try this."

Torya Blanchard is also unafraid of the future. She believes in the people she grew up with and in the advantages of urban living, especially in a future when high-cost energy makes a lifestyle built around the automobile too expensive and environmentally unsound. But as a young adult who never knew the thriving industrial Detroit, she's unsentimental about the past. Her vision for the city calls for consolidating homes and businesses to create a few vibrant neighborhoods, and turning bulldozers loose on blighted areas. Right now, she says, "Detroit is too big for its own good."

No one's self-image involves being a statistic or a data point in a survey, but Torya Blanchard represents several important trends that defy the negative assumption many experts share about Detroit and the future of the American economy. During the recession, 60 percent of the people we surveyed said they thought they were capable of starting their own business. This figure is higher than the number we saw before the recession.

This confidence also turned up when we asked people how they felt about the prospects of business competition: 49 percent of people in our survey agreed with the statement, "There is greater opportunity for individual business owners to compete with large companies now than there used to be." As shown in Figure 1.1, young people were more confident than others on this point, perhaps because they grasp the power of networking technologies that can give individuals and small groups access to big markets.

These responses suggest an optimism that doesn't appear in large-scale surveys of consumer confidence, which was very weak during the time when our BrandAsset Valuator surveys were being done. However it does appear in unexpected places where people who take a very pragmatic view of life are eager to try almost anything and will exploit whatever resources are available. In Detroit, the most obvious resource is space. In area, Detroit is 20

"There is greater opportunity for individual business owners to compete with large companies more now than there used to be"	
Spend Shifters Age Group	Percent Agree
22–28	53%
29–49	49%
50–67	48%
68+	37%

Figure 1.1. Optimism for Entrepreneurship

percent bigger than Boston, San Francisco, and Manhattan put together. With roughly one-third the population, it's easy to understand why the Motor City has so many empty buildings and lots that seem to be turning into urban prairie.

In the short term, and in the eyes of most visitors, Detroit's vacant lots and emptied-out buildings—estimated at roughly forty thousand properties—represent a kind of ending. This assessment isn't wrong. Detroit's reign as an industrial powerhouse and center of the world's automotive business is long gone. The city will also continue to shrink in population. By some demographers' estimates, there will be about 600,000 Detroiters when the exodus finally stops.[6] Shocking as this figure may be to those who recall when its population approached two million in the 1950s, it would still leave Detroit with about as many residents as Milwaukee, Denver, or Washington, D.C. It's a solid base for a new kind of settlement that, with a little planning, might make Detroit a magnet for people who seek an urban lifestyle—with all the culture and connection that implies—at an extraordinarily low cost.

This is precisely the model imagined by the American Institute of Architects when it conducted a special study of the city. As the Great Recession struck in early 2008, the AIA sent a team of experts in planning, design, technology, and development to survey the region and meet with local citizens. With no attachment to the old Detroit, they could see that municipal government was trapped in a cycle of trying to maintain the old-style city services with ever-declining tax revenues. Better to recognize that the old industrial city was truly gone, the experts reasoned, and embrace a new, more sustainable model by going with the natural flow of things but steering the city to a better destination.

The better destination, which the AIA offered in a sixty-page plan, calls for an interconnected group of nine "urban villages" surrounding a core downtown district where jobs, commerce, and public spaces like parks, theaters, museums, and sports venues would be concentrated. The villages would be less densely populated than the core, but not as loosely developed as a typical suburb. Imagine places where people can easily walk to shop, dine, attend church or school, and hop on mass transit to get to anything else. On these short trips they would pass through parks and restored open spaces (instead of blighted neighborhoods) that would await future development.

The AIA concept might sound like the kind of starry-eyed vision consultants have offered to cities in the past. (Did you ever see the "monorail" episode of *The Simpsons* TV show?) And anyone afraid of top-down social engineering would have doubts about master planning. But on close examination the proposal is not an attempt to impose a rigid blueprint on the city but instead a document that describes a way to leverage resources and initiatives already present. While many residents and businesses departed in recent decades, well-funded museums, medical centers, and universities remain. New stadiums have been built downtown for the Tigers baseball team and the Lions of the National Football League. And even General Motors' much-criticized Renaissance Center, a towering office complex, remains a substantial economic engine. Nearly five thousand people work at the "Ren Cen" every day, and as both Torya Blanchard and Charles Sorel know, they bring their lunch money with them.

Detroit also has leaders who have already begun to bypass the broken city government to support community renewal in specific neighborhoods. The most effective, a coalition of businesses and nonprofit organizations called the University Cultural Center Association, has used its financial and technical expertise to spark hundreds of millions of dollars' worth of activity in Midtown. The UCCA helps businesses and those who want to rehabilitate housing stock obtain grants, loans, tax credits, abatements, and all sorts of technical assistance. The small staff, which will cut through bureaucratic red tape for people who want to bring their ideas and energy to the ailing city, is led by a no-nonsense Detroit native named Sue Mosey, who is so low-profile that her name doesn't appear on the UCCA . People in the know, however, call her the mayor of Midtown.

"Okay, it's true, if you really want to get things done around here I'm the one you can call," says Mosey, who is fifty-five years old. She then adds a bunch of humble caveats. She's a Detroit native who is so in love with the place that she has spent most of her adult life working overtime to make it better, she says. Anyone who has put in so much time would naturally develop the skills and the contacts to get things done. Besides, she was raised in a family with nine kids and educated by Roman Catholic nuns. People with this kind of background are natural pragmatists who see what needs to be done and then get to work.

"The bottom line in Detroit is nothing new," adds Mosey. "However great the culture was when it grew, in its heyday, that culture stayed around way too long." As successive mayors and city councils failed to adapt to the decline in the auto industry and in high-paying jobs, the middle class departed, leaving behind mainly poor people who needed expensive services. With demand for help high and tax revenues sliding, the slow decline of the city became a fast-moving avalanche. But in the chaos groups like the UCCA could act on the neighborhood level, using the power of institutions like Wayne State University, with its thirty-two thousand students, to fight the trend. Like an army defending a country against rebel insurgents, Mosey and her organization can support new businesses that become little safe zones where neighbors can gather, shop, and see a semblance of normal life. Sometimes merely keeping the lights on at a café or the door open at a grocery store can provide enough hope to stabilize a city block.

The work is demanding, and the progress is incremental. "You have to like to live every day in a challenging environment," she admits, "but there are people who thrive in that. Those are the people who are here." These people, who are determined, imaginative, and relentlessly optimistic, inspire Mosey to keep going every day, no matter what the headlines say about layoffs and plant closings.

On the day that the European news crew departed the Inn on Ferry Street, Mosey commandeered a big oak table in the hotel lounge for a long chat about Detroit and its future. She was instrumental in the $8.5 million development of the inn, which was begun in 2000 with the renovation of six historic buildings. It was one of the first big projects Mosey helped direct for UCCA. The inn brought much-needed hotel space to Midtown—and twenty-five jobs. And Mosey doesn't mind playing host to journalists who intended to tell the story of Detroit as an urban wasteland. She has no illusions about conditions in the city and no interest in denying them. But she can also hope that visiting reporters will recognize that successful projects like the inn represent a brighter future.

Mosey is enthusiastic about what she calls "really small, credible efforts" that combine imagination and energy to fill a particular need in the community—whether it's a bookstore, a laundry, or a bakery. "Someone comes to us with an idea that will create maybe three or four jobs and we help them the way someone's mother-in-law might help," she says. The backing comes from UCCA's member organizations and government programs. "The idea is to have organic redevelopment from the bottom up rather than the top down. That way we call the shots ourselves in the local community."

A typical UCCA project is a small company called City Bird, which began as an online retailer for goods, mostly artistic and craft items, made by artisans in Detroit and the Midwest. Founded by siblings Emily and Andrew Linn (she's thirty-two, he's twenty-six), the company did well enough with sales on the Internet to expand to a retail shop. With about $8,000 in cash for stock and marketing help from Mosey they were able to renovate a storefront in an old brick building on Canfield Street next to a bustling brewpub. The space is big enough to provide for retail displays, an art studio, and a stock room and shipping operation. In the first few months of operation, City Bird's sales of jewelry, housewares, and art were already strong enough to pay the rent and create one part-time job. The founders, who grew up in the city, recognize their business success but take more satisfaction from being able to return to Detroit after college to make a contribution to the city's renewal.

"I'm not sure why I feel so tied to Detroit, but I do," confesses Emily Linn. "Being a part of it, having a stake in what happens, matters to me." And while others might see a depressing landscape, she sees opportunity for all sorts of creative projects. One of her favorites is an ongoing art project called The Lot on Cochrane Street. An empty space commandeered in the summer of 2009 by artist Kathy Liesen, it became a site for concerts, dance, displays of all types of art, and community celebration. Like the city's museums and City Bird, The Lot represents a kind of cultural capital that Detroit has in abundance as the low cost of living and welcoming atmosphere draws performers and artists of all types.

The same vibe that makes an artist feel at home transforming a lot into a public art space inspires one of the more creative business options being considered for Detroit: farming within the city limits. More than an oxymoron, urban farming is a way to convert ugly, dispiriting abandoned properties to a productive purpose. Because the crops are raised close to residential areas, practitioners must use the most ecologically advanced techniques for feeding, watering, and waste management. However, urban growers have the advantage of being located smack in the middle of their marketplace, so they do not have to pay for expensive transportation of their produce. They can also use greenhouses to extend their growing season.

So far just a handful of Detroit's empty lots have been transformed into gardens, but they are producing enough to supply local restaurants and other customers who want fresh produce that is organically grown but sold at a competitive price. The growers, some of whom actually scratch out a profit, sell much of their squash, lettuce, and other vegetables at the city's sprawling Eastern Market, as well as at public sales sponsored by Earthworks, a program sponsored by local Capuchin monks. Devoted to meeting basic community needs, the order operated a soup kitchen in Detroit since 1929, and during the Great Recession served as many as two thousand meals per day. Earthworks is an extension of this mission, an attempt to promote new uses for the land that would feed people, change the character of devastated neighborhoods, and raise employment.

"Food is a basic need in any community, and what we are trying to do is bring the producer and the consumer closer together," explains Patrick Crouch, manager of Earthworks. Crouch has a nearly foot-long reddish-brown beard, which covers a green sweater torn in places and patched over in others. He is Detroit's version of a Tennessee Mountain Man. On a cold winter morning Crouch's market has only a few fresh vegetables to offer in addition to locally made preserves and honey, but in warmer months the harvest from local gardens includes everything from asparagus to zucchini and the demand is greater than the supply. Through trial and error Crouch has helped city farmers learn which crops yield the greatest profit—and it's not always high-priced heirloom tomatoes.

"Kale, believe it or not, is a very valuable crop because the cost of labor is minuscule," he notes. Local farmers can also profit by planting unusual varieties that chefs might like to try. One recent hit was a type of turnip so sweet it could be eaten raw, straight out of the ground. Garlic and scallions can be profitable city crops, along with carrots, "but you have to be careful," he adds, "because they can be labor intensive."

Earthworks provides advice and marketing help free to the urban farmers, but Crouch imagines that the handful of properties now under cultivation will soon be profitable without any assistance. He is not alone in his optimism about urban farming. In the winter of 2009–2010 Crouch hosted a number of visitors from other cities who planned to start similar programs. Most prominent is Majora Carter, the dynamic founder of an environmental justice movement in the South Bronx. Carter is working on a national urban farming initiative called American City Farms that would deliver high-quality local produce at a profit. "By organizing local community growers into a worker-owned cooperative, we can help the poor while creating low-impact green jobs. There's tremendous passion among the community farmers here and an abundance of land, making urban agriculture a viable business model in Detroit."

After seven years of experience in Detroit, Crouch estimates that a three-quarter-acre plot could earn a grower $20,000 per year. This analysis lines up with a more hard-nosed assessment of urban agriculture by John Hantz, an investor and entrepreneur who intends to invest up to $30 million of his own money in Detroit to plant orchards and build truck gardens with greenhouses that can produce organic salad veggies eleven months a year.

Hantz, a money manager who oversees $1.3 billion in funds, has already made a personal investment in Detroit's future through the purchase and restoration of nine homes in the historic Indian Village community. He jokingly says he's part of the "I Live Here Movement," which means he is rooted in the city and believes that devotion and hard work will shape a bright future for its people. Hantz Farms would rely on the city to help put together enough land to make the world's largest urban farm. It would be set on a collection of sites, not one large swath of land, and it would be a for-profit, tax-paying enterprise. Agriculture experts at Michigan State University are advising Hantz on environmental issues—some urban plots are too contaminated for farming—and he's hired an international authority in food production to make his idea a reality—Michael Score, a soil scientist and sociologist, whose last project was in the developing nation of Zaire. John Hantz is expecting Score to use the same skills that made farms work in Africa to build a big enough operation in Detroit to supply not just the city but also the surrounding region.

Fanciful as it might sound—growing fruits and vegetables where assembly lines once turned steel into cars—the Hantz Farm proposal quickly gained traction after it was first aired in 2008. Recently elected mayor Dave Bing has taken an active interest, and business leaders who have at last accepted that old-fashioned heavy industry is gone actually see hope in the farm initiative. At the end of 2009 Doug Rothwell of Business Leaders for Michigan asked, "What do you do with a population of 700,000 in a geography that can accommodate three times that much?" In a time of crisis, growing food seems like a remarkably workable concept.

Crisis also makes people think in extraordinary and dramatic ways. Evidence of this arose in early 2010 when roughly a dozen young Detroiters drafted a pledge—"The Detroit Declaration"—that made public their long-term commitment to the city and outlined principles that should guide citizens, businesspeople, and political leaders who hope to shape the city's future. Beginning with the simple statement, "Cities are the greatest expression of civilization," the declaration calls for a "greater, healthier, more vibrant, urban and livable Detroit." The values and priorities set by the signers, among them City Bird founders Emily and Andrew Linn, include

> *Be welcoming and embrace our diversity.* Move beyond mere tolerance of our differences to a true commitment to openness, understanding and cooperation, and the inclusion of multiple perspectives both in our neighborhoods and at the highest decision-making realms.
>
> *Preserve our authenticity.* Celebrate and elevate that which makes Detroit unique—local art, music, food, design, architecture, culture—to build a stronger local economy.
>
> *Cultivate creativity.* Build an infrastructure to foster and promote emerging talent in one of Detroit's greatest strengths,

the arts: music, film, visual arts, design, and other creative industries.

Diversify our economy. Create a culture of opportunity and risk-taking, especially by investing in entrepreneurialism and small, micro-business.

Promote sustainability. Embrace the triple bottom line of economic, social and environmental benefit by retooling our infrastructure with green technology, adapting vacant buildings and open spaces for new uses, and creating healthy, family-supporting jobs.

Enhance quality of place. Create a comprehensive vision for transit-linked, high-quality, walkable urban centers in Detroit.

Demand transportation alternatives. Invest in an integrated regional transportation system that links communities and provides citizens with access to the jobs, health care, and education they need.

Prioritize education, pre-K through 12 and beyond. Create a culture that values the wide, equitable educational attainment necessary to produce both economic opportunity and stronger citizens.

Elevate our universities and research institutions. Create world-class education, new technology, and medical centers to attract and retain students and faculty from around the world.

Enhance the value of city living. Demand public safety and services to improve the quality of life for residents.

Demand government accountability. Reward civic engagement with responsive, transparent, and ethical governmental decision-making.

Think regionally and leverage our geography. Maximize our position as an international border city and a midwestern hub

between Chicago and Toronto. Forge meaningful partnerships between Detroit and its suburbs to compete globally in
the 21st century.

The Detroit Declaration may be a dreamers' document, but it also
points to a path out of the economic wilderness. More than anything, imaginative ideas for sustainable communities and businesses will be the wave of the future American economy, and as
they reflect on this reality the frontiersmen (and women) of Detroit
believe they have competitive advantages over other places. Office
and factory space cost half what they do on the coasts. Michigan
is also a great place to find skilled workers of any type, from
engineers to marketing people, who can be hired for less in part
because they live in a place where the cost of living is low. They
are also willing to devote themselves to projects that would seem
like long-shot gambles in any other environment.

Two blocks off Woodward Avenue, inside an industrial building on Burroughs Street, a half-dozen engineers who work for
Nextek Power Systems gather around a whiteboard where they
have scrawled notes based on readouts from a computer screen.
They are analyzing data on the performance of an innovative
power system based on Thomas Edison's preferred form of electric
supply—direct current.

Also called DC, direct current is the juice that comes out of
batteries, fuel cells, solar panels, and other sustainable energy
sources. Because it is difficult and expensive to transmit over great
distances, Edison's DC lost out to alternating current—AC—
when the electric age began. AC, promoted by George Westinghouse
and Nikola Tesla, allowed for a single huge generating station to
supply power for homes and businesses spread over hundreds if not
thousands of square miles. To make use of this system, lights, appliances, and motors were all built to operate on AC, and it became
the standard.

But the advantages inherent in this system came with some vulnerability. The huge and complex network can be brought down by an isolated incident—even a squirrel chewing through a wire—and big power plants are hugely expensive to build. Also, as much as half the power produced by generating stations is lost as electricity is sent to distant consumers.

As long as fuel prices were low and the grid didn't get overloaded with demand, the AC system worked well enough. Today, demand for power often surpasses the capacity of the big grid, and fluctuating fuel prices make it expensive. Add the problem of global warming caused by the burning of fossil fuels, and you've got three big reasons to seek more efficient, renewable energy systems. Nextek Power Systems staff talk about their technology with the fervor of evangelists because they see how it can be applied to solve these challenges. DC power generated close to where it will be used is almost 100 percent efficient. When the sun or the wind produces it, the fuel cost and carbon emissions are both zero.

Think of it as "organic power or organic electricity," says Nextek CEO Paul Savage. By *organic*, Savage means the electricity is made close to where it's used and is not processed in a way that reduces its power. "You naturally become more efficient," he says, when you see the entire infrastructure for electricity sitting on your roof. Over Paul's shoulder, a sign above the whiteboard proclaims the company's motto: "Edison was Right."

In the past, DC entrepreneurs couldn't take advantage of their superior efficiency because almost everything that used electric power was made to run on AC. Nextek is solving this problem in two ways. First, its systems can work with both types of current. Second, the firm is partnering with firms like Philips, which makes lighting and other equipment. Savage's biggest breakthrough so far has been with Armstrong, which makes a billion ceiling tiles per year. The company's ceiling systems are installed on metal racks. These racks can actually transmit power to lights that operate at low voltage. One big selling point for such a system, besides its efficiency, is safety. "The number one killer of electricians is working on lighting systems," notes Savage, adding, "This is lower current than what recharges your tooth brush."

As he conducts a tour of his lab and engineering shop, Savage speaks with the enthusiasm of an evangelist—and he has made converts of more than a few utility companies and industrial firms. More than a hundred corporations have agreed to participate in a Nextek pilot program to create a small DC power grid serving a one-square-mile section of Detroit, he reports. When completed, it will be the biggest DC network constructed since Edison's time. Just as important, it will put Detroit at the center of a potential revolution in electricity and the so-called green technology that is supposed to produce the jobs of the future. This development thrills Savage's wife and partner, Fay.

A native of the region, Fay Savage comes from a family that goes back four generations in Detroit, but she's not interested in resurrecting the industrial city of old. Instead she imagines a new community powered by imagination and creativity, which is less dependent on a few dominant industries.

"In Detroit the big systems failed," says Fay. By *big systems*, she means the auto industry, government, unions, and other institutions that failed to adapt. But in the wake of their failure, she adds, some "people see this place can be a great city but for new reasons. There's an opportunity here to reimagine and reenvision things." Detroit is the best place in America for anyone interested in bold ideas, she argues. Where else could you build a solar-powered DC system to supply energy at the lowest possible cost to an entire neighborhood? Where else would such an experiment even be possible?

You might say they are all dreamers. From Charles Sorel, who presides over a bit of Paris he planted on a blighted landscape, to

Paul and Fay Savage, who claim kinship with Thomas Edison, Detroit seems to be full of people who refuse to see what everyone else sees. In empty buildings and abandoned lots they see opportunity and hope. In the faces of Detroit's survivors they see a willingness to work, to experiment, to fail, and to succeed. They are not the only ones. An outsider who is open-minded (and open-hearted) cannot help but be inspired by the indestructible spirit of these Detroiters. Clear-eyed and realistic, they do not imagine their city as a renewed industrial powerhouse, but they do believe it can be a productive place where ideas are turned into innovations and communities can provide a graceful, interconnected, and humane quality of life.

Perhaps this is why a Gallup survey recently found that of all the respondents who answered questions about their well-being, farmers were the happiest and felt the most respected, even though they ranked last in pay.[7] This sense of satisfaction likely flows from the control they feel over their time and the sense of purpose they experience in their work. In our survey research, 77 percent of people agreed with the statement, "How I spend my time is more important than how much money I make," with the same number feeling they were "coping" or "living comfortably" on their present income. In Detroit, where people can see an asset's true value, they are not universally discouraged by the prospect of focusing on "needs" rather than mere "wants." Instead we found folks generally agreed with the 80 percent of Americans in our survey who said they were "more optimistic" now about their well-being than two years ago.

Fortunately, a few companies are already connecting to the Detroit ethos. We modeled an index of a basket of "indestructible spirit" firms, those top 10 percent of all brands in our U.S. study that score highest on being optimistic, innovative, progressive, and rugged. In this basket are companies and organizations such as Timberland, Google, General Electric, IBM, Sears/ Craftsman, Levi's, Habitat for Humanity, and the U.S. Army.

And in 2010 their index performance outpaced all other brands on key metrics:

One of my favorite brands	+121 percent
Would recommend to a friend	+113 percent
Worth a premium price	+109 percent
Use regularly	+91 percent
Prefer most	+79 percent

In all, the organizations that show indestructible spirit seem to be tapping into today's mind-set, which says that despite hardship, optimism and strength are the only way forward: only 13 percent of Americans in our BrandAsset Valuator study believe that "looking ahead, my family and I will be worse off than now."

The optimism reflected in these numbers actually guides the choices made by entrepreneurs struggling to make it in places like Detroit. Typical is David Armin-Parcells, who recently opened a wine bar and retail shop over a downtown restaurant. With just $20,000 cash and a lease that promised his landlord a share of the profits, Armin-Parcells was able to get into business with little risk. He takes real delight in the fact that Motor City Wines, which also features live music, is in a former speakeasy that can only be reached by a secret stairway. It is flanked by abandoned buildings, which adds to the playful air of mystery customers feel as they enter the club.

On a cold but sunny day, Armin-Parcells stood near his business on the corner of Woodward and Congress. He couldn't say when he might turn a profit at Motor City Wines, but then, his overhead was so low he could afford to wait. "My parents were optimists and I am one too," says Armin-Parcells. "I love where I live and I already have a great life." Behind him, in the window of a vacant store, his attitude was echoed in bright orange letters placed there by a local artist. It was a simple message that read, "Everything Will Be All Right."

Exactly one month after the European film crew bustled out of the Inn on Ferry Street and flew off with the story of a down-and-out Detroit, a new mayor took the oath of office. Sixty-six-year-old Dave Bing is a different kind of leader. Considered one of the top fifty basketball players in history, Bing spent most of his pro years with the Detroit Pistons and built up such an enormous reservoir of goodwill that when the city needed a leader who wasn't beholden to any traditional power brokers, he was the obvious choice. Smart, strong, and independent, he seemed to understand both the depth of the city's crisis and its potential. He spoke of restoring trust and repairing the damage done by decades of neglect. But he envisioned this as a matter of human values, not capital investment. Indeed, his agenda did not include a single public works project or neighborhood rehabilitation scheme. Instead he called for three shifts in values:

• A tough new ethics policy

• Reduced crime in the city's neighborhoods

• A long-term, big-picture approach to government

As a basketball player, Dave Bing was almost indestructible through sixteen college and pro seasons. Indeed, after suffering a devastating eye injury that doctors thought would end his career, he played five more years with only partial vision. In retirement he overcame early business defeats to build a conglomerate of Detroit-based companies under the umbrella of the Bing Group. Can Dave Bing inspire Detroit to a bright future? Fortunately, he doesn't have to. The city is already filled with people driving toward a renewal. Bing's election is a reflection of their spirit, and if you'd like to join them, all you have to do is stake your claim and make your commitment. If you're lucky, they'll get you started with a good breakfast at Le Petit Zinc.

Chapter Two

Don't Fence Me In:
Dallas, Texas

The Texas sun beats down on a mud-colored landscape. A hundred yards to the south a light breeze ripples the water in a shallow pond. A small herd, maybe twenty head, collects where the land dips toward the entryway to a large structure the color of pale red rock. At high noon an experienced hand shuffles warily to the entrance, unlocks a big door, and lets it swing open. The crowd that had been waiting so calmly presses forward and inside. Most follow the leader, who ambles straight toward the computers, self-help books, and résumé-building guides. After all, this isn't some cattle ranch. It's the Dallas Central Library, where the pond is actually part of a public fountain and the herd is a crowd of patrons eager to access the Job Resource Center.

With unemployment at a ten-year high of almost 9 percent, Dallas and the state of Texas began 2010 burdened by the weight of the Great Recession. Though hardly as crippled as Detroit, where joblessness was three times as high, Dallas was nevertheless confronted by uncomfortable realities as the worst economic downturn since 1929 pushed more people into unemployment than any preceding recession. Instead of the rapid growth and ever-burgeoning wealth symbolized by longhorns and oil wells, the region had seen layoffs at premier companies including Gulfstream, American Airlines, and Blockbuster. But the people here responded like Texans, taking responsibility for themselves and turning to traditional sources of social capital—family, friends, churches, and other local institutions—to find a wealth of support.

At the library, assistant director Miriam Rodriguez walks past the computer stations where men and women type application letters and study job listings. She wears a soft blue jacket, dangly turquoise earrings, and a matching turquoise necklace. Her short brown hair and glasses say "librarian"—but the way she greets patrons, with a warm smile and welcoming words, makes her seem like everyone's favorite aunt. The library is busier than it has ever been, and she likes it that way.

Like most libraries across the county, Dallas Central has seen a surge in visitors that began when the recession started and continued along with it. The Job Resource Center was opened in 2009 in response to the number of requests from people seeking help starting new careers. It has contributed to a 15 percent rise in attendance at library events and a 5 percent increase in the number of books in circulation. Nationwide, library use reached an all-time high in 2010, with the Library of Congress noting that a record 68 percent of Americans now hold library cards.[1] (Community colleges have seen similar increases as people seek to retool themselves to meet the challenge of the new economy.)

In hard times public libraries become a vital resource for people who want to respond to the challenges of the economy, improve themselves, or just find inspiration from a public lecture. In the coming weeks Central will host two different seminars that would appeal to almost anyone feeling the stress of the economy. One presentation on conflict resolution, called "Fight Fairly," would help people to get along in times of stress. The other, called "The Science of Positive Thinking," would offer evidence for the physical and spiritual benefits of optimism even in the face of daunting obstacles.

Although a local teacher would give the positive thinking lecture, Miriam Rodriguez would be qualified to offer it herself. Born in Cuba, she was so ambitious that she began working full time at an academic library when she was just sixteen years old. She fell in love with the work—helping people find the books, articles, and information they needed—and became a full-time professional when she earned a degree in information science from the University of Havana. The work was fulfilling, but she grew frustrated with the limitations of a society isolated by politics and controlled by the Communist Party.

Sponsored by members of her family who were already living in Texas, Rodriguez immigrated to Dallas in 1983. She worked as a baker, practiced English, and never let go of her dream of returning to library work. In 1989 she got a job at a Dallas branch library, where she worked mainly with Spanish-speaking patrons. Rodriguez earned a master's degree in library science at the University of North Texas (in 2005 she was honored as her school's alumna of the year), and she moved up the ranks quickly, becoming an administrator whose multicultural projects won her national recognition. But these days her work draws as much on her experience as a struggling immigrant as it does on her expertise as a librarian.

"We noticed people were asking about jobs and training," says Rodriguez as she describes the creation of the job center. All around her the library buzzes with more activity than anyone would expect on a midweek afternoon.

As Rodriguez recalls, patrons who had been laid off, and many who were just frightened about their future, flooded reference librarians with requests for help with writing résumés and responding to job openings posted on the Internet. Others were already pursuing new degrees so they could make themselves ready to shift into new lines of work. "They say, 'I'm taking classes at a college and I need the Internet to take a test.' Or they are connecting to remote sites such as YouTube EDU to take online college courses." The concept of lifelong education, long touted as the key to future employment, now seems to be accepted at all levels of society. "In the twentieth century people had one or two jobs in a lifetime," adds Rodriguez. "Today it's ten or fifteen. Learning is never finished."

Confronted with the challenge of so many people needing help to upgrade their job prospects, Rodriguez commandeered some space and some computers. "No investment was needed," she explains. "We pulled from the collection. We had computers and we got volunteers. The volunteers were crucial." They also arrived, in big numbers, as soon as Rodriguez put out a call for them. She was not surprised. "Dallas is a place where people take care of people," says Rodriguez. This spirit can be traced to many cultural influences. Living up to its nickname, "the buckle of the Bible belt," the state is steeped in traditional religion, which emphasizes personal responsibility and charity. Many Texans orient their lives around vibrant church communities that become like extended families. In many Hispanic communities, multiple generations live in close proximity, and it's not unusual for friends and neighbors to get directly involved when someone needs help.

According to local experts, volunteerism is strong in Greater Dallas because of the community's deep religious roots. At the Volunteer Center of North Texas, director Julie Thomas reports a surge in interest from individuals who are eager to help others. "This is a faith-based community, and people live what they were taught," she reports. Today, she adds, "life is more uncontrollable. There are terrorist threats, pandemics, and the economy. All of this causes people in their personal time to be more introspective, and realize it's not all about me." This sentiment reflects the hopeful news in data from the Bureau of Labor Statistics, which reported a small rise in the percentage of Americans volunteering during the first year of the Great Recession.[2] At the time the news was announced, many observers suggested that the numbers were swollen by the unemployed, who were turning to volunteerism to give themselves a purpose and a sense of contributing to the greater good.

This love-thy-neighbor ethic is in action at the Central Library in Dallas, where any given hour will find a retired businessman conducting mock interviews with would-be job applicants and student computer experts teaching middle-aged men who have been laid off from their jobs how to use online employment sites.

The urge to help runs so strong in the community that Rodriguez was able to open five more job centers around the city and quickly fill them with helpers. One year into the program, she even had a crop of formerly unemployed folks who had found new positions with the library's help coming back to act as trainers for those who are still in need.

"People have been beat up," adds Rodriguez as she reflects on the faces she sees coming through the door. Among those in crisis are long-time locals who have been caught in the economic downturn and out-of-towners who come from northern states or neighboring Louisiana because they believe Texas is still a land of opportunity. Many of these newcomers are in even worse shape, she notes, and wind up living in shelters for the homeless. For a time, during the very worst of the recession, her staff actually fed meals they brought from home to several families. Although that crisis has eased, they continue to provide a haven of free education, safety, and even entertainment for families that are hard-pressed to maintain the basic necessities of life. The need for these services is especially acute.

"Before, people had money to go on vacation or they went home to Mexico for a while. Many more are staying in Dallas." Instead of roller coaster rides and days at the beach, patrons are checking out books, attending forums, listening to authors reading their books, or attending concerts at the library. Young people can attend programs on everything from the Japanese literary art form called animé to money management. Perhaps the most innovative program is called Every Child Ready to Read, and it connects the library to future patrons even before they are born.

Developed, as Rodriguez says, to help break the cycle of inter-generational poverty, the ready-to-read program trains nurses at a dozen public health clinics who talk to pregnant women about the way that reading to a child helps both bonding and brain development. After a child is born, she adds, "The doctors who give vaccinations also prescribe reading to your child." The hope is that kids from poorer families will get the same exposure to books that children in middle-class families typically receive and will arrive at public school ready to keep pace with their classmates.

Funding for Ready to Read has remained steady, despite the recession, because donors favor grassroots programs that have an obvious impact on the community. They are also loyal to the library and its mission. For example, David J. Haemisegger and Nancy Nasher, the couple who own the region's most upscale shopping center—North Park Mall—were so impressed by the Dallas library's work that they donated a large space inside the mall for a children's library. (Actually it's leased to the library at $1 per year.) Called Bookmarks, the mall library hosts reading hours, puppet shows, and other events. It is the most popular attraction at the mall, which is also known for public art installations and cultural events ranging from magic shows to performances by string quartets.

Like Nasher and Haemisegger, many Dallas businesspeople and corporations have maintained donations to the library even as other nonprofits have seen losses in gifts because of the recession. Indeed, in one survey after another, local officials have found that the library ranks third (behind police and fire services) in popularity. This confidence, which appears in one American city after another, makes the library one of the few institutions that retains the trust of the people at a time when every other pillar of society, public or private, seems to be suffering in the eyes of the average citizen. (In early 2010 a majority expressed skepticism about the leaders of government, finance, industry, and the media, which as of 2009 enjoyed the confidence of less than one-third of the people polled.)

In this skeptical environment, libraries have defied those who predicted their demise at the start of the Internet Age. Instead they have become hubs for community activities and resources for individuals who want to learn new skills, advance their education, or conduct a job hunt. The support libraries provide free of charge has led to record-setting attendance at library events nationwide, along with increases in library visits that are so dramatic that people are actually wearing out the carpets in front of checkout desks. Libraries are so important to this community that when the recession forced reductions in the budget provided by taxes, patrons jammed public meetings to oppose any cut in services. Ultimately a compromise was worked out that leaves at least one library with a job center available seven days a week. Other services were reduced, but whenever possible programs that benefit families, especially mothers and children, were kept in place. For them, the library is a neighborhood sanctuary that provides relief from the stress of daily life in the Great Recession and a kind of enrichment that had nothing to do with dollars and cents.

As she considers how individuals are helped most by those closest to them, Rodriguez turns her thoughts to her own family. Her son-in-law, husband to her daughter (also named Miriam), was laid off from his job months ago. "With that comes shame and self-esteem issues," she recalls, "but there were also people who knew and wanted to protect the family." A plumber by trade, her son-in-law eventually decided to strike out on his own. Family pulled together to make sure he had a vehicle, and neighbors— some of whom weren't quite ready for bathroom renovations— went ahead and hired him. These jobs, which were both business arrangements and expressions of kindness, allowed him to establish a record of successful projects and show his work to future clients.

The openheartedness shown by Rodriguez's neighbors and friends recalls the unity that became a hallmark of other stressful periods in American history, most notably the Great Depression and World War II. During the Depression, hand-me-down clothes circulated from family to family, and charity was often delivered in the form of a meal handed out a back porch door. In the war years, rationing prompted people to share car rides and to pool coupons for meat and sugar in order to have modest dinner parties. During the Great Recession the Rodriguez family has grown closer by reviving old traditions—like Sunday dinners and board game parties—and creating new ones.

"We are definitely spending more time together, and my two girls are pulling our recipes. They used to go to all the restaurants. Now they go to Amazon.com and buy cookbooks. That's funny." More touching, to this mother of adult daughters, is the new respect she feels as her daughters recognize the struggle and sacrifice she endured to become an American. They now enjoy telling stories about the ancient (1960) Chevy that their father kept in running condition in the years when money was tight. "And my heavy accent, which was a bother to them when they were in school, well, now they appreciate that I sacrificed and learned my skills."

A trace of Cuba does linger in Miriam Rodriguez's voice, and this accent keeps her connected to a life story that begins in a place of hardship and struggle, and includes a great deal of striving for both autonomy and a sense of belonging in her new country. It is the quintessential American tale and holds timeless lessons. It is also being echoed across the Dallas area, as Texans confront new economic realities with their own definitions of success and a good life. They are doing this by reinventing themselves and embracing attitudes and values that often resonate with the past.

As we saw in Detroit, hard times have reinforced the virtues of practical skills, doing it yourself, and mending and repairing in order to make things last. On the national level, this trend is supported by real data. At the start of 2010, for example, the median age of cars on the road in the United States reached 10.6 years, the highest ever. America Online noted that the quality of cars, especially those made in America, is so high that many owners aim to keep them for 200,000 miles or more. According to the research firm NPD, 94 percent of consumers are planning to do the same amount or more amount of maintenance on their vehicle next year, and 56 percent of people intend to hold on to their car "until it dies." Lonnie Miller of the auto industry watchdog R. L. Polk & Co. put it more colorfully when he told AOL, "People are cooling their jets on buying new vehicles."[3]

The shift toward what we call "durable living" has powered the rise of an entire movement of makers, people who trade ideas for creating their own tools, machines, and technologies, attend giant "Maker Faires" in cities across the country, and devour magazines like *Popular Science* and the new magazine called *Make*. Founded by Phil Torrone, *Make* is published out of an office in New York that also houses Adafruit Industries, which sells a catalog full of do-it-yourself kits that help people make useful stuff like an iPod charger for pennies. Torrone and his partner Limor Fried promote what they call a "citizen engineer" approach to life that has attracted 100,000 subscribers for the magazine and millions of visitors to their Web sites. Their open-source approach means that every design and invention created in their community is made available free, and participants help each other in the way that neighbors once offered advice to their fellow backyard mechanics as they leaned over an engine.

"We went through a couple of dumb decades when people just didn't know how things worked," explains Torrone. (An intense fellow with a shock of long black hair, Torrone resembles the actor Johnny Depp.) "We're trying to show them that it's not as daunting as you think," he says. "If you come up with an idea, there are people who will help you make it work."

Indeed, new technologies like MakerBot, an inexpensive open-source 3D printer, make it possible for all sorts of people to create products on their own. "Hobbyists wind up realizing they can make things for a living," adds Limor Fried, an engineer who trained at the Massachusetts Institute of Technology. With the help of her Web site, DIY inventors and at-home manufacturers can offer their wares and accept credit card payments. Today their community includes retired engineers from Boeing and NASA who mentor young electrical enthusiasts. "We bring people together," she says. She and Torrone also help people gain confidence despite economic conditions.

Their success has overwhelmed their home and office loft, which is cluttered with laser-cutting machines, transistors, and packing boxes. Soon they plan to give up their bedroom for office space and sleep in their walk-in closet. After all, the spirit of the maker community is to tinker and optimize instead of sleep. And on occasion, tweak the nose of the establishment. Torrone recounts when he and Limor Fried went to a U.S. Department of Homeland Security conference and an analyst presented a vomit-inducing flashlight weapon called "the dazzler." Filled with pulsating LED lights, it promised to incapacitate an assailant for a mere $1 million each. Phil says, "We thought this was a terrible waste of taxpayer money. Plus the guy was kind of creepy." So they countered with their own "open source non-lethal weapons" project, featuring what they called "the bedazzler." The couple released the source code to their community at a price of $250, using Arduino software and a gutted giant flashlight from Sears.

America Retools

Eighty-four percent (of the people surveyed) agreed with the statement, "These days I feel more in control when I do things myself instead of relying on others to do them for me." Other key results from the 2009–10 BrandAsset Valuator survey:

- Sixty-five percent say, "Since the recession I am interested in learning new skills, so I can do more myself and rely less on others."

- Eighty-five percent agree with the statement, "Now I tend to be more of a DIY person."

- Seventy-two percent agree with the statement, "Nowadays I am more open to paying more for higher quality goods that last longer and won't fall apart."

- Sixty-nine percent agree with the statement,
  "Nowadays I am willing to repair things (shoes,
  handbags, appliances, and so on) so I don't have to
  replace them."

The results exhibit hopeful signs that America is moving from an acquisitive to an inquisitive society. The shift from dependency to self-reliance is achieved through the acquisition of new skills and knowledge, along with a philosophy of continuous betterment. In 2009 the Lone Star State's postsecondary student body reached an all-time high, with three-quarters of new students enrolling in community colleges.[4] Community colleges now account for more than half of all college students in Texas. While Americans cut back in other areas, they didn't stop spending on learning. In fact, spending on tuition, continuous education, textbooks, and private, community, and secondary graduate schools experienced the largest growth rate of all discretionary spending (followed by reading, personal insurance, and health care). Even the stock prices of education companies such as Pearson, Kaplan, and Devry surged by nearly 20 percent in 2009, while museum attendance rose by nearly two-thirds.[5]

In BrandAsset Valuator we examined the 2009 performance of a basket of "retooling" companies, those that are in the top 10 percent in our data on being "helpful," "reliable," "educational," and "durable." They include mentors such as LeapFrog, Curves, Weight Watchers, and Apple, as well as DIY brands like Home Depot, Craftsman, and DeWalt (tools). The basket also included brands that stand for vigilance such as DieHard and ADT home security systems, or durability like John Deer and Ford F150. Finally, we added betterment brands like the *Extreme Makeover* television show and Oprah's Book Club. And again, their performance against all others is notable:

Would recommend to a friend	+249 percent
Use regularly	+234 percent
Worth a premium price	+210 percent
Prefer most	+196 percent
Like and respect	+102 percent

All the retooling trends are national, and many benefit from advances in technology that have dramatically reduced the cost of communications, advertising, product development, and even manufacturing. In early 2010 *Wired* magazine reported on the extreme edge of this phenomenon as it profiled inventors and entrepreneurs who were making money and creating jobs by manufacturing custom-made goods, including automobiles, robots, and motorcycles. The most sophisticated among these industrial revolutionaries practiced "crowd sourcing" to get design concepts, and studied the bespoke methods used by the most efficient factories in China.

Of course a retooler doesn't need to learn high-tech tricks or travel thousands of miles to study complex industrial processes to succeed in the new economy. Sometimes, all it takes is the willingness to make something old—and very essential—new again.

If you want to see how the Great Recession has inspired people in Dallas to retool their lives, you can start with both the chicken *and* the egg. You find them in hundreds if not thousands of backyards, where do-it-yourselfers have built coops, installed hens, and begun harvesting their own eggs. At most of these homes you'll also see the modern version of the old Victory Gardens: small plots that produce crops all year long. It's all part of a more practical lifestyle that has emerged out of economic necessity and a desire to shift from take to make, or from consuming goods to producing goods. "People are scared," explains Leslie Halleck, who keeps a "Beware of Attack Gardener" sign on the wall behind her desk.

"They are scared to spend money and scared about losing money. We live in a fear-based culture."

One solution to this fear, for Halleck, is a flock of hens named Einstein, Honkers, Pecker, Eunice, and Phyllis, a Polish chicken with a shock of white feathers that makes her look like the comedienne Phyllis Diller. She bought them in 2008, as the Great Recession gained momentum, and then watched as people all over her neighborhood, a part of East Dallas called Little Forest Hills, followed suit. But no one would have noticed a serious social trend was under way if a black-and-white Dominique hen hadn't wandered away from her home. A homeowner who alerted the gardening writer at the *Dallas Morning News* discovered the lost chicken.

City officials got into the act, and pretty soon they were getting anonymous complaints about henhouses all over Dallas. Neighbors who were mostly worried about property values also raised concerns about bird flu, noise, and the potential hazards of chicken waste.

As Halleck recalls it, and the local press confirms, the chicken controversy blossomed in part because reporters love writing about animals and just saying the word "chicken" over and over again can make almost anyone laugh. It was eventually resolved when city officials realized that no ordinance banned backyard hens and that they have long been considered an accepted element of residential gardens. A hastily adopted rule against roosters eliminated concerns about noise, and nuisance laws assured that other complaints could be addressed on a case-by-case basis. Halleck says she was pleased by the outcome, and also intrigued by the outpouring of support she received. Many agreed with her argument that when Texans become afraid of livestock, there's something wrong with them.

It turns out that Dallas was at the center of a national boom in backyard egg production. As the *Dallas Morning News* reported, the area was one of the leading markets in the country for the almost-ready-to-lay birds called pullets.[6] One local supplier, Daniel Probst (of a little farming community called Poetry, Texas), reported a fivefold increase in sales between 2008 and 2009. Backyardchicken.com, a support group based in California, told the paper it was adding a hundred new members per day to rolls that already included thirty-five thousand people. In the meantime, cities and towns across the country were scrambling to craft rules governing the home-based layers.

When the legalities were settled, at-home egg-farmer Halleck recognized that the trend was also an opportunity. In the spirit of "teaching a man to fish" she could preach the gospel of self-sufficiency by offering classes on hen-keeping at her small business, North Haven Gardens. So many people wanted to learn about keeping chickens that her first Saturday class drew the biggest crowd her store had ever seen. With the parking lot overfilled, cars spilled onto the shoulder of North Haven Road. More than a hundred people crowded into a makeshift classroom to hear about the economic and nutritional benefits of backyard chicken-keeping and to learn about the care and feeding of hens, which turn out to be surprisingly low maintenance. Ten minutes a day is more than enough time for feeding and watering. Waste management can be handled in two or three scooping sessions per week, and the result, if composted properly, yields the best garden fertilizer around at an even better price.

An avid chicken-keeper, Halleck can wax poetic over the perfect cycle of feed, fertilizer, and vegetable production she achieves in her backyard. She has even turned her little Chihuahua into a helper who helps round up "the girls" when it's time for them to move from the yard into their coop. But even she was taken aback by the level of excitement at that first chicken class and the ongoing interest. Chicken supplies have become a profit center at her store, which has seen a 15 percent increase in traffic. And every weekend, Daniel Probst trucks in a hundred birds and sells every one.

Eight months after the chicken craze began, Halleck had developed a theory about what happened. It was the pits of the recession, she recalls, and people were wondering, "How horrible can it get?" She adds, "They have lost their jobs or their hours have been cut and they think, 'Maybe I can grow my own food.'" In fact, 23 million Americans grew their own food in 2009, a figure that represents an increase of almost 20 percent over 2008.[7] Home canning enjoyed a revival as well: sales of preserving products grew by 30 percent in 2008, according to the American Ball Jar Corporation. Seen in this light, a homeowner who decided to build a coop with some two-by-fours and chicken wire is actually responding to crisis in a functional way. "This is how you can take control of how you live your life," she continues, "it's fun and healthy and good for you."

The good-for-you part includes the soul, which may explain why it drew the attention of Rod Dreher, a conservative Christian blogger who writes a column for the religiously oriented Web site Beliefnet.com. Dreher writes about religion, economics, and what he has called "granola conservatism." He praised and then joined Halleck's grow-your-own movement as part of a lifestyle shift practiced by younger adults, especially those with families, who are trading the stress of highly competitive and now declining professions for low-cost rural living that is more consistent with the Christian view of stewardship for the Earth. Instead of granite countertops and home gyms this life offers daily doses of dirt and a schedule governed by the seasons and the weather.

The *Wall Street Journal* noted the flight to the farm in December 2009 when it reported that rural communities were seeing an influx of twenty- to forty-year-olds with families. At a time when other investments seem unreliable and jobs only temporary, they see farmland as both a source of income and more permanent wealth. Real estate agents who were seeing double-digit growth in sales across rural America cited these factors. This shift was powered, at least in part, by the romantic view of farm life held by most people who have never shoveled manure or built a wire fence. (Americans have always felt affection for the yeoman farmer ideal described by Thomas Jefferson.) And the *Journal* reported dutifully on the comical mistakes—trying to cook a rooster was one—made by these pioneers.

But behind the fantasies of a rural idyll the paper also found commitment to a social and economic life that might be sustained without regard for the vicissitudes of the global economy. Shane Dawley and his family, the people who tried to eat their rooster, also failed with their first vegetable crop, but they diagnosed the problem—acidic soil—and will plant again. Dawley's motivation runs deep, just like the feeling that drove Jesse Pltacek from Kuwait, where he made a solid salary working for an international company, to a sixty-two-acre farm in Montana. When asked why, he told the *Journal*, "I started to think about things, about what's real and what's not real."

———————

Real is a multibillion-dollar company that goes bankrupt.

Real is losing your job and having no options for a new one.

Real is a 50 percent cut in income.

Mike Courtney and Gary Watson faced these realities as their employer, the giant consulting firm Bearing Point, began to founder in 2007. As the Great Recession hit, they sought refuge in a similar company, Slalom Consulting, but that move only forestalled the inevitable. "People would ask, 'Is this company going to be stable?' and I was noticing that IBM laid off ten thousand," recalls Courtney. "That old level of security is not available anymore. Now, at the drop of a hat you're gone. That's true even with major institutions like banks that have been trusted for a hundred years and are gone, and with people's nest eggs too."

As business fell off at Slalom in mid-2009, Courtney was first required to lay off Watson. The decision was painful because the two men were not just close colleagues but friends. A kind of dynamic duo of consulting, they shared a can-do philosophy about life and had encouraged each other in the long climb to the top of their business. As similar as brothers, they even chuckle at the same things, which is what happens as Courtney recalls that he didn't have to feel bad for very long because he lost his job, too. In the fall of 2009 he packed up the pictures and knickknacks in his office and headed for home. There he gathered his family and began a long discussion, one that would be resumed many times, about their priorities and their way of life. Fortunately he had reason to be optimistic, especially when he thought about how his friend's family reacted when they learned that the breadwinner was coming home, perhaps for good.

"They had said, 'We don't need half the stuff we have, and we don't need to do half the stuff we do,'" says Watson. "The whole family decided to dial back and focus on what we need, not what we want." This spirit was probably best illustrated when his son began talking about getting a dog. For months when the boy asked, "Where do dogs live?" Watson had teased him by saying, "In other people's houses." This time he didn't have to say anything because his son said, "I think we should wait to get a dog after your work gets settled down."

Watson was surprised by how little his kids worried about themselves and how concerned they were about him. "Kids are such needy creatures that I was surprised they were so selfless. But they wanted to know, 'Are you going to be happy?' They knew there was going to be a big transition from being a consulting executive to working in your own house. They kept asking me, 'Are we going to drive you nuts?'"

Courtney nods as he listens to his friend talk. He and Watson have known each other as friends and colleagues for more than fifteen years and spent many a night on the road together dining with clients and telling corporate war stories. But on this Wednesday night at a favorite restaurant on the north side of the city, their stories are drawn from family life, church, and their attempts to build new businesses. As empty beer bottles—a local brew called Shiner Bock—pile up on the table, the two men marvel at the pleasures of life at half their usual income.

The irony, says Courtney, is that change was forced upon him by the job market. When things looked bleak, he started working his network to line up the next set of opportunities. "But for the first time in my career," he says, "I didn't have three opportunities I could pull the trigger on in a moment's notice. It caused me to stop and think, 'Why am I doing this? Do I really enjoy it?' I do it because it's what I've done, for almost twenty years, and I'm most likely to get the bills paid. But is it really what I want?"

A tall, lean, and weathered man whose voice and manner proclaim "Texas," Courtney broke out of the "job" box and designed a three-track approach to his working life. One has him working the phones and pounding the pavement to drum up clients as a freelance management consultant. The second track takes him to firms that do the same kind of work, where he might be asked to jump into projects. The third leads, he hopes, to a nonprofit organization that will use the Internet to build social connections for people trying to do good works. This last item on the agenda is Courtney's favorite, but he's wary of discussing it in detail. He doesn't want to jinx himself or give away the idea. However, there's no hiding his excitement. He's certain that he understands the current business environment and believes the key to his success will be found in the right mix of doing good while making profits.

"You can't make money at the cost of the wrong thing, including hurting the environment, damaging the community, being negative." The irony, he points out, is that companies are not as committed as they once were to the long-term welfare of their employees, but the marketplace is going to make them worry about the well-being of their customers and the communities where they do business. Referring to the respect and esteem of his community, Courtney adds, "I want to earn more than money." To explain that "more," he mentions the long-established concept of the "triple bottom line," which adds measures of social and environmental impact to a company's performance rating. To this he would add a fourth concept, "the bottom-line goals" of the nonprofit and social service groups he wants to serve. If he's able to help them reach their mark, whether it means serving more meals to the hungry or raising church attendance, he'll feel successful.

Sitting beside Courtney, Gary Watson nods when his friend talks about service to others. Although he had adjusted to the new economy with a combination of family belt-tightening and diverse freelance interests, Watson had struggled a bit in his search for clients and a stable routine as a work-at-home dad. He got some help when wealthy family members asked him to manage their investment portfolios, and a volunteer job at church, leading a capital construction fund drive, gave him a chance to work with others in a group, something he always enjoyed doing. Soon he was also doing financial counseling at his church as part of a new ministry. This work is being done at churches across the South as pastors and laypeople try to help the laid-off and underemployed reduce their expenses, learn new skills, and connect with prospective employers. All this is done in an environment that also stresses prayer and faith.

At church, and in casual encounters with friends and family, Watson has been struck by the more acute struggle endured by people who were less ready to approach a world where secure jobs and retirement are in doubt. Rounder, balder, and more soft-spoken than his friend Courtney, Watson has clearly taken to heart the suffering around him. "We have a responsibility to people who are not as comfortable freelancing but are comfortable being cogs," he says earnestly. Describing many of the people he works with as a volunteer career and financial counselor at his church, Watson says, "They beat their heads against the wall, applying for jobs, applying for jobs, applying for jobs. They don't look to the side and consider options."

In Watson's experience, suddenly unemployed workers have to reach a certain breaking point where they are willing to abandon old assumptions and try something new. When they reach this point and become more open to suggestions, he is able to help them see how their skills may qualify them for work they never imagined doing. A retail store manager, for example, may find that experience staffing a store and keeping track of inventory will also work in the parts department of an auto dealership. In other cases, clients at the church-counseling center may need to go back to school or consider a kind of semiretirement based on a scaled-back lifestyle and wise husbanding of what may be left of their assets.

Determined to help those folks who may have the most trouble adjusting to the new economy, Watson is organizing a service that will provide them with budget and investment advice, free of charge. He plans to fund this activity with a traditional tithe—10 percent charitable donation—from the revenues generated by his own family's investments. Tithing comes naturally to him since he was raised in a family that practiced it at church, and he has continued the tradition as an adult.

A different religious term comes to Mike Courtney's mind when he thinks about the values shift that has occurred in his family and friends. He calls it an "awakening." Historically, conservative Christians have looked forward to "awakenings" that signal a revival of religious belief, practices, and energy. Three "Great Awakenings" are recognized in American history, and in each case these revivals of faith and tradition led to profound social developments.[8] The First Great Awakening presaged the American Revolution. The Second Great Awakening seeded the abolition movement and the Civil War. The Third Great Awakening is credited with inspiring Progressive reforms, including child labor laws, Prohibition, and voting rights for women. Courtney hopes that a Fourth Great Awakening will occur so that Americans can save their country from decline. Everyone needs to say, "I can't wait for the government to write me a check. I'm going to have to go out and make something happen," he adds.

Courtney isn't sure yet whether the majority of the nation will adopt his attitude, but he can point to the small-scale awakening of old-fashioned values that has swept through his household. "Now my eleven-year-old will do chores for money, and my eight-year-old is dying to do a lemonade stand because he made $30 with one once and wants to do it again to get a video game. But this is the most telling moment," says Courtney. He sets down his Shiner Bock beer and lowers his voice, like he's telling a story around a campfire:

"My four-year-old daughter went with her grandparents to play putt-putt, you know, miniature golf. At the end there's a way to win a free game. It was some deal where you have to get a hole-in-one or something. Well, they won a free game and my Mom said, 'Good for you. You'll get a free game when you guys come back.' My daughter said to her, 'You know, we don't have that much extra money to play miniature golf. We might have to wait a while till we can afford that.' I was very proud of her that she realized things cost money and you can't put down a piece of plastic and magically do whatever you want to do."

Chores. Lemonade stands. Delayed gratification. For the American family that got lost in the credit binge, these developments may indeed signal an awakening. And if it is being repeated in other homes—and Gary Watson says it is—then it suggests that life in many households will actually be better because of the shift that finds folks spending less money but more time and energy on their relationships. Watson reports that he used to feel disconnected from the family a little, as though it was his job to make the money but then fade into the background. Now he sees his children every day. His own parents have moved into a nearby home, and they've bought a big dining table (at a consignment store) so everyone in the family can sit together for dinner. "We say a blessing," says Watson, because he believes he has much to be thankful for.

Courtney and Watson speak with gratitude about the lessons they have learned in the Great Recession. Necessity and crisis forced them both to examine their values and lifestyle and lead their families in a new direction. They found greater happiness than they knew before and, ironically, greater professional satisfaction. As Watson says, they are learning that the techniques they taught others when they were consultants really do work for them in real business terms. This realization validated the work they had done for others and gave them confidence as they faced the future. As in Detroit, the stress and challenge of the new economy seem to inspire creativity and entrepreneurial initiatives. One slight difference, in Dallas, is that individuals often cite their conservative Christian faith as one of their major inspirations. Rather than having a working life, a family life, and a church life, people are seeking more integrated, holistic lives, with spirituality and a renewed sense of priorities guiding their choices. Seventy-seven percent of Americans in BrandAsset Valuator now agree with the statement, "How I spend my time is more important than how much money I make." But when it comes to their determination to promote sustainable, local economic activity, no one shows more pride than these Texans.

Twenty miles north of Dallas, a no-nonsense woman with short blonde hair patrols the aisle of Legacy Books, a bookstore that is almost as big as a supermarket. Teri Tyler wears an earpiece and microphone that allow her to communicate instantly with any staff member on duty, which comes in handy when a customer asks for a title. Tyler is serious about customer service, and though she keeps 110,000 books in stock, the technology means she can connect a customer with just the right item in a matter of minutes. This responsiveness is one of the key values she has employed to buck a national trend—the demise of independent bookstores—in a time of severe economic crisis.

"I worked for Barnes and Noble and Borders for twenty years," explains Tyler. "The biggest difference [between a big chain and her store] is we have more control in an independent store, we can make a decision in our store very quickly. If someone wants to have a birthday party in the café when a children's author is here we can say, 'Yes.'"

This freedom is what Tyler thought about over the years as she designed the perfect bookstore in her mind and imagined what it could be. As the Great Recession approached, she agreed to open the new store for investors who wanted to create a first-class indy bookstore—comparable to the best in any big city—on the Texas plains. They found a highly visible corner spot in a busy Plano shopping center. The store opened in November 2008, just as economists were putting the final touches on reports that would make the crisis official. Remarkably, through a combination of service and design—the gleaming building may be the most striking bookstore in the country—she has managed to make revenues grow steadily, month by month.

Although much larger, and equipped with free wireless Internet and a café that serves beer and wine as well as varieties of caffeine, Legacy Books functions much like an old-fashioned independent bookshop. Customers get very close attention and are encouraged to make the store a kind of social hub. The connection Tyler feels with customers and the sense that she is responsible for her own destiny compensate, to some degree, for the 40 percent drop in income Tyler accepted when she left the big chains. But she talks more about the good feeling that comes from supporting the economy of her local community.

"If you shop in a Borders, your tax dollars go to Delaware. At Barnes and Noble they go to New York," she says. "Ours go to Plano, Texas." Tyler says her desire to keep both tax dollars and profits local is shared by many people in Texas who were stunned by corporate scandals like the Enron bankruptcy and have lost trust in distant officials whether they reside in Washington or Austin.

"People pay taxes and don't see where their money goes or don't like where it's going," says Tyler. When times were good, middle-class folks wouldn't pay attention, but now that money is tight, she says, "The whole center [of American society] is much more aware of the taxes they are paying and what they are doing with that money. What local independent businesses have done is say,

'Almost 35 percent more of your tax dollars spent at my location stays in the community.'"

This "Don't mess with Texas" (or taxes) attitude is especially appealing in a place where people have a strong attachment to their history, culture, and geography. With a huge supply of open, buildable land, and population growth fueled by immigration, Texas actually looks and feels a lot like the expansive America that has embraced waves of newcomers and grown strong as a result. The Texas economy would rank fifteenth in the world if it were an independent country. It has more Fortune 500 companies than any other state in the nation. And as the occasional—if hardly serious—rumblings about secession suggest, Texans also have strong feelings about their own competence. These are hardly unmerited. The state has a very low tax burden, compared with others, and the cost of living there is 25 percent lower than the national mean. The recession was milder in Texas than most parts of the country, and job losses came at just half the national rate. The Milken Institute, which tracks economic conditions across the country, suggests Texas's resilience is a function of its business-friendly climate, rising demand for gas and oil services, a vibrant technology hub, and a lucky lag in terms of housing overdevelopment.[9]

Of course Texas has problems—it ranks low in education and high in crime, for example—but it also has a culture that stresses adaptability and personal responsibility, which may partly explain why so many Texans bypass whining in the face of a crisis and go straight to transforming how they view their own lives and priorities. "From my experience, people are falling out of corporate jobs and downsizing and deciding to do their passion and really making a business out of that, whether it's a restaurant or a service or a bookstore.

"Has there been a values shift?" asks Tyler. "Yes."

Where once Tyler traveled widely to help manage a big chain of bookstores, she's now intimately involved with just one location, one set of employees, and one community. She relishes the deeper relationships that come from this more rooted life and the opportunity it gives her to promote her passion—literacy. "We did an event yesterday that had 350 parents and children and educators in the store," she explains. This reading promotion didn't bring a flood of profit to the store, but it supported parents, teachers, and kids in a way that could yield long-term benefits. It also allowed Tyler to put her passion to work for her community.

Similar acts of almost-random support for community can be seen every day, all over greater Dallas. And, Tyler insists, Texans don't limit their generosity to their families, churches, or local communities. After the 2010 earthquake in Haiti, she heard lots of people say they were forgoing purchases and dinners at restaurants, so they could donate money to the relief effort. Listening to her, and watching how Texans both reinvent themselves and maintain a sense of responsibility, it's hard to deny the positive shift in values that is emerging at the grassroots level in the wake of the Great Recession.

Chapter Three

THE BADGE
OF AWESOMENESS:
BOSTON, MASSACHUSETTS

"Before we go, can I get you something to drink? How about a tonic?"

With a single word choice, Jon Norton reveals himself to be a man of a certain age and of a certain place. The use of "tonic" instead of "soda" or "pop" is a mainstay for older residents of the most tradition-bound city in America—Boston, Massachusetts. Since Norton is a native and almost seventy years old, he can make a natural claim on this old-fashioned lingo. As a retired school-teacher in an era of economic crisis, he might also be expected to adopt a cautious routine, living modestly on his pension and enjoying the friendships built over a lifetime of service in his hometown of Everett, a suburb of triple-decker houses and winding streets that lies beside the Mystic River.

"Yes, I could have settled for a nice quiet life," confesses Norton, as he tours Everett by car on a cold winter morning. Well over six feet tall, he wears a plaid flannel shirt and green corduroy pants but no coat to protect him against below-freezing temperatures. He says he keeps warm by staying in motion. He adds, "When I discover something interesting, I like to go with it for a while, see where it takes me. I go with the flow."

The flow, in Norton's case, isn't an abstract figure of speech but instead the actual flow of garbage—or to put it nicely, "solid waste"—generated daily by Everett's roughly fifteen thousand households. With a land area of less than four square miles, the city collects as much as forty tons of solid waste on a given trash day. For years less than 10 percent of this burden was recycled, leaving a substantial amount to be disposed of at landfills or incinerators at a cost of roughly $75 per ton. With landfills and other trash-handling facilities already overburdened, the cost to taxpayers and the environment rises every year.

As an elementary school teacher, Norton had devoted many hours to lessons on Earth Day, the environment, and the virtues of conservation and recycling. As chairman of the city conservation commission he is deeply concerned about his community, and devoted to preserving its quality of life. And as a true New Englander, he has always been proud of the region's history as the cradle of American democracy, where civic duty is a serious matter.

"Do you know we still have three newspapers in our city," he says proudly, "and we're the only city in the country with a bicameral legislature?"

Norton is right. In what some may consider a spasm of democratic excess, the city's founders created both a board of aldermen and a "common council." With twenty-five representatives in all, the people of Everett may have a more representative city government than any on earth. They also tend to feel a sense of ownership about their community. For Jon Norton, this impulse led him to investigate the state of recycling in Everett. He discovered that in a good week barely 5 percent of the households in the city put out anything for the voluntary recycling program.

Jon Norton's initial inquiry led to a job as director of recycling for the city. The half-time position helped Norton cope with the Great Recession and gave him a compelling new career at a time when most people wind down their lives. But he had trouble making real progress on behalf of the environment or the city budget, which was ever more strained by the cost of hauling and dumping waste. More pressure came as the bursting of the real estate bubble, which preceded the recession, sent property values and tax collection plummeting downward. (After peaking at just over $300,000, the median home price in Everett fell to below $170,000.) Like many municipalities, Everett also faced cuts in state aid and rising obligations ($1 million per year) for health insurance and pension payments.

With his beloved community under all this stress, Norton attended the annual meeting of the Massachusetts Municipal Association (MMA), a nonpartisan group that serves city, town, and village governments. There, among the dozens of seminars and display booths, Norton found Ron Gonen. Not quite half Norton's age, Gonen had come to Massachusetts to promote a new business called RecycleBank that seemed, at first, too good to be true.

Working with a partner he had known since high school, Gonen had designed a system that involved outfitting trash trucks with lifters that could weigh the contents of specially designed plastic containers. The containers would be tagged with computer chips identifying the households they served. According to the plan, as trucks and a pair of handlers worked their way up and down city streets, they would record the amount of recyclables in each can and credit the owners. Every month a simple computer program would deposit a weight-based credit in each recycler's account. Those points could be used for discounts on products or services. (The companies honoring the points, Gonen figured, would be happy for the business and the goodwill that comes with encouraging a "green" project.)

Aid from Columbia University, where Gonen was working on a master's degree in business administration, had helped him turn his idea into a workable technology. After lining up a bunch of points partners—Coca-Cola, Starbucks, Home Depot, and others—Gonen asked city officials in his hometown of Philadelphia, where he was raised by a single mother, to let him run tests in one upscale area and one middle-class neighborhood. Within six months, 90 percent of the households in both neighborhoods were devoted recyclers. Prior to the test, recycling was practiced by about a third of the homes in the rich community and less than 10 percent of those in the modest one.

At the MMA convention Gonen explained his experience in Philadelphia and a few other communities that had adopted his program, and Jon Norton peppered him with polite (he always called him Mr. Gonen) but persistent questions. Was the technology reliable? Were waste haulers willing to cooperate? Were the corporations that awarded points in it for the long haul? Gonen gave him positive answers to all these questions, but saved the best part for last—the RecycleBank program came with no start-up cost for municipalities and was guaranteed to reduce both the volume of waste going to landfills and the city budget, by substantial amounts.

How could Gonen deliver what he promised? The key was in the incentives for households—they could earn $25 worth of credits per month—which would produce valuable recyclable cardboard, plastic, glass, and metal while simultaneously reducing the number of tons deposited in a landfill. The prices paid for recyclable materials do vary with demand, which could affect their value. But the savings wrung from so-called tipping charges at landfills, which approach $100 per ton in some areas, would be consistent. In the contracts RecycleBank offered cities and towns, the parties would share in both the revenues from the sale of the materials harvested on recycling day and in the year-to-year reductions in landfill payments.

When Jon Norton couldn't poke a hole in Gonen's idea, he took it to the Everett City Hall, where the mayor and other officials were weighing strategies to increase recycling and reduce spending on trash. Every other idea involved penalizing households that didn't reduce and recycle. One, called "pay-as-you-go," would have forced residents to actually pay for the disposal of whatever they set out on the curb. (This was going to be done by requiring them to buy official city-issued trash bags.) As a veteran elementary school teacher, Norton favored positive reinforcement—gold stars, or in this case RecycleBank points—to punishment and was able to persuade the mayor to at least experiment with the concept.

"I was thinking that we should go green in two ways," recalls Norton. "One was the green you think of when you're helping to save the planet. The other is the green that's in your wallet. People like both of those."

Norton makes his point about "green" as he gets out of the car on a side street lined by single-family homes, duplexes, and small apartment houses. It's a crisp, clear winter morning, and the sound of a garbage truck—revving engine, squealing brakes—echoes in the distance. Norton takes up a post in the street, peering in the direction of the sounds, and keeps on talking.

"We were collecting very little recycling when the trial began. We picked up maybe three tons on recycling days. With RecycleBank we saw an immediate increase in the number of households putting the buckets out, and it kept on increasing. Within a few weeks people who lived on other routes were asking if they could participate. We now recycle thirteen tons on pick-up days. People want those points because they can use them to go buy things or go to dinner." Many local businesses, including coffee houses, restaurants, hardware stores, and pizza shops, signed up to accept the points. The program brings them customers they might not see otherwise.

When the entire city was brought into the program, Everett realized annual savings of more than $150,000, which it shared with RecycleBank, which also generates revenues from sale of recyclables and advertising on its Web site. In less than four years the company has expanded to serve more than a million households in twenty American cities, and it has begun operations in the United Kingdom—where the landfill crisis is far more acute than it is in the United States. "They will run out of space by 2015," says Gonen, "and everyone knows it, so you don't have to talk them into trying something new."

As a company, RecycleBank has attracted big investors who seem prepared to back it until the volume of business is enough to create a profit. (All those lifters and scales on the trucks cost money.) In the meantime these supporters and points partners are basking in the positive attention the company has received, including recognition from the United Nations, which named the company a 2009 Champion of the Earth.

For his part, Gonen is realizing a dream he had as a youngster who heard "go green" messages in elementary school from teachers who were not so different from Jon Norton. A former consultant with Deloitte, a firm that advises companies around the world, Gonen always had a passion for technology and an eye for creative solutions to difficult problems. RecycleBank is an expression of these qualities and his desire to do something good and meaningful with his life. "Life really is about taking risks and doing what you believe is right," he says. "It can come at a great emotional cost, and it can come with some anxiety and the loss of security and wealth."

In Everett, Jon Norton has to be prodded to talk about the personal aspects of his successful one-man campaign to save the environment and serve his hometown. But as he warms to the topic, it becomes clear that he feels that he gets as much out of the work as he gives. He's proud of a charitable partnership with Coca-Cola that allows residents to cash in their points for dollars that go to local schools. He's also proud of his newly developed expertise, acquired in old age, as a public servant. "I wanted everyone to be happy with this program," he says. "That was my goal, and I think they are."

Although it's supposedly a part-time job, Norton's work as recycling director keeps him busy more than forty hours a week because he encourages residents to call him at home if they have questions or problems, and he answers every inquiry every day.

"Because of this job, I know someone on every block of this city," he says. Norton is proud of this second career, which he designed for himself and took to with remarkable ease and flexibility. He has done the same thing in his daily life, responding to the pressures of the Great Recession by reducing his consumption, especially when it comes to energy. "I bought a hybrid car that gets about fifty miles per gallon," he says with a grin. "I fill it up every couple of months. That's how you get by in this life," he adds. "There's not just one answer to everything. You have to adjust and adapt. There's always a solution."

————————

Although there's thirty-five years between them, Jon Norton and Ron Gonen express similar values, motivations, and talents. One young, and one old, they approach life with a problem-solving perspective that helps them to live in a flexible, free-flowing way. This strategy, which we call "liquid living," is being deployed by people who are thinking creatively, shedding excess overhead, and shifting their priorities in response to the changing economy. The feelings behind these shifts turn up in the data among the total U.S. population from the BrandAsset Valuator, where we have noticed results like these:

- Sixty-six percent agreed with the statement, "Since the recession, I realize I am happier with a simpler, more down-to-basics lifestyle."

- Seventy-four percent say they now keep track of their credit score and financial standing.

- The top 20 percent most simple and easy-to-use brands have 58 percent more preference and 53 percent greater usage than their competitors.

- Sixty percent say they own energy-efficient appliances (and 50 percent are willing to pay a premium for such items).

- Eighty-three percent agreed on some level that the recession will have a long-term effect on how they allocate both time and money.

The shifts in how people spend time and money can be seen in many recent trends. For example, we see evidence of a move from a credit society to a debit society. In 2009, American credit card debt actually declined by 20 percent, marking the first decline since 1998 as people shed the weight of excess debt.[1] In 2009 Visa announced for the first time that its customers were relying more on debit cards than credit cards for their transactions.[2] The FDIC found another spend shift—people were using earned rather than borrowed money to make purchases without running up debt.[3]

If the old American dream was "having things," now it's "having agility." And in many ways, people are finding that as they become less materialistic they feel freer, less encumbered, and more available to opportunity. To get these feelings, people have set about systematically eliminating fixed costs and overhead expenses, preferring pay-as-you-go living. Trends affecting two old-line institutions—the post office and the phone company—illustrate the move toward thrift and agility. In 2009 the U.S. Postal Service, which is creeping toward a fifty-cent first class stamp, experienced its largest mail volume decline in its 243-year history and has pulled up twenty thousand blue mailboxes from America's cities (officials are also considering an end to Saturday delivery in order to cut costs).[4] In this same time period, expensive "land line" phones have begun to disappear. According to Verizon's estimates, these sets, which once hung on almost every kitchen wall, will disappear by 2025.[5]

Fortunately, the spend shift isn't pushing aside every old-fashioned institution. In early 2010 a *New York Times*/CBS news poll found that due to the recession, people were spending more time with family and friends or pursuing hobbies. One of the more popular "hobbies" seems to be sex, as condom and sex toy companies report higher sales. Other data showed the decline of the large "McMansion" suburban house (which is expensive and time-consuming to maintain) and a move back to America's cities. *USA Today* noted the recession halted forty straight years of double-digit growth in suburban living.[6] The downsized home is another recent national trend. The U.S. Census indicated that the American single-family home declined in square footage, reversing five straight decades of expansion.[7] Surveys by the National Association of Home Builders found that 88 percent of its members plan to build smaller homes this year.[8]

Curious about the new nimble consumer, we modeled an index of "Liquid Life" brands and companies who represent the top 10 percent on imagery such as "simple," "independent," "adaptable," and "dynamic." These companies (such as Geico, Bit.ly, and Progressive) sell goods and services that are supposed to defeat complexity, encourage mobility and agility (iPhone, Google Maps, and Foursquare), and help you make independent choices (WebMD, Hunch, and Yelp). These nimble, simple, adaptable brands outperformed their competition in an exceptional manner:

One of my favorite brands	+456 percent
Feel loyal to the brand	+444 percent
Would recommend to a friend	+360 percent
Use regularly	+212 percent
Prefer most	+195 percent

As people stripped away excess and complexity, they also moved away from artifice and displays of ego. This all shows up in our data, where things like envy and lust for expensive cars and homes declined by 26 percent between 2007 and 2009. (Luxury brands declined by 19 percent.) Perhaps the single biggest symbol of this spend shift was the General Motors decision to abandon that 1990s emblem of excess, the Hummer. By the start of the Great Recession, auto buyers just didn't want a car that represented such conspicuous consumption. (Of course, they may also have been influenced by reports that Hummer drivers got nearly *five times* as many tickets as the average driver.)

Alongside these shifts is the way thrift has blossomed to produce a socially sanctioned frugal lifestyle. In 2009, 58 percent of Americans (and 67 percent of Millennials) reported that they used coupons to make purchases. Booz & Company found that two-thirds of consumers frequently use coupons, value price over convenience, and believe saving is more important than spending.[9] In another spend shift sign, dollar stores like Dollar General and Dollar Tree rose up in the ranks of the Fortune 500. And in BrandAsset Valuator, 95 percent of Americans believed that even when the economy recovers fully, they'll continue to put time and effort into finding the best deals possible (with 42 percent agreeing strongly).

All these numbers support the notion that people aren't waiting for government or corporate leaders to show them how to respond to crisis. They are, instead, moving almost reflexively, on their own, to adjust and adapt. This phenomenon is not dependent on gender, age, or even income level—all groups are participating—although the Pew Research Center has found that it is, understandably, less pronounced among the affluent. Nevertheless, Pew has seen enough of a spend shift to conclude that 80 percent of all adults have pared back their personal list of goods and services they deem essential to a happy life.[10] "Yesterday's necessities," Pew announced in April 2009, have "become today's luxuries."

With big and somewhat mysterious economic and political forces driving these shifts, even the most esteemed experts cannot predict precisely where public sentiment will go. A few miles southwest of Everett, John Quelch has been watching the fluid way people adapt to change from his perch as professor at the Harvard Business School, where he studies, among other things, democracy and the marketplace. Quelch is fascinated by the question of whether people will snap back to their old overspending ways or we're witnessing a permanent change.

"For those who have discovered that when they decide against buying a new car their self-esteem is not affected *and* their old car continues to run well, the Great Recession has delivered surprisingly upbeat news about their own resilience." The same people are also discovering that they can be happy after moving from a mini-mansion to a smaller house or even an apartment, or from a home they owned to a rental. As noted, in an abrupt end to a decades-long trend, the average new American house was actually smaller (by 10 percent) in 2009 than in 2008.[11] During the same period, home ownership declined while renting increased. In a market where selling a home can be extremely difficult, renting allows people to move more nimbly to take advantage of opportunities.

When these changes yield lower consumption, they can produce social benefits like reduced carbon emissions as a matter of course. Quelch notes that this people-driven shift happens with fewer struggles than when policymakers try to impose similar measures from the top. For a contrast he points to President Jimmy Carter's attempt to reduce American energy consumption in the late 1970s. "In fairness to Carter, he was trying to legislate this stuff," notes Quelch. Today, while conservation and global warming may be a key political concern for some spend shifters, far more people are taking action for practical reasons—and that group, adds Quelch, is growing because they are reaping the benefits directly. "Wise companies," he adds, "will make it easy for people to get information about how their products reflect this trend by saving them time and money while making the world a better place."

As experts like John Quelch note, we signal our values and our priorities every time we make a purchase or decide where to invest our time and energy. In contrast, we participate in elections every two years or so. This means political choices are very crude and lagging indicators of public sentiment. If you want to understand how people really feel, track them day-to-day in the marketplace.

And if you want to measure their long-term perspective, study their big investments in items like houses, cars, furnishings, and appliances.

Although some widely held stereotypes suggest that Americans are impulse buyers, in fact we tend to do our homework when it comes to big purchases—and the Internet has made this process easier and more rewarding. For example, dozens of sites make it possible to get accurate information on home prices, taxes, schools, shopping, services, and more in every American zip code. The Internet also makes it possible for anyone to get loads of information on home design, energy use, building technologies, and even the philosophy of a builder.

Rainy Day (her real name) depended on the Internet to get the home of her dreams at the height of the Great Recession, when almost everyone else was afraid to make such a big investment. However, she had a head start on her dream. In fact, she had been watching the development of low-cost, energy-efficient housing for more than thirty years, waiting for the moment when the architecture, materials, and price hit a certain sweet spot. That's when she discovered a new Boston area company called Blu Homes, which manufactures highly efficient low-cost homes that look like the pictures in *Dwell*.

Formed just as the Great Recession took hold, Blu Homes was founded to revolutionize the business of factory-built or so-called prefab homes, which had grown bigger and more expensive during the housing boom of the recent decade. Instead of offering traditional pre-fab houses that required expensive special haulers to deliver, Blu designed highly efficient, hinged modules that could be shipped cheaply on standard rail cars or truck trailers and assembled on site to make exquisite small to medium-sized homes. Designs called for recycled and recyclable building materials, low-flow plumbing fixtures, and a high-tech energy monitoring system. Houses would be delivered almost ready to occupy, with owners responsible only for providing a foundation—or piers to hold the structure—and hookups for utilities. And in true liquid living fashion, Blu homes are modular so they can be expanded with additions that make them suitable for the new adaptable lifestyle.

A bus driver who makes a modest salary, Rainy Day had the good fortune to own a perfect spot for a house on the piece of her family's farm in Charlestown, Rhode Island, that she got from her parents. After reviewing plans, she chose a Blu Homes model called the Element, which measures less than 1,000 square feet, but she gave herself a little extra space with a finished basement. She liked the house because it features a huge bank of windows, which she could position to face south to soak up solar energy and reduce the expense of winter heating and lighting. The little house cost exactly $85,000, and is so tightly built she should pay far less than her neighbors to stay cool in the summer and warm in the winter. Overall, her cost of living should actually be lower than it was when she rented a place. But more important, the house is a daily expression of her values.

"I was green before the word *green* was as popular as it is," explains Day, who remembers growing up on a working farm that produced milk and eggs and vegetables. "My dad grew up during the Depression. They were very thrifty. They reused stuff. My dad brought home rags from a dyeing mill where he worked. We had blankets made out of leftover rags, and my mother made most of the clothes we had as kids. She came from a family of sixteen, and she didn't remember having new clothes."

The careful use, repair, and reuse of items was a way of making ends meet, staying out of debt, and maintaining the Day family's independence and integrity. If it was "green" or an example of "liquid living," no one called it by these names. It was simply the practical way to stay in control of one's destiny and didn't require taking big risks. Indeed, in the 1970s when Rainy Day learned about alternative energy—solar electric and wind—she went to her father with the idea of setting aside some land for an "energy farm." As she recalls it, he appreciated her enthusiasm but told her the time wasn't right. "He would say that's in the future. It's not practical now. But now even the town of Charleston has passed a wind ordinance to allow individuals to have small turbines."

Because she saved her money and did not jump into the real estate market as it expanded like a bubble, Day was ready when the future her father had predicted arrived. She didn't get a wind-mill (although she's open to the idea), but she did get a house that employs passive solar energy and was built with earth-friendly materials and methods. Her willingness to plan with care and then make a bold, inspired decision makes her the kind of customer that Blu Homes founders Maura McCarthy and Bill Haney hoped would get their start-up company off the ground. An investor, Haney became McCarthy's first backer when she came to him with an idea for "green" houses that would be affordable enough for a bus driver but beautiful enough to attract wealthier buyers who might want to downsize or build a unique second home. She had good designs, but as McCarthy herself recalls, she needed to iron out several problems that have plagued factory-built housing com-panies for decades.

"A lot of companies had trouble selling direct to customers," says McCarthy, because most buyers liked to tinker with design and this tinkering costs money. They also ran into trouble when they delivered homes but needed local contractors to do extensive site work or to install heating, air conditioning, or plumbing. As far as McCarthy could tell, no one firm had ever succeeded at designing, selling, manufacturing, delivering, and completing homes at a customer's site.

McCarthy got around these problems with technology that allows her customers almost infinite options for designing their homes and seeing three-dimensional images of how they would look with no extra cost. (They use the same expensive and sophisticated software deployed by aerospace, automotive, and shipbuilding companies.) Her architects and engineers then devised ways to have virtually all of the work on a home's utilities done in the factory. On delivery day, connections for heating and plumbing just snap together as the structure is unfolded.

Technology allows Blu Homes to move as nimbly as a frugal New Englander responding to the forces of the world economy. As McCarthy explains it, Blu designs have been customized for use as office space, school buildings, country homes, and backyard granny flats in jurisdictions where property owners are allowed to erect small outbuildings on piers under flexible, low-cost permit programs. The folding design has made shipping so inexpensive that Blu Homes can actually send a unit cross-country and still beat local competitors on price. (For example, a television studio in Burbank, California, is using four Blu homes for dressing rooms on its lot.)

"The whole idea is that less is more," says McCarthy, who grew up in a small town in rural Michigan and now works in a Victorian-era schoolhouse that has been converted into office space in the Boston suburb of Waltham. She is surrounded by young engineers, designers, and businesspeople who bring a light-hearted sense of mission to their work. (In the conference room where McCarthy is telling the Blu Homes story, one bookshelf holds just two volumes—a book on carpet manufacturing and the *Indispensable Calvin and Hobbes*, a cartoon book.)

"We want to give people permission to downsize by providing them with a house they will love," says McCarthy, "and we want to give them the badge of awesomeness because it's built with sustainable materials and it's so energy efficient." McCarthy's ultimate dream is to make Blu Homes a national company that may even have a manufacturing center in a place like Detroit, where costs may make it possible to sell houses at prices that are affordable even in depressed Midwestern markets. "We want to make an impact," she adds, "on the entire housing market."

In the meantime, Rainy Day will be happy to make less of an impact on her local environment as she settles into life in her new home. "I can't save the world," she says, "but I can use whatever resources I have to save what I can." Toward that end she is thinking about ways to preserve her part of the family farm, which fronts on a small river that is one of the cleanest freshwater streams in southern New England. A local conservation commission has inquired about buying the development rights for the land so that it can be preserved. Day imagines she'll take their offer, or work with the state Department of Environmental Management, which has a similar program. Either way, she likes the idea of living in a home that is so inexpensive she can afford to make future generations—perhaps even the children on her school bus—stewards of her land.

"I think they will become much better shepherds of the Earth than my generation has been," she says with optimism. "Our grandparents were frugal, but the pendulum swung and we had too much given to us. People bought not what they needed but whatever they wanted, including great big vehicles that make us even more dependent on oil, which just slays me. Now I hope that necessity makes people more responsible. It's going to be up to individual people, not the government. The government has enough problems to deal with. Individuals and small groups—the minnows and the guppies—need to come up with the innovation and take action, and I believe we can."

As the Boston Tea Party reminds us, Yankees are the original American rebels, and they have a history of banding together behind ideas that can seem quite radical at their inception. When economic crisis struck, and people in the small towns west of Boston began losing their property, they turned to each other—and not some distant power center—for a solution. They formed protest groups and raised their voices and called for a new paper currency that neighbors and tradesmen could rely on to pay debts and build wealth.

The first time New Englanders followed this path of protest to monetary self-reliance, George Washington stood against them, and the movement, which was called Shay's Rebellion, was repressed after a bloody confrontation that saw four of farmer Daniel Shay's men killed when they attacked a federal armory. The second time came more than two hundred years later when farmers, merchants, and tradespeople in the Berkshire Mountains of Massachusetts banded together to issue their own money—a currency called Berkshares—and, without spilling a drop of blood, began setting their own economic course.

The idea for a Berkshire currency was born in 2006 when a handful of businesspeople, community boosters, and the local chamber of commerce began looking for ways to help local retailers, restaurants, and service people survive competition from national chains that were moving into small mountain towns. They were led, in part, by a nonprofit organization called the E.F. Schumacher Society, which is in the Berkshire town of Great Barrington. The society is named after a historically prominent British economist whose book, *Small Is Beautiful*, was named one of the most influential books of the past half-century by the *Times* of London. Schumacher, who died in 1977, was a vocal proponent of local economies and argued for balancing development with safeguarding resources and the environment for future generations. "Any intelligent fool can make things bigger, more complex, and more violent," wrote Schumacher. "It takes a touch of genius— and a lot of courage—to move in the opposite directions."

The Schumacher Society was founded by Robert Swann, whose experience as a child in the Great Depression led him to lifelong work promoting rural land preservation and strong local economies in places like the Berkshires. Home to ski areas, summer resorts, and many theaters, the region claims an unusual mix of residents that includes people of great wealth and fame who own vacation homes in the mountains and many natives who are relatively poor. With the decline of textile mills and other factories in the last few decades, workers came to depend mainly on tourists, who prefer to find unusual, one-of-a-kind shops and eateries when they travel instead of the same outlets they find at home. A currency that guaranteed a 5 percent discount for shoppers—100 Berkshares could be bought for $95—seemed like a clever idea to promote these local businesses to tourists. And since they are accepted only in the region, the program might encourage locals to give their trade—whether they are buying hardware, clothing, or a set of tires—to their neighbors.

Thirteen bank branches agreed to exchange dollars, and local artists designed Berkshares as elegant bills, in denominations from one to fifty. Each bill shows the figure of a famous person from the region: Norman Rockwell, Herman Melville, W.E.B. Du Bois. By 2010 more than $2.5 million worth of scrip had been issued and hundreds of businesses, from dentists to jewelers, had agreed to accept it. Berkshares worked the way their promoters envisioned. For example, Guido's grocery accepts the currency from customers and uses Berkshares to pay farmers for produce. The farmers bring the bills into town to buy their supplies. But in addition to promoting the local economy, the local currency gives people a sense of control over their own destiny.

"We actually think of it as a way to separate our economic destiny from the government," explains Susan Witt, who is executive director of the Schumacher Society and a leader of the Berkshares initiative. Witt is in her mid-sixties. She was educated at Boston University and the University of New Hampshire and counts the writer Jane Jacobs, an expert on urban life, among her greatest influences. But when she came to rural western Massachusetts, she was delighted by the countryside and the prospect of living in a place where deer wander through her backyard almost every day. She has lived in the mountains that line the state's border with New York for more than thirty years and appreciates the history and character of the place.

"We have a culture, and a tradition, of citizens' solving problems on their own and not depending on the government," she says. This independent streak doesn't keep people from banding together in groups, as the Berkshares experiment shows, but it does make them wary of decisions made at a distance, whether that's in the agencies of the federal government or the boardroom of a huge corporation.

"Here in the southern part of the county [Berkshire County] we have more than sixty restaurants and only four are national chains," adds Witt. "That means we have at least fifty-six local chefs who are creating their own menus and buying food from local sources. Berkshares help keep that going." Berkshares also help make it possible for a population of about seventy thousand, scattered across an area of roughly five hundred square miles, to support specialty businesses that might not survive in another place. Two of these unique companies, Tom's Toys and JWS Art Supplies, are tourist destinations owned by the same man, an artist and entrepreneur named Tom Levin.

On an icy February morning, Levin started his day, as usual, with coffee in the back room at a place called Rubiner's Cheese Mongers, which occupies a former bank building on Main Street. (The tables for the café are actually located in a former boardroom that is lined in heavy hardwood paneling.) Levin, who is fifty-eight years old, was born and raised in Manhattan, where his father was a lawyer and his mother was a writer and editor. He was educated in the arts and graphic design and made a living as an artist until his loft studio was consumed by a fire. He then took up building, doing custom construction. In 1984, Levin and his wife, Susan, a writer with a doctorate in psychology, chose Great Barrington as the place to raise their children, Sam, Will, and Jake. She went into teaching, and he worked as a contractor until "an early midlife crisis" led him to consider retailing.

As a member of the local planning board, Levin knew the businesses in the region and the real estate. "I had kids," he adds, "and I knew there were no toy stores around." A tall man with close-cropped hair that's turning silver, Levin speaks in a crisp, direct way. "I also had an affinity for toys," he explains. "Always have."

With a wide-open marketplace and a natural fondness for the products he could sell, Levin embarked on a thorough study of the business, visiting shops all over New England. He also had to consider the adjustment he would have to make as he moved from busy, physically demanding work as a builder to the confines of a retail store and customer service. Since construction also comes with undependable workers, unreliable subcontractors, and clients who sometimes resist paying their bills, Levin ultimately made the switch. He stocked a storefront with the kinds of toys he knew were well made and that encouraged active play—no electric stuff and a minimum of plastic—and put up bright signs that announced "Tom's Toys" in red and blue letters set on a crisp white background.

Tom's Toys succeeded by offering what chain stores do not: carefully selected stock from a worldwide network of craftspeople and quality manufacturers. The shop also provided a level of service one might expect at a high-end jewelry store but not a place where you buy rubber balls and army men. Ironically enough, the conservative economic theorist George Gilder occupied the office above Levin's store. Gilder once promoted a vision of a utopia built on high technology that could hardly be more opposed to the locally focused philosophy behind Berkshares.

By the end of Levin's first Christmas season he knew the store would work. He opened his second shop—JWS Art Supplies—in 2000, hoping that the artists who flock to the region in warmer months would give him a boost in income when toy sales were slow. The attacks of September 11, 2001, came in that first year, and he feared it would hurt his business, but he continued to prosper. It turned out that many people turned to art, and crafts, in response to the stress of the attacks.

When Berkshares were introduced, Levin's shops were among the first businesses to accept them. The discount may bring some extra business his way, and he uses the scrip himself, to buy groceries and other items at a discount. However, the business benefits are not more important to him than the statement he makes using a local currency instead of dollars from the government. "The idea is to encourage people to support the local community, and I think it works," he says. And as an artist, he thinks the Berkshares are far more beautiful than anything ever issued by the U.S. Treasury.

But as the Great Recession bore down, trust evaporated and so did the credit flows for small businesses. During the crisis, Berkshares functioned as a covenant for the community, distinguishing trust among buyers and sellers and reinforcing a "we'll get through this together" spirit. Others seem to appreciate Berkshares as an instrument of self-determination. In early 2009, as the Great Recession swept across the developed world, businesses in the poor London suburb of Brixton began accepting a new currency called the Brixton Pound. The group that issued the currency, which was inspired in part by Berkshares, said the local notes would plug the "leaky bucket" effect, which is how they referred to the practice of many national retailers who spend the profits from operations in Brixton elsewhere. The British press describes the Brixton Pound as a big success during the Christmas season, as neighborhood shops bustled with business.

Whether they are turning trash to treasure or issuing their own money to address the needs of their local economy, stubbornly independent New Englanders seem capable of responding flexibly to meet their needs and express their values of practicality, creativity, and thrift. They don't need large institutions or politicians to lead them toward solutions. They are willing to take risks on new ideas.

This free-flowing approach to economic challenges may seem idealistic, but it is not just softhearted do-goodism. In Everett, Jon Norton and Ron Gonen make recycling profitable for the community, the planet, and themselves. In Rhode Island, Rainy Day's Blu home is a statement of eco-friendly values—but it's also a canny investment that will allow her to live securely on her family's farm. And while Berkshares may seem like a fanciful notion—Hey everyone, let's create our own money!—they have clearly contributed to the economic stability of western Massachusetts.

Eighty miles south of the Berkshires in the swanky Connecticut town of Westport, another highly creative Yankee uses real money and the traditional tools of finance to help old-fashioned companies thrive without becoming dependent on Wall Street or national banks. One of the funds operated by Main Street Resources is so committed to personal relationships and local development that founder and managing partner Daniel Levinson won't lend to a firm that he cannot drive to in a few hours. Referrals come by word of mouth, and Levinson won't even consider making a deal if a company isn't a "good citizen." By this he means that its managers must be devoted to their communities and their workers as well as the bottom line. Twenty percent of the profits from the fund go to charity.

"For the most part we back companies that do 10 to 50 million dollars in business a year and have 50 to 250 employees," explains Levinson, who works in a small office building that looks like a three-story New England clapboard house. "They are stable companies, and they are growing, but it's lonely at the top for the founder or the CEO. Morgan Stanley doesn't care to help him if he wants to make an acquisition of a competitor or grow in a way that requires some capital." Levinson won't be interested unless the owners are willing to welcome Main Street as advisers as well as funders. His money comes from a network of one hundred local executives who call themselves "The Guild," and they are eager to mentor the firms they fund.

"Once a month I have two or three members of our board come in and beat the hell out of me with advice," laughs Levinson, who has curly brown hair and looks ten years younger than his age (forty-eight). "We do that for all the companies we invest in because it helps them. Of course, they have to be open to the coaching, and we understand that we're not always right. But we are there with them as a resource because we want them to succeed, not for the short term but for the long term and in every way that benefits them, the workers, the environment, you name it."

Levinson studied applied mathematics and economics at Brown and has a master's degree in business administration from Stanford, so he understands numbers and management—but what he really values are the personal bonds he makes with the executives at the companies in his portfolio. When we met, he had just attended a funeral for an executive of Disc Graphics, Inc., a printing company that he helped go private in a $20 million deal. The company has won numerous awards for the quality of its work and eco-friendly manufacturing process, but the funeral service reminded Levinson why he left a fast-track career on Wall Street to start his own nimble fund devoted to smaller local businesses.

"Everyone who was at that funeral had a personal connection to the company and was there because they cared so much about each other," recalls Levinson. "It reminded me of the time, when the recession started, and I suggested to the owner that he cut the workforce by about 20 percent. He said, 'I can't do that. If I do, I'll go home and my wife and daughter will be crying.' These are companies that care about their workers. They provide health care and security and they make money. It's done on a personal scale that's sustainable, and I like that because it's what will work for the long run."

Observing Yankee ingenuity from a slight distance, Robin Chase sees signs of future development around the world. Co-founder of the famous Zipcar company, which pioneered networked car rentals in America, Chase has become a renowned expert on sustainable businesses and communities. Zipcar, which was based on the assumption that people could be trusted to share vehicles that were scattered across a city, was one of the first businesses to succeed using an Internet-only sales and operations model.

Chase left Zipcar but remains in the Boston area, where it was started, and continues to work on transportation issues including a new venture called GoLoco, a ride-sharing social network. Chase is constantly searching for ways to help people live in ways that are more efficient and less damaging to the environment. She notes that attractive urban communities, like the new Brooklyn, will be part of the solution because they allow people to get out of their cars. Smaller homes, lowered oil consumption, and more mass transit are also in Chase's prescription, but she acknowledges that many people will have to be persuaded to pay for these spending shifts, especially if they require reduced consumption or an invest-ment of tax dollars. Here she sees a place for Madison Avenue–style marketing.

"There are several categories of people who adopt change," explains Chase as she sips tea in a Middle Eastern restaurant in Cambridge. (The daughter of an American diplomat, Chase spent many of her childhood years in the Middle East.) "You start with the people who have a real belief in the need for a change. They can be the trendsetters, who are followed by people who do some-thing because they perceive it to be cool. After them you get the laggards, who will eventually come along because they see that the new thing is working."

The trendsetters in Chase's equation are often wealthier people seeking status symbols. In the wake of the Great Recession, says Chase, "we are in a trend space." In that space, she believes, effi-cient cars and homes and products made from eco-friendly sources will be the new status symbols. Like the other new Boston start-up Relay Rides, which allows people to rent a car from other car owners in their neighborhood by the hour or day, a thriftier life-style "will signal status without consumption."

A similar change occurred in America in the aftermath of the Great Depression as the big flashy cars and mansions of the Roaring

Twenties became symbols of wretched excess, and simple pleasures like crossword puzzles and miniature golf became nationwide fads. Unlike other social analysts who criticize advertising and marketing, blaming them for the hyperconsumption of decades past, Chase prefers to focus on how they can be used to promote the better ideas of the future.

"People like Rachel Maddow and Paul Krugman are skeptical of marketing," adds Chase, referring to two prominent political commentators whom she admires. "I think marketing can be brought under control and used to show us how to do more, better, and get Peoria aligned with the West Coast. We did that with Zipcar by doing a great job of branding that made it appeal to people all over." Other innovations can be promoted in the same way if their stories are told well. "Anecdote can move people forward," adds Chase.

A fifty-two-year-old with gray hair and intense brown eyes, Robin Chase exudes optimism and confidence when she talks about a future filled with innovations based on technology and individual creativity. As she travels the world consulting with companies and nonprofit organizations, she continually refines her thinking based on what she observes and discovers. She expects that the best life, for the most people, may come out of a strategy that combines American individualism with a Buddhist concern for community. Adding a twist to an old slogan, she calls this "thinking globally, but acting individually." In New England, this is a tried-and-true concept.

Chapter Four

AN ARMY OF DAVIDS: TAMPA, FLORIDA

It was a typical autumn day in Tampa, where Florida's most reliable asset—the sun—brought the kind of balmy weather that was in large measure responsible for the absolute mess that was the state's economy.

Without the sun's blessing, Florida could never have attracted a thousand immigrants a day and seen the enormous real estate bubble and bust of the past decade. The sun had beamed down as loose mortgage lenders poured cash into the hands of unqualified buyers, many of whom "flipped" newly bought homes in days or weeks for double-digit price increases. It warmed the workers who labored year-round to build massive subdivisions—and then, when the bubble burst, it kept shining on abandoned houses and empty lots where weeds and scrub trees grew so tall that the for-sale signs and abandoned furniture soon disappeared from view.

By November 21, 2009, the Tampa Bay area was so mired in the Great Recession and so well identified with the real estate crisis—few places suffered more—that it would have been hard to find someone who couldn't offer a fairly accurate analysis of all that had gone wrong. Like the rest of the state, this four-county region of three million-plus people had depended on immigration and real estate development for economic growth. The economy was so imbalanced that when the bubble burst and construction stopped, workers had no alternatives. They couldn't even pick strawberries or citrus. The farms and orchards had been sold to developers. As people stopped working and then stopped buying stuff, the businesses that used to sell to them—like car dealers and retail stores—closed. Malls emptied out. Shopping centers were abandoned.

As social service agencies strained to help, food pantries and homeless shelters were overwhelmed. Catholic Charities actually opened a tent city, like the ones used after natural disasters, to house the displaced. Called Pinellas Hope, the colony of tents was soon filled with 250 occupants. By the fall of 2009 the average tent stay had grown to seventy-five days. The agency was proposing another tent city. The local press was filled with reports on the plan and opposition from neighbors. These stories appeared along with articles about the region's poor prospects for recovery. Soon the prestigious Brookings Institution ranked Tampa Bay near the very bottom in its assessment of the economic conditions in the one hundred biggest metropolitan areas in the country. "Recovery Won't Arrive Here Soon," read the headline on a local news Web site.

Brianne Swezey knew all about the trouble in Tampa. Having fled frigid Minnesota in 2003 (at the age of twenty-three), she had lived through the boom and bust and struggled to find steady employment, often working two or three jobs just to pay the rent. But on this Saturday morning she was immune from the tension and anxiety of the Great Recession and the ennui that might be evoked by the sun-washed landscape of vacant buildings and empty streets. Driving toward a business park on the west side of town, she thought about the event she had planned for the day. With her help, a dozen young artists and designers would forget their own troubles and get lost doing what they love for the benefit of others.

"The funny thing is that in this economy I've thought about volunteering more, not less. Even though I don't have a lot, the situation makes you appreciate what you do have. And I'm not the only one. Instead of being down about how I need money for this and money for that, we'd rather just start doing something for other people."

A bright-faced young woman with blue eyes, straight blonde hair, and a penchant for the super-caffeinated jolt of Red Bull, Swezey talks and moves in a way that makes you believe her when she says, "I just like to get things done." Designathon 2009, which allowed artists, designers, and Web designers to donate their services to worthy clients, was a perfect example.

Born of a brainstorming session with fellow members of the group Tampa Graphic Design/Meetup.com, Designathon went from idea to event in less than six weeks. In that time scores of nonprofit organizations and struggling local businesses applied for consideration and a dozen were selected. When the big day arrived, the artists and clients gathered at the International Academy of Design and Technology, which donated space, computers, and other facilities for the day. In a marathon session that ran into the night, the "creatives" (as they were called) went to work for groups including a shelter for battered women, a charter school, and the YWCA.

At the end of the Designathon, beneficiaries left with custom-made Web sites, new logos, designs for literature, and even sample advertisements. The artists and technology specialists got the satisfaction of doing good work for good causes, formed friendships with their peers, and began relationships that might lead to employment in the future. In a region and a business where job seekers often outnumber available positions by ten to one, the chance to show one's work was a great opportunity.

"These were groups that needed visibility, and in some cases they were affiliated with national organizations that had photos, Web access, and other resources that they just hadn't accessed. We helped them to do things like that," explains Swezey. "My job was mostly support, you know, running for food. But it was a great day in the spirit of Thanksgiving. Our Meetup group hadn't done anything for public service. At the same time there were designers who said that getting a chance to work with people like that helped them form relationships that would have never happened. It worked out well for everyone, I think."

Swezey is a natural organizer and optimist. Her energy made it possible for a community of young artistic types to come together to perform a public service without any political or corporate leader issuing a call to action. But she would be the first to credit social media technology providers like Meetup.com with giving her the tools to rally scattered groups of less-than-powerful citizens into a potent force—an army of Davids, if you will—to make an attack on the Goliath of despair that dominated the mood in Tampa Bay.

Although they exist in the online realm, the social media— Twitter, Facebook, Foursquare, Meetup, and other services—allow groups to share ideas instantaneously, form communities without regard to time and space, and organize actions that can affect people in very real ways. They provide the means for isolated individuals to achieve on a scale what would otherwise be impossible and to defy the dystopian view of society that some critics of technology once offered as they considered a future dominated by virtual reality. So while it is true that much of what distinguishes modern life—suburbs, cars, and the various screens we stare at for much of the day—can isolate us, the Internet can alleviate loneliness and help people collaborate for the greater good.

"It is hard to find anything or connect with anyone in Tampa because the city is so segmented," explains Swezey. "There's Tampa, Clearwater, and St. Petersburg, and all the smaller suburbs. There's not a real downtown in Tampa. It is really the kind of place made for Meetup, and it has helped me realize there are hundreds of people like me here."

To be more precise, at least 592 people in Tampa Bay consider themselves enough like Brianne Swezey to join the Meetup organization she discovered when she moved to the region. Tampa Graphic Design Meetup counted just twenty members in 2003, and its activities involved little more than the occasional cocktail party. As a recent graduate of the College of Visual Arts in St. Paul, Swezey was well versed in both the technology and the potential of the nascent social media world. She also comes from a generation that was schooled in both volunteerism (many schools require students to volunteer) and a certain nothing-to-lose approach to life. They are skeptical about big organizations—government, corporations, mainstream media—but confident in their own abilities. Within a year she was leading the Tampa group and building it into an active resource for a community of newcomers and old-timers.

Swezey energized the group by inviting experts to offer programs on everything from poster art to Web design. She shifted venues, so that participants could gather at theaters, cafés, workplaces, and even the local IKEA store. And she created themed events for holidays to provide more structure for the remaining social gatherings. Connections made online and at monthly meetings helped participants find both freelance work and full-time jobs. As word of the group's success spread, it attracted new members by the hundreds. For a small annual fee—$12 as of 2010—they got relationships, daily buzz about their business, and the equivalent of a never-ending continuing education course.

The evolution of Brianne Swezey's Tampa group from an online social hub to a complex support network that could rally a battalion of do-gooder artists would delight the big thinkers behind Meetup. As the chief community officer for Meetup Inc., Douglas Atkin spent years thinking about the purpose of the technology, which allows people with shared interests to meet both online and in their real communities, and how people could use it to make their lives, and the world, a better place. He learned most by observing what the truly successful groups had in common.

First and foremost, he discovered, "was that they had to have a distinct purpose." Next came "a minimum number, perhaps four or five, of truly committed people who showed up consistently" when a group moved from online communication to in-person gatherings. It didn't matter if the gathering took place at a coffee shop, a country club, or in someone's living room. What did matter was that this core group stuck with it long enough to interact and form relationships.

"This purpose plus interaction equals 'stickiness,'" said Atkin when we interviewed him via Skype (he was vacationing in Costa Rica when we explored Tampa). "After a few years you also have to have an organizer [such as Brianne Swezey]," he added. These organizers help set a positive tone, keep a group focused on its purpose, and maintain the members' interest by giving them interesting material and activities.

Atkin, who had recently stepped down from his management job but remained a consultant to Meetup, comes from the world of advertising and marketing. In his 2004 book *The Culting of Brands* he describes how products sometimes attract consumers who feel an all-but-religious devotion to them. In some cases—Harley-Davidson motorcycles or Apple computers, for example—the passion lasts for decades and passes from one generation to the next. In others, like Vans sports shoes, the attachment may rise and fall. A bit like members of cults, brand fanatics often seem to be looking for a way to both distinguish themselves and identify with others who like the same thing.

The book, which marked a high point in Atkin's career as an advertising executive, gave him a chance to offer managers around the world insight on how they can help customers turn shared interests into relationships and communities. Atkin saw that the Internet was going to bring people together to share their ideas about everything—from politics to products—and he tried to show businesspeople how to not just survive but thrive in this new environment. He turned out to be right about the public using technology to trade information on marketplace decisions. According to our BrandAsset Valuator surveys:

- Sixty-four percent often talk with friends and family about favorite brands.

- Fifty-six percent rate products and services online.

- Fifty-one percent rely on online consumer reviews when deciding what to buy.

- Forty-seven percent rely on recommendations from family and friends about what to buy more than before the recession.

We modeled a brand basket of companies that define community building. These are the top 10 percent of companies and brands in BrandAsset Valuator that score the highest with consumers on being "social," "socially responsible," "visionary," and "down to earth." Within this basket are brands such as Whole Foods, Ford, Olive Garden, Wii, Facebook, Twitter, McDonald's, Disney, and eBay. And these "Army of Davids" brands outperform all other brands on key metrics:

One of my favorite brands	+263 percent
Would recommend to a friend	+218 percent
Prefer most	+142 percent
Worth a premium price	+135 percent
Use regularly	+126 percent
Like and respect	+73 percent

When he moved from the advertising business to work for Meetup, Atkin was able to devote himself entirely to understanding how people built enriching and satisfying groups without worrying about their commercial implications. In a paper he published in 2010 on Forbes.com he noted that our media-saturated environment predisposes people to capriciousness. By this he means that we are exposed to so many images and ideas that we are vulnerable to distraction. However, when we focus on a group, especially one that gives us a sense of purpose, we are more likely to settle into a more comfortable and stable routine. Online this might mean visiting the same sites every day. Offline it could mean attending meetings or stopping at the same coffee shop every so often to be with like-minded folks. Like everything that depends on human nature and social interaction, the way that groups are created, grow, and live cannot be quantified. However, the mystery can be observed, and as a longtime observer Atkin offers a "community checklist" of elements that must be considered as you evaluate a group's potential:

- Does it satisfy a real need? Do its members learn more, have more fun, get more done, or get support?

- Does it have a clearly articulated purpose?

- Is it clear about who belongs and who doesn't?

- Is there interaction between members?

- Do members form enduring relationships that go beyond the original reason for connecting?

- Do members contribute, do they participate, do they work together to achieve the common purpose? An audience is not a community.

- Do members feel responsibility for each other and the community at large?

- Are there roles, responsibilities, and jobs performed by the membership?

- Is it self-policing? Do people censure or eject unruly or unreasonable members?

- Are there guidelines, rules, or norms of behavior?

The designers and artists who gathered together under the banner of Tampa Graphic Design Meetup satisfy Atkin's criteria perfectly, and he has seen hundreds and perhaps thousands of effective groups arise even in the last two years. Many have pursued political agendas independent of major parties or elected officials (in fact, the largest Meetup groups in the Tampa area are part of the so-called Tea Party movement), while others promote specific causes like protecting children from violence or supporting breast cancer survivors. Meetup even hosts a "Random Acts of Kindness" group.

The social media that allow people to build local groups have given individuals one more kind of resource that can be used to improve the quality of their lives in a direct way outside traditional institutions, many of which are out of favor, and with little or no financial cost. All this occurred just as the pain of the Great Recession motivated millions to seek a definition of success that was less dependent on status symbols and wealth. Although this desire may seem to require some sort of grand gesture or big life transition, it is more likely to involve something much smaller. The army of Davids benefits from a big supply of foot soldiers, but it also needs generals. In fact, in Tampa we found a very active community of "Meetup Leaders" who come together to swap stories on how best to build and sustain their groups. This leadership is essential as it gives individuals the courage to step out and know that others will rally around their convictions. People like Brianne Swezey make this dynamic possible.

More ways to enlist are coming. In 2010, for example, one of the creators of the social network giant Facebook launched Jumo (the word means "together in concert" in the African language

Yoruba) to connect individuals who have time, money, and talent to nonprofit organizations involved in helping people around the world. In concept Jumo would help someone in New York who knows how to build water systems go to a community that needs her services and donate them. Similarly, Jumo could show a retiree in Denver who would like to donate a slice of his monthly check to a cause he holds dear—child health, for example—how to do it.

Chris Hughes, who built Jumo, discovered the power of this kind of organizing when he created MyBarackObama.com, a Web site that collected 13 million participants who helped decide the 2008 election. The site was eventually taken over by the Democratic Party, which failed to capitalize on its energy. In spring 2010 Hughes told TheDailybeast.com, "It didn't remain an independent organization, which I think it should have. In the language of the campaign, we saw a movement of people who were hungry for change. They were much less concerned with the Democratic Party."[1] With Jumo he hopes to organize and channel the concern and generosity of millions who don't want to affiliate with a partisan political party into ongoing involvement. Others, including Facebook, have offered ways to accomplish a similar purpose but only as part of a sprawling set of services and connections. Jumo is for social activism only, and participants won't be distracted by other functions. "People have a genuine desire to be more involved in the world around them," Hughes told TheDailyBeast.com. "But the Internet and opportunities online haven't yet caught up with that desire for people to meet and engage."

Jumo and other sites that seek to turn positive impulses into action are precisely what Meetup's creators had in mind. Having read Robert Putnam's 1995 landmark book *Bowling Alone*, which warned of the decline of "social capital" represented by dwindling civic life, they tried to create a technology to reverse the trend. Atkin looks at today's social media landscape and concludes that Meetup and the others are succeeding. The change will take time as Americans rediscover the organizing skills lost when they stopped joining fraternal organizations and clubs, but the restoration of the neighbor-to-neighbor connection has begun.

"The recession slapped people in the face and forced them to consider what is important," says Atkin. "All the stuff you can't afford and the things you bought because you thought they would make you happy aren't it." The "it" that Atkin believes people are discovering is the powerful bond that comes when people work together to achieve a worthy goal, like boosting struggling non-profits with free design, advertising, and Internet services. Of course this generally happens when online gatherings shift to real-world, face-to-face meetings. The two great benefits of this, he adds, are less loneliness and more direct actions that make things better at little or no cost to the individual.

———————

Perhaps the most innovative method for organizing people to do good outside of the normal channels of charity and government service emerged in San Francisco in 2008, when a local activist named Brent Schulkin organized hundreds of people to shop—that's right, shop—at retailers who agreed to invest more than 20 percent of the profits they earned from the group shoppers in energy efficiency. Called Carrotmobbing (carrots symbolize a positive incentive as opposed to a stick, that is, a boycott), the campaign had its first success at the K&D Market, where Saturday profits tripled thanks to the mob and the owner used some of the extra profit to pay for new energy-saving lights.

Schulkin doesn't promote his concept aggressively. Instead he offers his Web site as an organizing tool and encourages others to conduct their own Carrotmobs wherever they happen to be. After his K&D success, locals organized buying sprees at retailers and restaurants in Portland, Kansas City, New York, and half a dozen other U.S. cities. In each case businesspeople agreed to invest in some way that would benefit the greater good and were then rewarded with a flood of sales. This buying-with-a-purpose brought long-term benefits in the form of first-time customers who would become regular patrons. It also gave participants a way to use dollars they were going to spend anyway to make the world a little bit better.

In Tampa, a young entrepreneur named Kim Pham was hoping to raise about $1,200 to make her little shop—Kaleisia Tea Lounge—more energy efficient. She identified ways to improve lighting, ventilation, and water consumption and made a proposal to Carrotmob headquarters. They liked the idea and helped some allies in Tampa organize a mob, but when the day came most of the forty or so participants turned out to be her regular customers. The event did not generate the revenue for energy improvements, but it was not a total failure. In fact, it brought into focus the special challenges posed by Tampa's sprawl, and it affirmed the depth of connection Pham had already established on her own. After all, those regulars who *did* show up came because they care about her.

A Vietnamese immigrant, Pham comes from a family of entre-preneurs; her mother, a successful businesswoman, encouraged her to forgo a formal business education and instead learn by doing. She came to Tampa in 2005 with the idea for a teahouse that would be both a business and a kind of haven for the community. The location, just off the interstate highway that links downtown with northern suburbs, offers customers a perfect spot to take a break either before or after work. Pham decided to call the place Kaleisia Tea Lounge (*Kaleisia* is a combination of the words *kalei-doscope* and *Asia*), and she decorated in bright colors. The menu was built around what she calls the "wall of tea," where more than a hundred canisters of leaves from around the world allow for an almost limitless number of mixtures. Simple foods and pastries make it possible for customers to have a light lunch or dinner.

Pham's goal was not to maximize earnings-per-patron but rather to build repeat business by establishing a spot that was a soothing antidote to the stress of life in a transient and splintered community. (Florida is second only to Nevada in the number of residents born somewhere else.) Pham, who is twenty-nine, is succeeding not just because of her ideals but also because of the conversations and relationships that flow from her business philosophy. The more interactions around your business, the better you understand your customers (and vice versa). Like the bartenders in the TV show *Cheers,* "where everybody knows your name," she made a point of learning all about her customers and making sure their orders were perfectly executed.

Free Internet access, live performances, free workshops, and artwork by locals also built Pham's business, but the shop's value as a focal point for the community became most evident when she started focusing time and money on community projects. Profits from her retail tea packets—called Tea Drops—go to fund the preservation of a local park and to art programs for children. Every spring Kaleisia hosts a festival of music and art—bands, belly dancing, free food, a silent auction—to benefit Community Stepping Stones, a nonprofit that conducts programs for children and adolescents. This activity, which Pham undertook as an expression of her values, was according to BrandAsset Valuator perfectly aligned with what consumers prefer. As our surveys found, 73 percent agree that they are "willing to pay a premium for companies that contribute to my local community."

By offering ways for people to be generous and involved, Pham used tea to improve life in Tampa just a bit and to strengthen relationships. As her customers became friends, they caught her spirit of engagement. One day she arrived at her shop to discover a few regulars, who were talented painters, decorating the wall near the shop door with a mural showing Asian-style slanted roofs with mountains rising behind them. In a blue sky the words "Kaleisia Tea Lounge" were written in a graceful script alongside a pair of delicate tea leaves.

"Nobody asked them to," says Pham. "They just did it. They were just kind, and they really did support us."

A petite woman with long black hair that she parts in the middle, Pham projects a mix of amazement and self-confidence. She's amazed that she has succeeded in building a beloved and successful local business despite intentionally doing the opposite of what others might do. (Giving away profits, inviting people to linger over inexpensive orders.) The confidence comes through when she talks about how her customers respond to her. For proof she can point to all the books and magazines that customers have brought to the shop and left for others to read, and to the back wall of the shop interior where other artists, inspired by the mural outside, used tea leaves to spell out *communitea, opportunitea, humanitea,* and so on.

When she opened her shop, Pham deliberately ignored a lot of the lessons taught in books about how to succeed in business. She bypassed conventional wisdom about selecting her location, avoiding busy sites where national retail stores were clustered. And instead of rushing to open, she took months to outfit and decorate the space. But the care she poured into the effort impressed her landlord so much that he gave her half a year rent-free. When she finally opened, the mood of the place and quality of her food and drink won her a loyal and ever-growing customer base. "We make sure that we are friends with the customers," says Pham, "and they can say, 'I know the owner.' Our customers have taken ownership of the store."

After five years, Pham has proven that her instincts about business, community, and making a contribution to Tampa were right. Even through the Great Recession her business has grown, and she has reached the point where she is ready to give it to employees who are willing to maintain the army of Davids model. "It would make me happy to give it to them," she said. "I trust them." Her plans call for a move to Charlotte, North Carolina, where she believes the market is ready for "a place to make tea as it's supposed to be consumed all day every day for everyone." Once again she will make a commitment to support local nonprofits and provide an environment that is a refuge and a resource. She has learned, she says, "If the customers stay happy, you can keep going." Making them happy doesn't require a large amount of capital or a big commitment to expensive marketing. The main investment comes from the heart.

The experience of Kim Pham and the Carrotmobbers reveals how customers can be inspired to help a business grow when they get the opportunity to use their dollars for some higher purpose. Groupon.com, which arose at about the time when Schulkin conducted his first mob, mobilizes the masses with a more direct, pocketbook appeal. It says to consumers, "Join together in big enough numbers, and we'll give you an amazing bargain." In an era of high unemployment and widespread belt-tightening, Groupon's ability to save lots of people money while helping a business keep its doors open may be considered a real public service. Groupon.com offers daily deals on products, services, even meals at restaurants for members who check the Web site. The steep discounts—typically half price or less—only kick in after a certain number of people agree to pay for the coupon or "groupon" that gives them the special price. For consumers the site means low prices. For businesses it is an ingenious way to create or expand a market at low cost.

Groupon evolved out of an earlier effort that was quite similar to Meetup. Called Thepoint.com, it offers people a central place to organize campaigns and raise money for everything from environmental protection projects to disaster relief. Some campaigns on Thepoint.com involve individuals seeking donations to pay for college or rebuild after a fire. Others are devoted to raising funds for bigger causes, like medical research. The name—Thepoint .com—was inspired by Malcolm Gladwell's best-selling book *The Tipping Point*, which examined the ways that a certain idea, invention, or concept can become a widespread phenomenon once it reaches a "tipping point" where a sufficient number of people embrace it. Thepoint.com had yet to reach its own tipping point when its founder, Andrew Mason, hit upon the Groupon.com concept.

Mason began in his home city of Chicago, where he felt like he was stuck in a consumer rut, never going to eateries or shops other than the ones he was already familiar with, he told us by phone. He hunted down businesses that would be willing to offer discounts in exchange for a big surge in customers. He then began selling vouchers for these discounts online. The way Groupon works, businesses won't honor the vouchers until a big enough group signs up to buy. The number guarantees a volume of business that will justify the price cuts. It's an ingenious model that keeps people coming to his Web site every day looking for deals. (Some participants who are eager to get their vouchers will even refer friends to the site, which means they help Mason build his membership list.) Founded at the end of 2008, Groupon grew so fast that by 2010 it served forty cities, claimed 1.5 million members, and was recently valued at $1.35 billion.[2]

Although Mason's organization does distribute discounts, he sees it as both a group buying club and a new media outlet that tells members about all sorts of places—theaters, restaurants, spas, hotels, and other business—they might enjoy. "We're less a modern version of a coupon than a modern version of a city magazine that exposes you to interesting things," he says. "Groupon gives you that extra, powerful incentive to go out and try it." In Chicago alone Groupon has 325,000 members who get a notice every day. When the offers are good, as many as ten thousand people click on the "buy" button. With friends telling friends about the great deals they get on the site, membership continues to grow. "We'll be the biggest daily circulation service in Chicago before long," he adds.

In Tampa Bay, the second entrepreneur to offer a Groupon discount was Wendy Longman, co-owner of a boating company called Windsong Charters. She offered four hours of canoeing or kayaking, which normally cost $42, for just $15. She sold more than enough coupons to hit her target—and with just 42 percent showing up to redeem the coupons she sold, the cost of the program was less than she expected. She considered the experience a big success and will do it again. In meantime she promotes discount group sales and "Wacky Kayak Wednesdays" on other social media sites that drive both tourists and locals to the marina where she operates.

Windsong's sailboats, kayaks, pontoons, and other miscellaneous boats are moored and racked in a marina north of St. Petersburg in New Port Richey. Driving there from the south, on State Road 55, we passed through a landscape of dead strip malls, abandoned auto dealerships, and billboards touting dental miracles, religious academies, and "cash-4-gold." The company occupies a trailer on a patch of what used to be the parking lot of a dockside restaurant that closed years ago after a fire. Racks of yellow kayaks stand near the trailer, and when we arrived an ancient terrier was sunning himself on the pavement. A plaque mounted on the side of the trailer announced that Windsong was the Pasco Chamber of Commerce's 2010 Business of the Year.

Wendy Longman greeted us with a big smile and an offer of coffee and locally grown tangerines. A square-shouldered woman in her forties, she wears a brown polo shirt with the Windsong logo on the breast, sunglasses, and khaki shorts. She has the tanned and freckled face to prove she spends plenty of time on the water.

"My philosophy when I started Windsong was a Henry Ford/ Bill Gates attitude," she says. "Henry Ford said that everybody will be able to afford a car in their driveway. Bill Gates said everyone will be able to afford a PC in their house. Wendy Longman said everybody will be able to have an affordable day on the water."

Longman's passion for the sea is at the heart of a business strategy that has helped her start-up company thrive despite a so-so location, a barebones facility, and a business climate that is the worst in sixty years. She is a frequent user of Facebook and Twitter and posts bright and enthusiastic reports on sailing conditions, special offers, and her experiences at sea. (She's a Coast Guard certified captain.) Longman is so ingenious that she got a state license so she could conduct weddings aboard her sailboats, which brought a lucrative new line of business, and she's very effective when it comes to communicating the benefits of her services, which many people might consider a low-priority luxury. Her pitch, ironically enough, focuses on value.

"Say there's a family of eight of you, and you're all going to see Mickey Mouse," she told us. "It's $75 per person for the ticket, and you get to stand in line for six hours for a twelve-nanosecond ride. You come to me, stand in line for twelve nanoseconds, and you get to have an eight-hour ride." Longman will also charge the family about $200 less, for the day, than they would pay at Disney World.

All the details for Windsong's offerings appear on a highly interactive Web site, which she updates frequently with new services. In addition to weddings, which she performs every week, Longman also helps people with marriage proposals, holiday celebrations, and even memorial services at sea. With each new customer she adds to the network of people who receive her online updates and makes herself more a part of the wide Tampa Bay community, which is far more valuable to her business—especially in hard economic times—than the sporadic tourist trade. This networked approach helped her increase revenues throughout the Great Recession and build a happy life.

"I hate my job," she says with a laugh. "Can't you tell?"

———————

Delivering a message through social media helped Wendy Longman and Kim Pham enlist support for their businesses, which in turn sustain the local economy. Pham takes it a step further and contributes directly to projects that benefit the community. For Eric Sturm, messaging via social media is not a tool for reaching a market for a product. It is, instead, the product itself. And he intends to make both a living and a serious political impact with it.

"I am one of those people who can't afford to leave and is having to innovate in order to stay," explained Sturm in the spring of 2010. "I bought a home that is now worth less than my mortgage. My bank was bailed out with my tax money, but I haven't missed a payment on my loan. I work for myself, which means I'm 100 percent responsible for what happens to me, and I live in a place where the powers-that-be have screwed up the economy so badly that the only way to grow is to do something online. But I try to keep my sense of humor. Some days I even think, 'This place is so pathetic maybe they'll decide to make me emperor one day.'" Sturm already is an emperor of sorts in the online realm he has built at a site called 83DegreesTampaBayMagazine.com.

At first glance, Sturm's 83 Degrees Web site looks like a booster-y, Chamber of Commerce–type news site devoted to promoting a sunny view of Tampa Bay. A brainy-looking "economist" stares out from a photo in center of the homepage over a caption that notes he is "professor Dr. Joe Dieppe of the prestigious Bastogne School of Business." Under a column labeled "Top Stories" the site promises an "in-depth jobs report" as well as news about a proposal for a new stadium to house the Tampa Bay Devil Rays baseball team.

But look a little closer and you'll discover articles touting "The Awards for Awards" and declaring "Florida Needs Bernie Madoff." Dig deeper and you'll find out that the Bastogne School of Business is a fiction and that everything on this Web site is satire intended to rouse the public to change local politics.

Thanks to attention from other media and word-of-mouth buzz, Sturm's site gets heavy traffic—and has made him a bit of a pariah in more traditional business circles. "It resonates," he says, "because people know that things here are a lot worse than the media and the government told us they were. When we were losing fifty thousand jobs a month, the state and counties were telling us we were still growing. Now we're the second-worst for personal bankruptcies and near the top of the list for foreclosures and unemployment. It's time to have a real discussion about how we live, how the economy here is organized, and what has to be done to make things better. We can't wait for some outside force to come tell us what to do or help us. We have to do it ourselves."

At age thirty-nine, Sturm says he belongs to a generation that never expected to see a Social Security check and always assumed that everyone has to take care of themselves. When the economy seemed to boom, he says, "It didn't matter as much that people in big corporations and government were incompetent and there was some corruption. I mean, we could afford it."

However, he adds, in times of economic crisis incompetence and corruption become harder to ignore. At his old job for a large corporation he'd rather not name, his contributions to efficiency saved stockholders $54 million—but still weren't enough to guarantee any security. He decided to strike out on his own as a publisher of regional entertainment guides just as the Great Recession struck. (He based his business plan on faulty economic reports that were later "updated" to show the drop-off in business activity.) As the unemployment rolls swelled and his own prospects dimmed, his resentment grew. Finally, when local officials used taxpayer dollars to pay a firm to develop a "good news" Web site about Tampa Bay, Sturm's concern became outrage.

"This propaganda site was planned to use our taxes to put up articles about how great things are," fumes Sturm. "First of all, things aren't great. They are all screwed up, and it's the fault of our so-called leaders. But besides that, I don't think we need to be using public money to put out the same old message about real estate and tourism and sunshine that got us into trouble in the first place."

Deciding to fight fire with fire, Sturm purchased a domain name that nearly matched the one selected for the government's promotional media site. (The name, 83 Degrees, is a reference to Tampa's average temperature in April.) Sturm went live with his site on the same day that the subsidized Web site was posted and got wide attention for his spoof. "It was done to punk or culture jam what they were doing, and it worked." Indeed, within weeks the local business press was pointing to a "credibility gap" in the government-sponsored project, and after a few months state officials began investigating possible ethics violations related to the contracts awarded to producers.

As an activist, Sturm was such a smashing success that he was completely shunned when he attended a gathering of local political figures who used to rely on him for information about what is going on around the community. As a businessman, he's struggling to make money on his Tampa Options entertainment guides, which depend on advertising and downloadable subscriptions. People who are unemployed, struggling to make ends meet, or just worried about the future tend to lose interest in nightlife, restaurants, and diversions that are featured in Tampa Options. Recognizing this, and the possibility that many years may pass before the region recovers from the recession, Sturm is looking for opportunities, especially in political activism.

"The problems in Florida have been brewing for a long time," says Sturm, "and maybe the pain has to get even worse before people will consider doing what's necessary." What's necessary, he thinks, is a better system for raising tax money, investing in infrastructure, and encouraging innovative businesses that will take advantage of Tampa's port, its labor pool, and its climate to produce goods and services for a global market. "We missed the industrial revolution, but maybe we can take part in the next big wave, the innovation evolution."

Support for political change may come outside the current two-party system, and Sturm can imagine helping to organize disaffected locals to contribute in small ways—using dollar bills and votes—to change the status quo. He sees an opening in a recent proposal to create an elected mayor—to replace the current appointed chief executive—for Hillsborough County. Home to the city of Tampa, the county is the fourth largest in the state, and the job would come with real power to influence the future of the region. Years may pass before the position is created, but just to be sure, Sturm has bought the domain name www.hillsboroughmayor.com.

"I may be homeless and blogging from a public library," quips Sturm, "but if that job ever opens up, I'm going for it."

———————————

The power of a man (or woman) with a laptop is not to be underestimated. This truth is illustrated every day by the growing power of Web-based publishers who are offering ways for writers and journalists to reach big audiences without the cost of creating or distributing printed journals or traditional TV programs. One of the most successful sites of this type, the Huffington Post, was launched in 2005 and grew like wildfire to become the second-most-popular online news outlet. Founder Arianna Huffington told us that despite its relative size, her operation had much in common with local bloggers.

"There is no question that new media tools have empowered the little guy—leveling the playing field between the media haves and the media have-only-a-laptop-and-an-Internet-connection crowd," she says. "It's definitely allowed individuals to have a voice, make an impact, and hold the powerful's feet to the fire." Long a vivacious and assertive presence in politics, Huffington moved into media with many powerful allies. But her site hosts reports from thousands of contributors, many of whom have no other outlet for their views.

"For individuals hoping to find meaningful connection in a complex world, blogs and news sites offer astounding opportunities," adds Huffington. "This desire for self-expression transcends borders," she says. "For instance, the HuffPost's live-blog coverage of the Iranian protests following that country's contested presidential election last year was only made possible by the contributions of Iranians on the ground—from videos posted on YouTube to tweets conveying what was happening in the streets. Self-expression is the new entertainment. People are not satisfied with passively being told what is 'news'—they want a seat at the table. Especially if it has a laptop on it!"

No development in generations has had a bigger effect on the flow of information than the Web, which has forever changed the balance of power. Today, people can't be fooled into liking something. In this age of transparency, a scandal or piece of negative news will spread quickly, affecting the level of trust consumers feel for a company.

"But the good news is that it can be rebuilt. People respond well to honesty. If a company finds itself in a crisis situation, it's imperative to acknowledge responsibility—to genuinely acknowledge how one's actions were to blame," says Huffington.

"Take, for example, the housing bubble that was fueled by the Wall Street casino. Even though we now know that people in the Fed were warning of big trouble ahead as early as 2004, the warnings were ignored—and when the bubble burst in 2008, the experts were all too happy to fall back on the 'Who Could Have Known?' defense. There are two lessons in all this: it's important to communicate forthrightly, and actions matter. You can't fake good behavior or a good response—people will see right through it."

––––––––––

While Arianna Huffington and her site empower a thousand bloggers on a national level, in Tampa, Sturm, Pham, Longman, and Swezey prove there are many ways to play the David role and confront the Goliath that is the current economic environment. The time when size gave businesses a huge advantage is passing. The Davids are thriving because they can readily establish common interests and deep relationships with both customers and suppliers. These contacts provide the information and insights they need to maximize their profitability while minimizing costs. While they each flashed a unique style and chose a different emphasis, they also had much in common. They were all playful, passionate, and highly skilled communicators. They were optimistic by nature, comfortable working with all kinds of people, and unafraid to share their ideas. Three out of the four were under forty years old. The one who was past the age of forty—Captain Longman—was truly young at heart.

———————

Pauline Ores would not be surprised to find that the Tampa Bay Davids share certain personal qualities. As the lead social media analyst for IBM Market Insights, Ores has made a deep study of how tools like Facebook, Groupon, Meetup, and Jumo affect communication in a broad sense as well as the marketing of goods, services, and ideas. A dark-haired woman with blue eyes and a wry sense of humor, Ores speaks with the blunt style of someone accustomed to being the only woman in a room full of male engineers. Although she works for a huge corporation that most people immediately identify with high technology, she focuses intently on human-scale values and behavior. She's widely quoted by the social media cognoscenti. Among her more quotable insights:

> "In the social media world, the most powerful person is the one who shares the most."

> "Control in social media is like grabbing water. The stronger you grab, the less you hold."

When we met with Ores to discuss what we had learned in Tampa, she began by observing, "Only human beings can listen. With other animals it's called hearing." By this Ores means that as social creatures we must depend on our ability to listen and understand others. If we use this ability, we quickly learn what our fellow human beings want us to know. But be careful, she says. Sometimes the most important information lies in what people refuse to say. To illustrate this point she tells a story about her mother, a Holocaust survivor, who was surprised when she visited Eastern Europe and tried to speak Russian with the people she met. Because their countries had been subjugated under the old Soviet Union, most had been taught Russian in school. But when given a choice, they refused to speak it, even with a tourist, in order to demonstrate their independence. In general, adds Ores, people do not like being dictated to by anyone, whether it's a boss, a salesperson, or a family member. However, people do enjoy being heard or being invited to share their views or participate in a project or community endeavor.

Whether by design or instinct, the Tampa entrepreneurs have opened themselves to others, signaled they would listen carefully, and invited responses. They have also adhered to some of the other essential elements of social networking Ores has observed:

• Having someone specific manage the community.

• Enabling people to have conversations themselves.

• Staying true to their ideals.

"There can be no faking it," she says, "because the online world is so vast and the people in it are so alert that scams, deceit, and deception will inevitably be uncovered."

The honesty and transparency that come naturally to Longman, Swezey, and the others will be essential to every business enterprise of the future, says Ores, who has studied communities and technology for fifteen years. "The platforms [like Facebook and Twitter] may come and go, but the sharing of information is never going back into the box," she adds. In the age of social media large companies with lots of employees will have to foster honesty and openness in order to deal with complaints or criticisms coming from the outside. To do this well, managers will have to be receptive. "They will have to be willing to be influenced if they ever want to have influence on others."

The good news in the analysis that Ores makes is that fearless and ethical operators will thrive in the future marketplace, wherever they are located. "There are many ways to win with this," she observes. Perhaps as many as you might find in an army of Davids.

Chapter Five

BLOCK PARTY CAPITALISM: BROOKLYN, NEW YORK

Consider, if you will, the lowly pickle.

Five thousand years old (well, at least the pickling process is that old), the cleverly preserved cucumber delivered in a bath of salty brine, oil, or vinegar is actually more nutritious than it was when it was picked on the farm, and it is decidedly more delicious. The spices added to the jar make the vegetables—cucumbers are just the beginning—savory, sweet, salty, or even fiery. They also connect you, from that first bite, directly to the product's source. If you were chowing down at a couple of friends' home in Brooklyn, that source could be in distant Holland, Michigan, where Heinz operates the largest pickle factory in the world, or it might be a restaurant kitchen a few blocks away, where a young entrepreneur works through the night to turn humble vegetables into delicacies that include hot heirloom cucumbers, Moroccan beans, and minted eggplant.

Brooklyn Brine would be your hosts' choice if they were pickle connoisseurs and devoted residents of the brownstone borough that hums with life in the shadows of Manhattan's skyscrapers. In recent years Brooklyn has become a kind of pickle paradise, with more than a dozen new producers opening for business—including Brooklyn Brine. The ultimate artisanal enterprise, this tiny pickle company was started, literally, on the power of a skateboard and the strong right leg of Shamus Jones.

"It started with an idea without a strategy," says Jones, during a break from deliveries. "I knew the community was interested in new things and that I could take local vegetables that are only in season for a short time and use pickling to make them available year-round. I asked the guy at a restaurant across the street from where I lived if I could use his kitchen at night when he was closed. I didn't have any credit, so I couldn't fill out his credit application or anything like that, but he just trusted me. A lot of people were like that."

A Brooklyn native, Jones had lived and worked in Seattle for a while, where he had figured out how to use pickling to preserve the exotic (and pricey) chanterelle mushrooms that grow wild in the Cascade Mountains. Chanterelles are not well suited to Brooklyn, but the borough has vibrant ethnic communities that prize all kinds of pickled vegetables. Inspired by the potential market, Jones began experimenting with recipes. Finally, on a sunny morning in August 2009, he loaded some samples in a backpack, grabbed his skateboard, and hit the sidewalks.

Gliding from block to block, trailing the faint scent of garlic and dill behind him, Jones stopped at food shops in Greenpoint, Williamsburg, and other neighborhoods. As he met one proprietor after another, he ceremoniously opened his jars and invited them to taste. He got an order at almost every shop. Within months he was selling a thousand jars a week and Brooklyn Brine was becoming an institution. The success was built on taste, as Jones discovered ways to make eggplants, beets, and other vegetables into concoctions that would complement a meal in the way that a wine might. His most startling breakthrough—pickled garlic stalks—won an award at the 2009 International Pickle Festival, and soon calls from eager retailers were coming from distant Manhattan and then Boston.

In some cases, the interest from customers may have been aided by the fine print on Brooklyn Brine jars, which notes that every ingredient inside is New York grown and certified organic. Going local and all natural fits Jones's own values. Shamus Jones is a vegetarian who worries about the environmental impact of shipping food hundreds or thousands of miles. He is also eager to live out his values—what he feels inside—through his work and business. "But we don't want to be seen as pushy environmentalists or hippies," he insists. Decidedly apolitical, Jones is willing to take a stand, personally, but he wants his company to succeed because it makes good pickles. It just happens that the freshest and best-tasting ingredients come from local organic farms. The same equation explains his devotion to small-batch production methods. "We are succeeding by doing this on a scale that allows us to hand-pack each jar," he says. "That is how we have become successful in a short time, and we intend to keep it that way for a long time."

At age twenty-nine, Shamus Jones says he is certain he has found both the work he wants to do for the rest of his life and the place where he'd like to live. In fact, he doesn't separate his work from the other elements—a sense of place, friends, family, fun, and so on—that go into his definition of happiness. In his mind, and his heart, a life well lived is a seamless blend where he can find connection and relationships that cut across every aspect. He wants to sell his pickles to his neighbors and see them when he goes out for the evening. And whether he's doing business or shopping for groceries or clothes, he likes the idea of expressing his values in everything he does. He's skeptical about big institutions, including government and corporations, and stubborn about living on his own terms.

"I was raised just by my mother, and she was a person who always stressed the positive side of things and understanding that every choice you make has consequences. I started getting into skateboarding in 1989 and 1990. That was a rogue kind of thing where you are with the weirdos and the misfits, but it's also political. My peers opened my eyes to the idea that you don't have to do it like it was always done before. Don't believe you have to have 2.5 kids and live the way other people live. For me it's more important that I think for myself, and live in a way that is sustainable and fair to everyone."

This post-partisan, ethically sensitive view makes Jones almost a poster child for his generation. His has come of age in a time when money and career are no longer easy avenues to an identity. Indeed, even as the Great Recession was beginning to ease, many experts were forecasting an extended period of high unemployment, especially for young adult males. The main reasons for this pessimism revolved around lower consumer spending (Americans are still recovering from their debt binge) and tight credit, which would limit the job creation that happens when businesses expand. The trend means it will be that much harder for young adults to build a life with a sense of purpose. The answer for individuals will lie in the kind of creativity, innovation, and energy that arises from within to meet a challenge.

Shamus Jones's generation seems well equipped for the challenge. These Millennials—born roughly between 1980 and 1998— take a more holistic approach to life and seek meaning in everything they do. As first noted by demographers Neil Howe and Williams Straus in their book *Millennials Rising,* this generation is more ethnically, racially, and religiously tolerant than any in American history. Millennials have a live-and-let-live attitude, leading all groups in their support for gay marriage and the rights of immigrants. They are more engaged in community life, as evidenced by their high rates of volunteering and voting, and (perhaps due in part to the 9/11 attacks) remarkably patriotic. And as the first generation raised in the media-saturated Internet age, they resist marketing hype and they hunger for authenticity and creativity.

At roughly ninety million, the Millennial Generation is 20 percent bigger than the post–World War II Baby Boom cohort, but is distinguished by much more than its size. As a massive survey published in 2008 by the tech entrepreneur Eric Greenberg shows, this generation is remarkably optimistic, with almost 80 percent saying they have more opportunities to make the world a better place than previous groups, and 85 percent saying they feel they must lead society toward positive change.[1] Millennials in many ways view the post-crisis landscape as a clean slate. After all, they had less to lose to begin with. According to DEMOS, a Washington, D.C.–based research group, 34 percent of eighteen- to thirty-four-year-olds do not have health insurance coverage.[2] And while others may fret over their 401(k)s and depleted bank accounts, Millennials are 24 percent happier than other generations in American society. Fifty percent of them believe they "will be better off in a year from now."

Jones, who cracked the chain store market with an order from Whole Foods, talks excitedly about hiring his friends at good wages, providing health insurance, supporting Brooklyn's economy, and promoting public interest in distinctive, high-quality pickles. "People are starting to understand that food can be like an art form," he says. "There are nuances and subtleties to food that make a real difference, and I like being able to offer people that experience."

Although he didn't know it at the time, when Shamus Jones wheeled around Brooklyn with his pickle samples, he became part of a trend that has been reshaping life and business in the borough for more than a decade. At 95 Broadway he arrived at an important landmark in this movement, a modest-looking butcher shop with a blue and white awning. Called Marlow and Daughters, it sells the highest-quality beef and pork available in all of New York City and a wide variety of made-in-Brooklyn products. It is also one of four businesses started by a pair of young entrepreneurs—Mark Firth and Andrew Tarlow—who are widely regarded as pioneers in the borough's renewal. Since 1998, when they opened a restaurant because there was, literally, no place to eat in their neighborhood, they have played a key role in the renaissance of Brooklyn, and, more important, a carefully constructed way of life built around urban neighborhoods.

Their values—authenticity, craftsmanship, honesty, and the common good—read like a code of honor, not a capitalist manifesto, but they match the sensibility of the customers they hoped to serve. Like Brooklyn itself, they are no-nonsense people with a sometimes ironic sense of humor. After all, Brooklyn has always stood in the shadows of powerful Manhattan and carried a chip on its shoulder because it feared being regarded as second class, a "dems and dose" kind of place where immigrants, tradesmen, and middle-class families have always found support and encouragement without the artifice and pretension of Park Avenue or the Upper East Side.

Tarlow and Firth settled in Brooklyn for the same reasons everyone else did—the borough offers reasonable rents, easy community connections, and relief from the more-is-better mantra that dominated Manhattan in the debt-fueled run-up to the Great Recession. Their first business, called simply "Diner," occupied a long-shuttered prefabricated Kallman diner that had been sitting in the shadow of the Williamsburg Bridge, on the corner of Broadway and Berry Street, since the Great Depression. It was surrounded by a solid neighborhood of working-class families and young adults who were pursuing their dreams in the big city, but who couldn't find a fair-priced bite to eat within walking distance of their homes.

"It was a no-man's land down here," recalls Tarlow, and opening the place "had everything to do with [serving] the community." In fact, when he and Firth started Diner with $100,000 and lots of elbow grease, they were trying to establish a shelter of sorts, where neighbors could find comfort foods like soups, stews, and hamburgers, as well as the comfort of a kindhearted staff and fellow patrons.

The menu, which also includes fancy daily specials, was built on locally grown meats and vegetables and fish from local waters. This choice was partly a matter of the owners' sensitivity to environmental and energy issues. Tarlow notes that food transport is a major contributor to greenhouse gasses, which makes locally grown supplies a better choice for the Earth. But the policy was also based on taste. Locally grown stuff is always fresher, and Tarlow was determined to give his neighbors the best possible ingredients. It's not a marketing strategy. "We don't use language like free-range chicken, and it's very rare we say on the menu where it [the food] comes from," he explains. However, the quality comes through, and when someone asks, the staff at Diner will happily explain where every ingredient came from, and how a dish was made.

The open attitude is another part of the Firth-Tarlow business model. They hire people for their personalities as well as their experience, because they want to build positive, long-running relationships with their customers. Turnover at Diner is so low that the typical employee has been on the job more than four years. Most like the place so much that they show up for meals on their days off. The pattern holds at the food shop, Marlow and Daughters, as well as at the company's two other Brooklyn restaurants, an Italian eatery called Roman's, and Marlow and Sons, which the *New Yorker* describes as "a commissary/newsstand/tavern/oyster bar." It's a busy, noisy place that is too loud for most people, admits Tarlow, adding, "And too crowded. But based on this space we can only be what we are. In that way would it work for Texas? No. It also wouldn't work in a mall. In those ways it is very Brooklyn."

Tarlow is a fit-looking man with blue eyes, brown hair, and a soft, friendly face. At age thirty-nine he's a bit older than the Millennials who make up his customer base. But he expresses all of their values and could be considered one. On a Wednesday afternoon he sits at a big table in the back of Marlow and Sons, watching as his staff tend to the lunch crowd, which includes a steady stream of people fetching to-go orders at a counter. The bustle suggests a profitable operation, and Tarlow allows that all of his businesses do make money. However, he only recently installed a system for tracking profit and loss in a very deliberate way. Until then he was satisfied to know that at the end of each pay period his employees were covered, to draw his salary, and to give away 7 percent of every day's revenues in free food and drinks.

This relatively loose approach to finance can be traced to the values Tarlow and Firth brought to their enterprise. "The intention wasn't really to make money," he says, adding, "[Only] in this past year have we tried to prove that we could buy these ingredients, offer the food at this price, and still make a profit." The prices at Marlow and Sons are slightly higher than what patrons might expect to pay at a chain restaurant. A lunch sandwich made from grass-fed beef is $9.50, for example, and at dinner a chicken entrée is $22. But patrons seem to understand that they are paying for better ingredients, better service, and the intangible benefits of having such a unique and welcoming business in the neighborhood.

While they may not explain it this way, their willingness to consider values beyond price prevents the so-called race to the bottom that can be so destructive in times of economic crisis. The classic example of this can be seen in Japan, where a long period of economic stagnation prompted noodle shops to chase customers with ever-lower prices. As prices were slashed, so were maintenance, worker wages, and benefits. As noodle shop employees lost earning power, the economy was further damaged, and communities suffered. With this example in mind, it is easy to see how Tarlow's approach—provide both a high-quality product and a positive presence in his neighborhood—helped him find a sweet spot in the market. It's why, as he says, someone would rather spend $15 once a week at Marlow and Sons than grab three $5 sandwiches at a fast food joint.

This success is a point of pride for Tarlow, and it allows him to show anyone who's curious about the practicalities of community-based business just how it can work. But from the start he's been more interested in making his life work in a locale where he can feel meaningful connection with his neighbors. When the Great Recession arrived, he heard the worry and discouragement in their voices and brought his staff together to discuss how they might help.

"I really impressed upon my staff that the only thing we don't want to talk about here is the recession," recalls Tarlow. "People need to sit down and relish the humanness of the experience of dining. If they're only going out once a week, or a month, we want them to at least come to us instead of going elsewhere."

The ban on glum talk is fully consistent with Tarlow's human-scale sense of purpose. To him, quality starts on the inside with an attitude of compassion and empathy. He's better able to live this way in a place where people live close together, see each other on the street, and prefer to eat a meal made by familiar hands. It's a life quite close to the one his grandparents knew when they, too, lived in Brooklyn.

"I grew up in Long Island," explains Tarlow. "My grandparents had been in Brooklyn." When he reached an age when he could choose where to live, he joined many in his generation who went back to urban centers. This move is yet another expression of the Millennials' affection for the Greatest Generation and their interest in traditional American values like community pride, civic engagement, and the can-do toughness found in old city neighborhoods. As they say in Flatbush and Canarsie, "It's not for nothin'" that the borough has always stood for the quintessential melting pot, a proud place where newcomers have always been able to make it. (Even today, one in five Americans can trace their ancestry back to someone who settled in the borough as an immigrant.[3])

As they have moved to Brooklyn, the Millennials have helped a storied community recover from a long period of decline—symbolized by the loss of the Dodgers baseball team in the 1950s—and grow in wealth, population, and diversity. Much like the Detroit that planners envision for the future, the borough offers genteel neighborhoods with affordable housing, great shopping and entertainment, and all within a subway ride of Manhattan.

It is such an expression of the Millennial Generation's hopes and dreams that thousands are putting down deep roots as they buy homes and start families. Andrew Tarlow and his wife are raising three children in a house they bought in a neighborhood near Diner, and they intend to stay. "The Long Island [suburban] thing was for my parents," he says. "I say I'm from Brooklyn."

The value of this lifestyle becomes most evident, in Tarlow's eyes, when he's able to provide a setting where his neighbors can mark their most important occasions. Birthdays and anniversaries and holiday celebrations are staples at his neighborhood haunt, but he's actually more deeply affected by the times when his customers seek the comfort of Diner or Marlow and Sons when their needs are more profound. "If there's a death in the family," says Tarlow, "we would like them to be here with us."

Days before we met, a customer who played in a local band died, and his bandmates, family, and friends came to mourn at the same place where they had gathered at least once a week for many years. Tarlow fed them all, and poured drinks into the night, and when they tried to pay the bill, he just wouldn't give them one. "That's a sign of community," he says. It's not a business strategy, he adds, but it is part of an approach to life that finds value and meaning in every moment.

―――――――――――――

When Andrew Tarlow talks about the joy and sorrow he shares with his customers, his voice rises and falls in a soft rhythm. It's almost like he's singing a love song. According to his customers and neighbors Porter and Hollister Hovey, he's got perfect pitch.

The Hovey sisters (Porter is twenty-seven and Hollister is thirty-one) don't need a sermon about free-range chicken when they read a menu, and they don't require a complex back-story on the fennel in their soup. What they *do* want, and what they came to Brooklyn for, is a chance to live in a place that feels established, almost permanent, in its authenticity and character. The history of the place dates back to Dutch settlers and the Revolutionary

War. Its famous sons include both Walt Whitman and Spike Lee. Some ancient homes remain from colonial times, but most of the borough's stone and brick buildings were built between 1860 and 1930, and the trees that shade certain blocks are old and leafy.

As experts in community will tell you, the architecture makes a difference. Solid and traditional apartment blocks and row houses invite people who want to put down some roots and like the idea of living in a place that has sheltered the middle class for a century or more. A local historian, Francis Morrone, likes to say that the strong neighborhoods contribute to the borough's reputation for stubborn persistence. "The allure of Brooklyn has to do with survival," adds Morrone, whose walking tours of the borough amount to a strolling seminar on its development and growth. Participants, who are likely to see kids playing in the streets and catch the aromas of a dozen dinners being prepared in a dozen kitchens, immediately sense the timeless feeling of nurturing neighborhoods.

The feeling is as much a matter of architecture as anything, says Morrone. Mostly overlooked during the period of massive redevelopment programs that occurred after World War II, Brooklyn held onto its grand old buildings, which meant that they could be claimed and rehabilitated by successive generations who enjoy high-density, distinctive neighborhoods. When sturdy brownstones and apartment blocks offer spaces big enough for families at rents far below Manhattan prices, they invite people to settle in for the long run.

The lifestyle, built around walking instead of driving, encourages daily trips to the butcher shop or the greengrocer rather than weekly pilgrimages to a supermarket. This rhythm of life brings everyone into the market and fosters reliable, supportive relationships. It's the conversations that begin with "How are you today?" that represent the deeper values of a Brooklyn life. It's the daily contact with someone who comes from a different part of the world and may even speak a different language that makes life more interesting.

This diversity is recognized around the world, as the Hoveys learned when friends from Scandinavia came to visit. Instead of crossing the bridge to visit Chinatown and Little Italy, their guests preferred Brooklyn's ethnic neighborhoods, which include Hispanic, Caribbean, Asian, South American, and Orthodox Jewish communities. In these places they discover unique shopping districts filled with one-of-a-kind stores and restaurants instead of chain stores and fast food outlets. As Porter Hovey explains, nothing here feels too fabricated.

By *fabricated*, Porter seems to refer to a service or product that comes with a false sensibility. In this way Italian names—*grande*, *venti*—for drinks offered by a Seattle-based coffee shop chain can seem fabricated. The same is true for knock-off "antique" furniture sold at big-box stores or imitation vintage clothes displayed at suburban shopping malls. Whenever an item is marketed in a way that denies its true origins, she can sense the deception, and it's this deception, not the product itself, that makes her uncomfortable.

Porter doesn't mean that everything she buys should be hand-crafted. Instead, she says, she wants authenticity. Recent Kia car commercials that describe the automaker's beginnings as a bicycle maker ring true to her. (Kia doesn't have to make bespoke cars, just be true to its story.) IKEA furniture communicates in the same way, adds Hollister. "You don't have to buy antiques everywhere or have every piece unique . . . you just need a few things to make it your own."

As Porter Hovey explains it, she is not "anti-brand" in a way that suggests a total rejection of consumer goods. Instead she wants the things she uses and accumulates in her home to convey her values. Sometimes this means shopping at IKEA for a mass-produced bargain, but sometimes it leads her to pay more for a custom-made or locally sourced item. This greater need for intrinsic meaning to consumerism is evident in our latest BrandAsset Valuator data:

- Eighty-five percent (total population) are willing to pay more for higher-quality goods and services.

- Only 24 percent (total population) preferred to buy name brands. (Among Millennials, this is only 21 percent.)

- Only 15 percent (total population) are willing to pay more for brands that enhance their social standing.

This pattern can also be seen in data on consumer behavior in the years leading up to the recession, as shown in Figure 5.1. In 2005 and 2006, Americans abruptly shifted their interest away from things that made them look good on the outside (status and ego), toward purchases that made them feel better on the inside (truth and meaning). We discovered this by modeling a factor analysis of purchase drivers from our data. And even while the economy was humming along, consumption shifted from

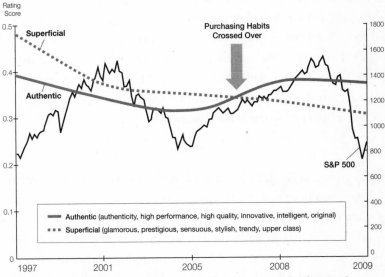

Figure 5.1.   Were People Conscious of Their Excess and Adjusting?
Source: BrandAsset Valuator 2009.

conspicuous to personal enrichment. This suggests that perhaps society was becoming aware and concerned about its indulgences. Put another way, we shifted our mind-set *from what we carry* to *how we carry ourselves*.

Brooklyn is an icon of an America that is dismantling ego and artifice and peeling back the layers of excess and façade to reveal the foundational truths about what makes people truly happy. While brands still perform that function, their value is no longer so explicit. As noted, these days only 15 percent of people are willing to pay more for brands that "enhance their social standing." Instead, ego gratification is more nuanced and satisfied from within. You get it from expressing your values, from close relationships, the ideas you embrace, and your own creativity.

Although they have serious corporate day jobs in Manhattan, the Hoveys are known in Brooklyn for their avant-garde photography and their devotion to antiques. They share a loft filled with taxidermy, art, and furniture from several different centuries, including apothecary cabinets and dressmakers' dummies. In Brooklyn they can afford a space big enough to hold a full-size couch and all the other objects and decorations that make a place feel like home. They can find this stuff, as well as handmade clothes, crafts, and jewelry, at shops throughout the borough and at the weekend market called Brooklyn Flea. It is yet another manifestation of the character of a place where urban life is enjoying a very particular kind of renewal.

The Flea, as locals call it, resembles the weekend markets that have occupied piazzas and vacant lots in cities across Europe for many generations. (Milan has the Cormano. In Brussels it's the market at Place du Jeu de Balle.) In fair weather months, the Flea operates at two locations—one in Fort Greene and the other in a neighborhood called DUMBO, for Down Under the Manhattan Bridge Overpass. Hundreds of vendors participate, selling everything from architectural salvage to vintage clothing.

The founder of the Flea, Eric Demby, is yet another young Brooklynite who grew up somewhere else (Maine) but recalls grandparents who lived in the borough neighborhood of Crown Heights. He says that at first he settled in Brooklyn simply because it was cheaper, but he quickly realized that the community was evolving as a place where people with shared values were seeking a very specific way of life.

"I sense a lot of intention in the people who move to Brooklyn now," says Demby, as he takes a break from his workday to sip coffee at a café called DUMBO General Store. He's dressed for work in a plaid shirt and distressed jeans. His eyes are framed by fashionably clunky glasses with black frames. "People are pursuing a way of life specific to Brooklyn, or that they believe is specific to Brooklyn," he continues. "It's a sense of place and togetherness that people are constantly amazed exists in New York City. The idea that 'Oh that's so Brooklyn' is growing. There's a critical mass of similarly minded people pushing these ideas forward."

As Demby sees it, the ideas that animate the new Brooklyn are deeply personal and can be seen in the way people interact at his market. Customers enjoy meeting the artisans, or in the case of antiques and salvage, the "hunters" who bring unique and beautiful items for sale. At the Flea they get to know about the materials used to make jewelry or the history of an old chest of drawers, and they get to haggle over price. "There is an old-fashioned town square-ness about what we are doing," he adds. "People are craving public space. People want to participate. We are a big operation and supportable because people have been turned off by their retail experiences. The price at the Flea is determined by what you want to pay."

The public square is not just an intellectual concept for Demby. A former political activist, he has worked in public relations and as a writer covering political affairs, music, and culture. Before he started Brooklyn Flea he wrote frequently for the Brownstoner, an online journal that was founded to report on real estate and renovations and quickly evolved to cover, as editor and founder

Jonathan Butler notes, "all the tangential topics that impact life inside and outside the home in Brooklyn." The site offers a business directory, restaurant reviews, links to media outlets that cover the borough, and dozens of Brooklyn-centric blogs, including one devoted to the proposed construction of a sports arena in Flatbush.

Although the Brownstoner's success—1.5 million page views per month—is a remarkable triumph of local blogging, what Demby and Butler recognized was that a local online community could be translated offline. "What we saw was that everyone went online to seek community, and then in the past two years, they have come off again." Demby and Butler were pioneers in exploring the virtuous circles of growth and engagement between online and offline communities. The success of this strategy is borne out in the Amazon Alexa Web traffic reports for Brownstoner, which show traffic tripling from its 2009 starting point. The marketplace Demby and Butler created drew more than 150 vendors and 20,000 shoppers on its first day, in April 2008, and its popularity never waned. The mix of dealers who sell antiques, household knick-knacks, old clothes, and art gives the Flea the feeling of a weekly scavenger hunt, and two dozen food stands offer an astounding variety of treats. Among the most popular are Asia Dogs (hot dogs with Asian toppings), Milk Truck (a gourmet grilled cheese stand), and the Red Hook Vendors, who offer the kind of street food you'd get at a fiesta in El Salvador or Guatemala.

The food and the merchandise are so unusual that culture critics actually report on the Flea for local TV stations and newspapers. And the @brooklynflea Twitter hashtag lights up each weekend. But the main attraction is the crowd itself. The Flea is a good place to look for celebrities—famous actors, artists, and musicians can be spotted there every weekend—but regulars relish the opportunity to bump into friends and share their news about a special find they uncovered at a market stall piled with items. (In the very first newspaper article about the Flea, *New York Times* writer Guy Trebay reported on a customer who bought what he believed was a famous Roseville vase for $12. If authentic it may have been worth ten to thirty times as much.)

When customers have one of those *Antiques Road Show* moments, Demby knows that he has done his job well. He chooses vendors in the same way that a curator might put together a collection of art. "We are very attuned to where we live and what Brooklyn is. We are very methodical about what we do, and we always wanted the Flea to be democratic." In his mind, *democratic* means both open to all and responsive to marketplace demands for certain goods and better prices reached through the most direct application of the principles of supply and demand.

True to the spirit of the borough, Demby says it's not enough to simply bring buyer and seller together and feed them nicely while they practice momentary street-level capitalism. "We don't want to be viewed as interlopers," he says. Instead, he wants to create a lasting institution that will contribute to Brooklyn's vitality. And he believes he has done this. "The Flea has this way of erasing that feeling of being second fiddle. If you want Brooklyn in your brand, at this point, your brand needs to be world-class." Making a world-class community that retains its livable qualities may be the ultimate goal for everyone who has made a commitment to the place. As they succeed, they are actually making Brooklyn-ness into a symbol of authentic value that can be respected and prized around the world.

The original "Brooklyn" shirt was a replica Dodgers baseball team jersey sold in the Sears catalogue in the 1940s. It sold best in the region around New York, but when Jackie Robinson broke the color barrier in 1947 and the famed "Bums" finally won the World Series in 1955, the white shirt with blue letters was briefly popular across the country.

In 2010, shirts decorated with the word "Brooklyn" are prized around the world. Fashion-conscious hipsters wear them in

Berlin and London, and so do teenagers on the Tokyo subway. Brooklyn means something to almost everyone in the world. At Brooklyn Industries, a twelve-year-old company that has made Brooklyn shirts for, literally, hundreds of thousands of buyers around the world, it stands for an approach to life that can be boiled down to three words: *Live. Work. Create.*

More than a slogan, these words were the basis for Brooklyn Industries' creation in 1998, when two artists—Lexy Funk and Vahap Avsar—met at the Omi International Arts Center in upstate New York. As Funk remembers it, she was coming to grips with two of the major problems artists face—relevance and money. Where relevance is concerned, she had begun to notice that a business, especially one that offers a well-branded everyday product, can have as much impact on the culture as any writer or artist. (To understand this all you have to do is consider the way carmakers define the American landscape or Victoria's Secret affects our view of sex.) On the money side of the equation she had seen that the traditional ways to turn creativity into income—selling through galleries or other venues—work well for precious few. "How do you really make a living as an artist?" she asks rhetorically. "You do these odd jobs and feel distressed."

Beginning with a design for a messenger bag that would be made out of vinyl recycled from billboards, Funk and Avsar rented a huge space in an industrial building near the old Brooklyn Navy Yard. The former sheet metal fabricating plant was so big it could hold entire billboards, which were peeled apart, cut, sized, and fashioned into bags. The couple lived in the same space, without heat or air conditioning, in part because they wanted to prove that "You can live and work and create in an integrated way. You don't have to live your life in a dichotomy where there's work and then there's life."

Doing all the design, sewing, and peddling themselves, Avsar and Funk sold what they made by word of mouth until they opened a retail store in Williamsburg. Like the bags, and the clothing that followed, the store was something they designed themselves. The feel of the place appealed to their customers, who came in great enough numbers to provide the cash flow for steady expansion. Never blessed with outside capital, the firm has grown slowly by offering products with a certain message. The stuff decorated with the word "Brooklyn" and other themes that evoke the borough communicate their love for a certain kind of urban lifestyle. Other items, like T-shirts with political slogans, combine a values statement with quality merchandise.

"Traditional marketers speak down to customers," says Funk, who is a young-looking thirty-eight-year-old woman with long strawberry blonde hair and blue eyes. "We want to speak directly, and we're not afraid about coming down with an opinion." Other companies that sell affordable fashion, she points out, tend to play it safe and be unintellectual. "Idea-driven fashion stays in the purview of high-end designers. We are affordable, *and* we present ideas."

The ideas promoted by Brooklyn Industries mirror the Millennial Generation's sensitivities. They include equal rights for men, women, and every sexual orientation as well as support for the environment and local communities. The company has distributed gay pride T-shirts and devotes some of the revenue from sales to organizations that promote recycling, low-carbon transportation, and the development of urban recreation areas like the famous High Line Park, which was recently opened atop an abandoned elevated railway track in lower Manhattan. Inside the company, Funk and Avsar have emphasized worker security and benefits and followed a slow-growth plan that they believe will allow them to gain efficiencies of scale without sacrificing quality. Their factory workers in Brooklyn are mainly immigrants, and they have always been paid above prevailing rates. (In lean times they were paid on weeks when Funk and Avsar were unable to pay themselves.) As demand outstripped the available workforce, they considered outsourcing production to China. With the help of a

Chinese neighbor who manufactured bags, Funk found factories in China where she could get high quality from operators who treat their workers well. She says she is committed to monitoring the factories and will, if necessary, use her relationship with suppliers to improve working conditions.

With an alert approach to outsourcing, Funk believes that Brooklyn Industries can make every part of the world that it touches just a little bit better. To pursue this broader mission, she and Avsar slowly expanded their retail chain, spreading first to different neighborhoods in the borough and then venturing into Manhattan in 2006. In 2008 they opened a store in the Bucktown neighborhood in Chicago. Another store opened in Portland in 2009 and then Philadelphia in 2010. An arrangement with National Wind Power, which builds wind turbine projects, has allowed Funk to power all the stores, along with her headquarters, with wind energy. Furnishings are made from recycled materials, and the stores are continually involved in community projects that range from donating book bags for needy kids when school reopens in the fall to boosting literacy with book parties and supporting charities with the profits from specially designed T-shirts. (One of these projects involved a graphic shirt bearing the message "NYC Is Still Dying." Proceeds went to homeless people with HIV and AIDS.)

Brooklyn's advocacy work and slowly spreading influence (from Philadelphia to China) create what founder Funk calls a "sense of agency" for everyone at the company. "A store is an essential part of a community, a meeting point, a hub," she adds. She intends for her stores to spread a little bit of that Brooklyn feeling— neighborliness, creativity, responsibility, passion—far and wide. She expects to find receptive customers and communities almost everywhere because the values that drive Brooklyn Industries are universal. "Berlin is not the same as Brooklyn, but there's similar energy in Berlin," she says, her voice rising with excitement. The same feeling exists in certain parts of London or Portland. "It helps form a collective unconscious that is different." The difference is a hunger for authenticity, connection, and quality as it's found in her home borough. "Brooklyn is the name and a place," she concludes, "but it's also an inspiration."

If Brooklyn is not just a place but also an inspiration, what would be the ultimate expression of Brooklyn-style authenticity? Might it be an organization that could help anyone in the world build a life around personal creativity and values? If so, then it's called Etsy, and it operates out of a loft space in a bustling neighborhood that is wedged between the Brooklyn and Manhattan Bridges and a narrow stretch of the East River.

Up a few flights from a business service shop called Copy Rite, Mr. Grit dominates Etsy's reception area: a ten-foot-tall sculpture made of cardboard layers like shingles. Blessed with wide eyes, an orange nose that looks like a carrot, and tiny arms with clawlike hands, the thing resembles a *Tyrannosaurus* with an owl's face. Beyond Mr. Grit young staffers work at computers where they manage the sprawling Etsy Web site, and artisans practice their craft in brightly lit workspaces. Presiding over all of this is twenty-nine-year-old Rob Kalin, a boyish redhead wearing jeans, a cardigan, and a blue silk scarf made by a friend.

Born and raised in Boston, Kalin got the idea for Etsy when he worked for an arts and crafts Internet site that offered advice and community support for people who made things by hand but that did not provide them with a way to sell their work. (A craftsman who works with wood, he was also struggling to find people who might be interested in buying his own creations.) Beginning in 2005, Kalin and his partners began developing an online place where any artisan in the world could display work and sell to any buyer in the world. Within five years the company had 300,000 vendors—the majority were women in their twenties and thirties—and the site was visited by millions of shoppers every month.

Revenues came from the twenty-cent fee charged to list an item on the site and a sales commission of 3.5 percent. Even at these low rates, the company grew to be worth an estimated $100 million in 2010.

Although Etsy is based on the Internet, the most advanced global medium in history, Kalin argues that his success is based on the oldest form of communication—storytelling. "It's part of human nature to want to know where you buy from, what you are buying," says Kalin as he snacks on granola and milk at a big table in the Etsy break room. "I don't think this is a trend, or a movement. This has always existed." The only difference here is that stories are told via Internet-based tools that create and activate a connection between the creator and the customer. These digital connections are not dissimilar to the human moments experienced by patrons of the Brooklyn Flea.

Outside, a Q train rumbles by on its way across the Manhattan Bridge. Kalin raises his voice a bit to be heard over the noise, talking about the sense of satisfaction that comes from working with your hands—"In my mind everyone should be making stuff"—and competing with ideas about what defines *value* in commerce.

"Large faceless corporations want consumers to believe that value is just price and convenience," he says. "That's bullshit in my mind. Value to me is what something means to your life, and then there's value to the planet and the environment, too."

Food is the perfect example of a product that has been sold on price and convenience, he says. Thanks to chemicals and carbon-producing transportation networks, food prices have been pushed steadily downward. However, when personal, social, and political concerns are brought to bear, people often make the choice to pay a bit more for something locally produced. The key to moving a customer is a good story.

"I'm not going to say, "Hey, you *have* to care about our values. I'm going to tell compelling stories in as compelling a way to as many people as possible." Before the Industrial Age made it possible to manufacture goods and ship them great distances, people generally knew the story behind the table or teapot they bought because they knew the craftsmen who produced all the goods sold in local markets. These relationships established bonds between buyers and sellers, which gave everyone incentive to deal fairly.

The stories that Etsy tells in an effort to reestablish the values of the old marketplace may be contained in the description of a piece of jewelry and the woman who made it. Others are told in little films called "video portraits" that the company produces to highlight certain vendors. Whatever the format, they depend on the basic human hunger for narratives and the accessibility of the Internet to establish relationships.

"This is the beautiful subversive power of the Web," adds Kalin, pointing out that you can get straight to the person who is producing the item you want to buy. The next step for Etsy will take the company into cities, towns, and villages to help people meet together in the old-fashioned way: face to face. "We help them find people in their area who care about making things. Some rent commercial space to sell together. Others have craft fairs and meet-ups"—creating places where they can get to know each other. The point is to use the tools of the Web to benefit people, communities, and the environment on many levels.

Where does Brooklyn fit into the paradigm that powers Etsy? Kalin notes that everyone who works at the company lives in the borough and that because it is "dirtier, noisier, grittier, and every day is a bit of a fight," they are accustomed to setbacks and even "a little bit of destruction" every day. The combination of daily gains and losses contributes to the creative process. But in the end, he says, the Brooklyn spirit, which values what's on the inside of a person or a business, can be seen almost anywhere in the world. His favorite example is an Etsy guitar vendor.

Handcrafted out of wood, Armor Guitars are made by musicians who welcome contact with people all over the world who share their passion for music and instruments. Thanks to Etsy, James Peters and his entire family make a living by crafting everything from banjos to a large guitar they call the Jumbo. They accomplish all of this from a little red barn and woodshop in Springfield, Tennessee, a town of seventeen thousand that's a lot more like Brooklyn than you might imagine. But then again, thanks to Etsy, so is the rest of the world.

The tales of Brooklyn virtues represented by a skateboarding pickle man and the global reach of Etsy are so varied but also so consistent in their message that it's hard to refute the idea that a values revolution is under way. We understand, however, that stories aren't enough if you are a businessperson who wants to understand the post-crisis economy. Fortunately there's ample evidence from the consumer marketplace to support our notion that Americans are reorienting their investments of time, energy, money, and emotion—that the *spend shift* is real.

The proof is seen in a basket of the brands that consumers surveyed in BrandAsset Valuator associated with integrity and meaning. These brands represent the top 10 percent that score the highest on being "authentic," "kind," and "straightforward." These companies speak with a voice of clarity and sincerity and include Dove, Colgate, J&J, Burt's Bees, and National Geographic. And again, they outperform the competitive landscape:

Feel loyal to the brand	+277 percent
Would recommend to a friend	+214 percent
Worth a premium price	+177 percent
Prefer most	+155 percent
Use regularly	+147 percent

The idea that self-worth is a matter of inner values like integrity, character, authenticity, and even modesty is nothing new to

Americans. These ideals were revered by the people who first colonized the eastern seaboard and were carried by the pioneers who pushed ever westward. They are especially helpful in times of struggle, when you can't afford frivolous distractions and the easy comforts that can be bought with a dollar. After all, it doesn't cost anything to be a person of good character who meets others with honesty, kindness, and empathy. This truth got people through the suffering of the Great Depression and the horror of World War II. But since then, Americans haven't been challenged by such a widely shared crisis. We haven't been forced to sort out our values. Until now.

Chapter Six

THE QUALITY OF THE LION: LAS VEGAS, NEVADA

"Hi, this is Krystle—how may I help you?"

"Um, I need a pair of sneakers just like the ones I had. Is that your department?"

"Well, I'm sure we can take care of that. Can I have some information so I can look up your account?"

With her hands poised over a computer keyboard, twenty-eight-year-old Krystle Bone listens carefully, types in the name and address she hears through her telephone headset, and watches as all the information for a customer in Florida pops up on her computer screen. She has brown hair and eyes and a warm, infectious smile. On the wall of her cubicle a black puppy, part Labrador and part pit bull, gazes at her from the photos that decorate her space in a customer call center near Las Vegas. At the cubicle next to hers a coworker dons his headset and answers a call with a cheery, "It's a wonderful day at Zappos! How may I help you?"

Bone needs just seconds to find the information she needs. She asks, "Is this Frank in Florida?"

"Yeah, hi."

"Are you talking about the Keds Champion leather CVO?"

Frank confirms the key information and, without prompting, explains that yes, these are women's shoes he's ordering for himself—quickly pointing out the recent order for a size seven, in the same model, "which I got for my girlfriend."

Some men have an intense interest in ladies' shoes, and clearly Frank is worried about the unstated subtext that inevitably arises when a man asks for footwear that is labeled "for women." Bone is discreet and sympathetic, and she tells Frank in Florida that she can see he has been buying the same sneakers, in two different sizes, for years. "You must really like 'em," she says cheerfully.

"I used to wear them as a kid—I'm sixty-two now—but they don't make them for men anymore, so now I buy the women's size twelve." Imagining a middle-aged couple walking a mall some-where in the Sunshine State in summery clothes and identical, gleaming white shoes, Krystle Bone smiles to herself and responds not just to the content of Frank's comment but to the tone, making an effort to join with him.

"I have a friend in New York who's a costume designer," she says, "and when she worked on *High School Musical 3* they bought a lot of things for women that were made for guys and a lot of things for guys that were made for women. You go with what works, what fits, right?"

Reassured by this kindness and respect, Frank explains that he's been calling 888-926-7671 for shoes since 2005. Although he could order through the Internet, he likes talking to the people at Zappos.com. And while he might be able to find what he wants elsewhere (with a little effort), he knows that Zappos will always have the shoe he wants in the size he wants and he'll get free shipping even for returns. As he relaxes, Frank lets a little of his old New York City attitude come out and starts pretending that he wants the company to send him a check if he ever finds the shoes he bought at another retailer for a lower price. Bone says she's sorry the company can't do what he wants and tells him how much she appreciates his business. Then Frank lets her off the hook.

"I'm just bustin' your chops," he says. "I'm old-fashioned. I *trust* you guys."

There it was, the magic word.

Trust.

Of all the elements at play in the marketplace, and indeed, in all human relationships, trust is the most essential. Elementary as it may sound, trust is so important to our interactions with each other, and to our very survival as individuals, communities, and even nations, that it deserves special consideration.

In the animal world, trust can be observed in all social species, from dolphins that take turns feeding as a group rounds up a school of fish, to birds that signal each other when a predator approaches. Cross-species trust is also more common than you might imagine. Frans de Waal, a biologist affiliated with Emory University, has written quite persuasively about hippos that trust monkeys to clean their teeth and sharks that allow themselves to be entranced by the massages administered by little cleaner fish (called wrasse) that feed on their skin parasites.[1] The cleaner fish live in dangerous reefs, and as they bask, the sharks risk being injured by the rough coral. Yet they trust the wrasse and the wrasse trust them.

Among human beings, trust is the grease that makes every one-to-one encounter work, and it is the basis for all social organization. Because we are empathetic creatures, able to sense how others feel, we employ trust quite naturally. It is so ubiquitous in our daily lives—governing such basic things as family life and how we treat our neighbors—that we hardly think about it until it is violated. And therein lies the problem.

Over the past twenty years, and especially in the run-up to the Great Recession, Americans have felt their trust betrayed in countless ways. The big events—the banking crisis, the housing bubble, and Wall Street's meltdown—are easy to recall, but they are only part of the story. Alongside these major outrages, people experience the continual erosion of trust whenever they feel they haven't been treated fairly. Unexpected fees that pop up when we book an airline ticket or check out of a hotel make us feel wary. Hearing about cars that won't stop when the driver presses the brake pedal makes us feel unsafe. Products that fall apart or fail to perform as advertised make us feel cheated.

Those of us who follow marketing and retail trends have watched warily as people lost their trust in the mainstream companies they deal with on a regular basis. Not too long ago, consumers generally trusted national brands, companies, and institutions, while also taking them for granted. People didn't give this vote of confidence much thought. When we surveyed trust with BrandAsset Valuator, it invariably turned up as one of the most important elements folks weigh when making a decision to buy something. It ranked second only to quality. But in the past it wasn't something people thought about in an active way. If a product was made by a well-known company, consumers trusted it automatically.

The trust dynamic began to shift about fifteen years ago. The trend showed up in our BrandAsset Valuator survey of three thousand brands done between 1997 and 2001. During this time we saw that the number of products and companies rated trustworthy dropped by 12 percent. The decline accelerated in the era of the corporate scandal—Enron, WorldCom, Tyco—which tarnished the image of all big corporations. In the period between 2001 and 2005 an additional 43 percent of brands fell out of favor, leaving a majority in the negative column.

We believe this happened in part because the vast majority of people knew that leaders in both the private and public sectors were selling a false vision of reality. Even as we signed up for home equity loans, we knew in our hearts that the value of our houses had been artificially inflated. With middle-class incomes stalled but consumption continuing to rise, everyone understood, intuitively, that the apparent wealth of the consumer economy was based almost entirely on borrowed money. How reasonable was it for companies to sell us on consumption and loans in this period?

How realistic was it for the politicians to cut taxes, continue spending, and nearly double the national debt?

Reassurances about self-correcting markets and "new economic paradigms" that meant we shouldn't worry about overheated stocks and rising debt may have soothed certain sectors of the public for a while. But even during the economic expansion of 2002–2007 the vast majority of Americans—80 percent—lost real income. Surely these people knew they were falling behind and that all the talk about how they weren't was not based on realistic analysis. Accordingly, the next big decline in trust—another 12 percent loss in trusted brands—began in 2007 (before the Great Recession struck), and continued through 2009.

With the real estate and banking crises, the nagging fears became a reality. The collapse of Lehman Brothers and Bear Stearns exposed the recklessness at companies that were supposed to be rock solid. Who, a decade earlier, would have imagined taxpayers becoming shareholders and being forced to bail out the likes of Citi, GM, and AIG? With the Great Recession, the small reservoir of trust that remained seemed to evaporate all at once. The BrandAsset Valuator data showed that trust in financial institutions declined 58 percent as the public questioned their role in causing the financial crisis. Fast food restaurants, suffering from negative publicity due to food contamination scares, saw a 25 percent decline in trust, and U.S. automakers— GM and Chrysler both took bailout money—went down 18 percent.

You might say that, after all, the finance, fast food, and car industries all suffered from particular scandals, so their decline in public esteem should hardly be considered a sign of anything larger. If only that were the case. Dig deeper into the numbers and you see the loss of trust affects every corner of the economy, as Figure 6.1 shows.

If you step back and look at the entire consumer marketplace, it looks like a virus has entered the system and devastated it. Even

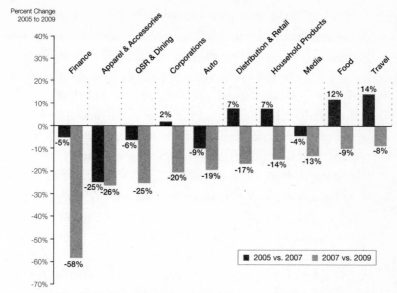

Figure 6.1.   Trust Decline Across Industries
Base: BrandAsset Valuator USA 2005–2009 All Adults; change in the percent of brands with greater than 20 percent endorsement on the Trustworthy attribute.

when you include the most favored entities, overall consumer trust declined by 25 percent. This problem is not restricted to America. In the same period we have seen trust declines all over the world:

The Trust Virus Pandemic

Mexico: –37 percent

Singapore: –45 percent

France: –49 percent

China: –60 percent

Brazil: –61 percent

Italy: –63 percent

Source: Individual country BrandAsset Valuator studies 2007–2009 all categories.

And sadly the trust virus has spread beyond commerce. In this age of instant information we have seen an explosion of scandals. From politics to sports to religion, the public has been exposed to a startling variety of stories about abuses of power and the violation of trust. Of course, scandals are nothing new. The difference today is the number of scandals and the pace of the reporting. For much of the past century quiet social bargains struck with the press protected the powerful—from philandering presidents to addicted movie stars—from public exposure. The collapse of this old order combined with the rise of new technologies (blogs, Twitter, Tumblr, and the rest) that make everyone a potential journalist has deluged society with discouraging and even dispiriting truths about the character of our leaders and heroes. In a time of plenty people might have been able to regard these outrages as entertainment, but with the economy in shambles and unemployment at its worst in decades, it's hard to see anything funny in the abuse of public trust.

In early 2010 analyst Michael Maoz of the highly respected Gartner consulting group surveyed the wreckage and declared, "Trust in institutions is dead."[2] Maoz was writing for people in the business of serving consumers, and what he meant was that no one can assume the people believe in their products, advertising, or public statements. "The network knows your secrets," he said, warning of the power of the Internet. "Hiding, skating atop, papering over the facts used to be much easier, but a new reality is out there: better to be more self-critical and earn back trust than show the peacock feathers of hubris all over again and get slammed by online communities.... Trust *qua* Trust lives, but as something unearned and taken for granted it is only a memory. Customer relationships have never been more important, nor have their intricacies ever been as complex."

Tony Hsieh (pronounced *Shay*) would agree with Michael Maoz on the profound importance of trust and second his argument that it must be earned and never taken for granted. But he wouldn't say that maintaining trust in a relationship is a complex challenge. He sees it as a very simple matter of designing a culture of respect for a company and making sure it is established and embraced by all before anyone ever tries to sell anything to a customer. For anyone eager to create long-term success, "Money has to be number four of five on the list of priorities," Hsieh says. It comes behind relationships with others, the desire to create something worthwhile, and having a sense of control over your own life. In other words, money doesn't make you happy, but happiness can make you money.

"Going in, we didn't really know what we were doing," explains Hsieh as he settles into a swivel chair in a conference room one floor down from where Krystle Bone works in a call center. The meeting room is decorated in a skateboarding theme, with boards on the wall and a collage of skater images covering the ten-foot-long conference table. A lanky, boyish-looking thirty-six, Hsieh is the son of immigrants from Taiwan. Raised in California and educated at Harvard, he seems to see his life as a kind of playground that promotes creativity, relationships, and excitement. "I was really most interested in designing a lifestyle for myself. It was selfishly motivated."

Selfish or not, Hsieh had followed his instinct for making himself happy with business to develop an Internet company called LinkExchange that was worth $265 million when he sold it to Microsoft in 1998. After financial backers and others got their share, he walked away with tens of millions of dollars and started an investment fund called Venture Frogs. Hsieh believed that running a fund that was involved in dozens of projects would fit his attention deficit disorder tendencies. In fact he found himself drawn to get deeply involved in just one of those companies, an Internet retailer called Shoesite.com.

The story of Zappos (a takeoff on the Spanish word for shoes, zappatos) would fill a book. It's enough to say that after a stumbling start and many near-failure experiences, Hsieh and the founders of the company hit on a winning strategy. (He says, "We sat down and thought about what we wanted to be when we grew up.") They decided they would stress customer service above all other values and gear their hiring and training programs to develop a workforce that would focus on creating trusting relationships with customers. The key here would be establishing an environment in which the employees themselves felt safe and trusted. In other words, you can't make people be nice and helpful and charming with a regime of monitors and punishments.

Building their company around service meant locating the call center—the people who would handle both phone orders and problems that couldn't be handled online—in the same place as the managers. (Anyone who has struggled with call center operators located half a world away, who don't quite grasp American idioms, will appreciate this strategy.) Las Vegas was chosen for many reasons including real estate and a favorable tax climate. And because its main industry is hospitality—casinos, hotels, entertainment, and the like—the local workforce is filled with people who are both inclined toward customer service and trained to provide it well.

Even in a city where "concierge" is a common occupation, Zappos has adopted a very picky approach to hiring, rejecting at least a hundred applicants for every two or three who get an offer. Once brought into the company, recruits undergo four weeks of full-time training, just to learn how to answer the phone. On the job, call center workers are given wide authority to solve problems. They can accept returns and grant refunds up to a year after a customer makes a purchase, and they can authorize payment for shipping with every new order and every return.

Zappos pays no commissions, so workers have no incentive to pressure customers to make extra purchases, and no one holds a stopwatch on their performance. In fact, call center reps are encouraged to chat for as long as customers desire. More than one call center employee can report that a lonely customer actually kept them on the phone for an entire shift.

The practices that became the Zappos culture weren't devised formally but grew out of an attitude of openness and acceptance. The founders invited input from every employee and intentionally hired people who were, in Hsieh's words, "a little weird," because they brought fresh perspectives. Fueled by Red Bull and frequent parties, the early associates worked extremely long hours, making the company the focus of both their work lives and their social lives. Although authority eventually rested at the top, everyone in the company was encouraged to offer criticisms. In this way, peers actually policed each other, to make sure that customer service was kept at a high level, and workers who couldn't maintain the right attitude would be pushed out. "We were willing to fire people," notes Hsieh, "and not just in the call center."

The focus on making sure employees fit the Zappos mold is as strong today as it was when only a dozen people worked at the company. In fact, an information technology specialist brought to work at Zappos headquarters at great expense was recently fired after just a brief tenure. "He didn't fit with the culture," adds Hsieh, "and we find it's easier to hire the right kind of people and give them the technical training than to try to get someone from the outside to fit the culture if it's not natural for them." The "culture" eventually became codified in a formal declaration that could be used by any organization hoping to build employee commitment and trusting relationships within the firm and with customers. Hsieh invited all Zappos employees to participate in developing the company's list of "core values," and they spent a year on the task. Here is the list they came up with:

Zappos Core Values

Deliver WOW Through Service

Embrace and Drive Change

Create Fun and a Little Weirdness

Be Adventurous, Creative, and Open-Minded

Pursue Growth and Learning

Build Open and Honest Relationships with Communication

Build a Positive Team and Family Spirit

Do More With Less

Be Passionate and Determined

Be Humble

Even a quick study of the Zappos list reveals that it includes all the values expressed by spend-shifting consumers in the post-recession economy. As they welcome change, the Zappos crew is expressing the stubborn spirit of reinvention seen in Detroit's indestructible entrepreneurs and the folks who are retooling at midlife in Dallas. By doing more with less they are living the liquid life, and by working as a team they make themselves an army of Davids who are attacking problems with a sense that together they can prevail. Their passion and humility echo the values of the pickle man in Brooklyn and the block party dads in Kansas City.

The mix of team orientation and individual creativity suggested in the Zappos creed is evident inside the company headquarters, where only the lawyers who deal with sensitive matters get private offices. Everyone else, including the bosses, get cubicles on one of two wide-open floors. However, even though they must accept a certain regimentation, employees are also allowed, even encouraged, to express their individuality through decorations. As a result, most Zappos cubicles overflow with knickknacks, pictures, toys, and talismans. Some—like the ones dominated by science fiction action figures and posters—have definite themes. Others reveal obsessions and fantasies ranging from sports to cartoon characters. Hsieh's own cubicle is decorated with toy monkeys, a cowboy hat, and a sign that announces he is Chief Golf Officer. (Monthly company golf outings are a tradition at Zappos.)

In total, the effect of all the tchotchkes and posters is a cross between a college dormitory and an elementary school playground. (The place has a nap room, and on the day we visited there was even a giant inflatable bounce house set up in the parking lot for employees to enjoy on their breaks.) But no one should worry that serious business isn't being done. Sales have risen every year as the company continually upgraded stock and added clothing, handbags, and accessories like watches to its offerings.

By refusing to cut customer service, the company thrived during the Great Recession, reaching new heights in sales. In the summer of 2009, while news of bailouts still swirled around the banking and auto sectors of the economy, Amazon.com, the champion of online retailing, approached Zappos about a merger. Although the company was privately held and thus exempt from public reporting, the price finally announced when the deal was set was a bit over $1 billion, which suggests that annual sales were in that neighborhood.

In his memo to employees on the day of the sale, Hsieh reassured them that their jobs were as secure as ever. He said that Zappos would continue as an independent brand; having a large and sophisticated partner in Amazon would enhance its growth. The press may declare, "Zappos sells to Amazon," he wrote, but other headlines would properly convey the spirit of the transaction. "I personally would prefer the headline, 'Zappos and Amazon sitting in a tree…'"

Ever an evangelist for the business culture that has arisen at Zappos, Hsieh insisted in his statement, "Just like before, we are in control of our destiny and how our culture evolves." This sense of control is a key ingredient in the psychological mix that makes Zappos run. Although Hsieh first employed it as a matter of instinct—he's just naturally assertive—experts in psychology and organizational theory generally agree that we all feel better and work better when we have a sense that we can affect our own fate. Hsieh got confirmation of this when he began a more formal study of the relatively new discipline called "positive psychology" *after* Zappos became successful. In a business setting, positive psychology suggests workers will do better in environments where they are supported, have the tools and authority to solve problems themselves, and feel emotionally connected to coworkers. The Zappos culture is designed to promote all these elements both inside the company and outside it, so that the firm's motto—*Delivering happiness*—is more than mere words.

Hsieh is such a believer in the value of a positive work culture that he has created a new venture—Zappos Insight—that teaches his blend of Zen capitalism to other companies. The offerings range from a subscription service ($39.95 per month) that offers management tips and videos to a two-day "boot camp" at the Nevada headquarters that includes counsel from Hsieh and his team, as well as a party with the Zappos staff. Launched in late 2009, the boot camp service was quickly sold out for the first half of 2010.

Hsieh is also eager to test his ideas for building trust-based businesses in the brick-and-mortar setting of downtown Las Vegas. Once the center of both gaming and commerce, downtown Las Vegas, which is dominated by Fremont Street, declined as "the strip" along Las Vegas Boulevard boomed with the construction of massive casino resorts. Nineteen of the twenty-five largest hotels in the world have been built in the strip district, and they have drawn almost all of the tourist business away from downtown—leaving the old city center with too many vacant storefronts and struggling businesses. Hsieh sees promise on Fremont Street, but instead of trying to devise a big plan for its redevelopment—something that has been attempted before—he would like to open a handful of restaurants, bars, and nightclubs of the sort he would like to visit.

If you look past the glitz and the gambling, "Las Vegas has a small town feel," insists Hsieh, "and it grows on you as soon as you are outside the strip." While city and state leaders tried to address the decline of downtown with a massive project called the World Market Center, this convention and trade show complex is isolated from downtown by highways and did not revive the old commercial center. Hsieh believes that a modest effort to "create an area with a few places where we would want to hang out" is more likely to make locals feel like eating, shopping, and even living in the old city center. He's looking at this idea not as an investment but as an expression of his commitment to the community and his values. If it works out as well as his effort to build a company he would enjoy in Zappos, Las Vegas could get the kind of boost it desperately needs.

The Las Vegas that Tony Hsieh wants to serve is not the one that stars in advertising campaigns that remind the world, "What Happens in Vegas Stays in Vegas." *That* Las Vegas is the one inhabited by Cher, Celine, and high-limit gamblers known affectionately as "whales." Hsieh's Vegas is home to year-round residents who find themselves struggling to maintain a middle-class standard of living. As the Great Recession began with a real estate crisis, Nevada was struck by the highest foreclosure rate in the country. The average value of homes declined from more than $330,000 in 2006 to $120,000 at the start of 2010.[3]

When we visited in February 2010, Las Vegas had finally gotten some good news on the real estate front, as thirty-nine straight months of price drops ended and a slight increase was noted. Sales had also ticked up slightly due to a number of trust-related factors— builders were offering smaller "right-sized units," lenders were providing better service and terms, and the inflation created by speculation had been wrung out of prices. KB Homes, for example, adopted a new custom-order process that helps buyers limit amenities and extras to reduce their costs. KB Homes have gotten smaller, on average, and nationwide the company's median price has settled at $216,000.

Both KB and D.R. Horton, another major builder in Las Vegas, were reporting that they were finally turning renters into first-time buyers as people began to feel more confident about their jobs and believed the housing market had reached a stable bottom. On the east side of town, where building had ceased two years ago and moonscapes abut new home developments, business was brisk at a Horton project called Hollywood Ranch. So many customers were inspecting model homes that Brian Frabbielle only had time to smile and brag a bit—"I've had four closings in the last month"—before he ran off to meet with some extremely motivated buyers.

With prices ranging from $87,550 to $135,800, Hollywood Ranch offered new attached houses with garages in a gated community with desert landscaping and a community pool. These prices were as much as 50 percent lower than the prices charged for comparable homes when the real estate balloon was fully inflated. With a down payment of 10–20 percent, buyers could own a home for less than $800 per month (below average for renting in similar neighborhoods) and feel confident that their budgets would stay balanced over the long term. Prospective buyers got more assurance from the builder, who distributed a tip sheet intended to steer people away from financial disaster. Where sellers once routinely pushed first-time buyers to stretch the limits of their pocketbooks, Horton advised them to research their credit scores, devise a long-term budget, and get approved for a mortgage *before* even considering a purchase.

Officials at one major lender in Las Vegas who promoted a responsible, old-fashioned approach to home mortgages and personal finance echoed this caution. Marketers for the Nevada Federal Credit Union deliberately sought the business of people who had bad credit scores or, thanks to bounced checks and other mistakes, had mangled their relationships with banks. With personal advice from a credit union staffer and special products like "New Start Checking," people who were supposedly bad risks got a chance to rehabilitate their records.

Credit unions already enjoy a positive image, but Greg Barnes, NFCU's vice president of marketing, decided to build trust by appealing directly to the feelings of his target group. He bought space on eighteen billboards to get out his message: "This Economy Sucks, We Don't."

As Barnes told a trade journal, "This is Vegas, so we were able to push the envelope a bit more" with the ad campaign. Combined, the new level of service and promotional effort brought thousands of new customers into branches. NFCU did a record volume of mortgage business in 2009, when the overall market was shrinking, and increased membership at a faster pace than ever before. Even the institution's credit card business grew by more than three thousand accounts at a time when millions of Americans were actually cutting up their plastic.

Low rates—8.25 percent for credit cards, less than 4.5 percent for a fixed fifteen-year mortgage—attracted many customers, but Barnes and his team worked to hold onto them through open communication. Customers and members are invited to post their comments online on public Facebook, Twitter, and Bebo accounts. Negative or critical comments are permitted and preserved on the site and actually receive active responses, which shows the credit union's commitment to having long-term relationships. At one point in 2009 NFCU had more Facebook friends than the local newspaper, reports Barnes. The pace slowed when the novelty wore off, but the credit union held to its policy of answering every comment openly. When one customer complained about limited services, Barnes's group didn't back away from the issue and took the opportunity to reinforce the credit union's image as a trusted resource:

> We're not a big bank with unlimited resources and bailout money.
> We do our best to keep convenient hours for all our members. Our Contact Center hours are 8:00 AM–5:00 PM Monday–Friday. P.S.T. Our branches stay open until 6:00 PM Monday–Friday. P.S.T. Of course, in the event

of an emergency like you lost your credit or debit card or they were stolen, you can report those 24 hours a day every day of the year. You can also access your account 24 hours a day every day of the year via online banking.

When another angry customer who wanted lower interest on her credit card wrote, "You are now on the list of banks/ credit unions that SUCK!" the credit union calmly replied, "We keep our rates as low as we can—but we do have to generate income to continue to provide low cost products and services to our members."

Realistic, honest, and direct, NFCU's approach to lending stands in stark contrast with the practices of the lenders who contributed to the mortgage crisis that came with the Great Recession. Those big lenders followed predatory practices—falsifying records, bypassing normal safeguards, or pushing loans on consumers who didn't understand them—and they became icons of destructive greed and lost public favor. Their sins were cited by some underwater borrowers who chose to simply walk away from their homes. At the peak of the Great Recession the *Christian Science Monitor* reported 10 percent of those who owed more than their homes were worth chose this option.

Fears of a massive "walk away" swept financial institutions in early 2009 as half the homes in Nevada and California dropped below their mortgage value. Not surprisingly, a study published by the University of Chicago Booth School of Business and the Kellogg School of Management at Northwestern University reports that as losses in value spread and deepened, more people chose a "strategic default" to get out of their payments.[4] However, even under the worst circumstances, most people—more than eight out of ten—feel a moral duty to maintain their obligation because a lender *trusted them* to repay a loan, and they were loath to break that trust. Democrats and Republicans were equal in their commitment to this moral view and, most remarkably, anger at cheating or incompetent corporate and government leaders did not make people more willing to abandon their values.

As they explained the walk-away dynamic, the authors of the study revealed that the most trustworthy homeowners are middle-aged residents of the Midwest, salt-of-the-earth people who have typified core American social values for generations. As trust leaders, they were determined to fulfill their obligations even as they saw corporations seeking bankruptcy protection and bailouts. Residents of the West and East, who were under greater debt burdens due to real estate price bubbles, said they were more likely to default—but the differences were not great, and as time passed it turned out that they were trustworthy too. Indeed, the number of new mortgage defaults leveled out and began to decline at the start of 2010. At the same time, bankers were surprised to see that the number of households making late payments actually declined for the first time since 2007.

With homeowners doggedly struggling to keep up their end of the mortgage bargain, the press in Las Vegas reported that some banks were following the credit union example, putting more time into relationships with their customers, delaying action against delinquent borrowers, and finding alternatives to foreclosure. "Short sales," in which lenders allow a borrower to sell a house for less than the value of the mortgage and then walk away, increased substantially in the first quarter of the year. This trend pointed to a wave of negotiations in which banks may accept short sales or reduce principal or interest rates (or both) so that more mortgage holders can stay in their homes.

With just the beginning of improvement visible in early 2010, it was not reasonable to conclude that the crisis in housing and mortgages was being brought under control. Some lending experts still predicted a new wave of defaults as adjustable loans were reset. However, hope could be found in Washington, where an effort was begun to encourage the faster resolution of the mortgage crisis on a house-by-house basis. Responding in part to voter complaints that banks and other institutions got generous help to survive the financial crisis while families did not, the Obama administration announced a program that would pay both lenders and borrowers to complete short sale agreements. Critics pointed to many flaws in the program, but among them we found acknowledgment that economic recovery could be stalled if borrowers felt that they were held to a tougher standard than lenders who got federal bailout money. As real estate expert Jonathan Miller wrote in *Business Insider,* "The only way out of this crisis is a solution with principal forgiveness in the equation."

It might seem counterintuitive to look for a cure for the trust virus in the much-maligned housing and mortgage sectors or, for that matter, in a city built on gambling profits. But in fact the depth of the economic pain in places like Las Vegas seemed to inspire the commitment and determination that are essential to trusting relationships. At Zappos, Krystle Bone says that she and her husband, who works for a security company, have become very good at appreciating their jobs, their community, and their friendships. Like many in Las Vegas they own a home that is mortgaged for more than its value and could not relocate without losing a substantial amount of money or ruining their credit scores. They are, in essence, trapped by the economy.

"We bought a house for $167,00 and they made it 'easy-peasy' for us to do it," chirps Krystle Bone. "Now it's worth under $100,000 and we couldn't sell it if we had to."

Determined to meet their obligations, the Bones have committed themselves to their jobs and to making things work in Las Vegas. She is part of a larger national trend that Joel Kotkin from *Newsweek* calls "the new localism," which seems to be reinforcing connections between people and places. In the seventies, nearly 20 percent of the population moved annually. But by 2006 (before the Great Recession) that number had declined to 14 percent. In 2008 the total number of people who moved was less than it was in 1962, when the nation had 120 million fewer citizens. In 2010, American families changed locale at the lowest rate since the 1940s.

Krystle Bone counts herself fortunate to have found a supportive employer that pays well enough for her to enjoy a decent standard of living in a place that feels more like an old-fashioned hometown every day. She is, in her own way, a pioneer of trust who is living out her commitments. Millions are following the same path, rejecting—in part out of necessity—the disconnected and transient lifestyle that was once the subject of ominous predictions about a lonely and unhappy society of the future. Instead we are more likely to see individuals, couples, and families choosing more of a rooted lifestyle that finds them working, shopping, and socializing in ways that support their local community and reinforces trusting relationships that reward them with feelings of security and loyalty.

The value of trust is not lost on businesspeople. As we traveled around the country, we did encounter some who began fighting the trust virus well before the Great Recession. In San Francisco the Giants baseball team managers reviewed for us a multiyear strategy they have followed to build trust with their fans. It began with the team recognizing that not all games are equal. A weekend battle with a pennant contender or long-time archrival like the Dodgers is worth more to a fan than a midweek night game involving a cellar-dwelling opponent. With this in mind, ticket prices were scaled according to demand.

The strategy, which the Giants call "dynamic pricing," is not a new concept, says Russ Stanley, who is in charge of client relations for the Giants. "I think the Romans did it at the Coliseum, setting prices according to the quality of the lion."

We met with Stanley during the off-season, on a morning when San Francisco fog hung over AT&T Park and a cold breeze blew in off the bay. Stanley is a playful, young-looking man of forty-five who has worked for the Giants since 1989. A romantic when it comes to the game and the team, his eyes fill with tears when he recalls that first season when the team went to the World Series, the Loma Prieta earthquake interrupted the third game, and the Oakland Athletics won the championship. The Giants wouldn't return to the series until 2002—when they lost again.

With a dearth of championships (the franchise last won the series as the *New York* Giants in 1954), keeping faith with fans is vital to financial success. In their trust-building campaign the Giants have introduced programs to help season ticket holders sell their seats for games they cannot attend, and assigned specific representatives to make sure these fans are happy with their experience at the ballpark. Each season ticket holder has the name and phone number of a team official, and their requests are answered immediately. This approach, borrowed from major casinos that assign a concierge to important gamblers, builds bonds that cannot be created without such a personal connection.

"We give them the name, phone number, and e-mail address of a real person who is responsible to them," explains Stanley. "We deal with problems immediately. If a person says they had trouble with a ticket that didn't scan at the entrance and they missed an inning or two, I give them an invitation to another game." When fans take him up on this kind of offer, Stanley will find them in the stands and make sure they're having a good time. In the future, these fans will feel like they know someone in the Giants organization—and, in fact, they do. As far as Stanley is concerned, there's no reason why anyone who comes to a game shouldn't be able to greet a member of the staff by name and stop for a chat. Relationships like these breed trust that encourages fans to come out for a game even during a losing season. They are also credited with making the Giants the favorite sports team in the region.

"Giants fans are like East Coast fans. They know the game, and they can't be fooled. The team understands this and has really learned how to treat them right."

This assessment didn't come from a season ticket holder, a Giants executive, or a baseball industry analyst. It came from Rich Walcoff, a thirty-year veteran San Francisco sportscaster at KGO Radio, who took his share of shots at the team when it occupied the old Candlestick Park and neglected the faithful who suffered with bad seating, bad food, and bad service. "Sports should be a sanctuary, a safe haven from the cold hard realities of life," Walcoff says. "Fans don't mind if you don't win it all, but they have to see you are making a commitment to win and to give them the best you can. I think the Giants do that."

Another firm that confronted the issue of trust long before the recession brought about the great spend shift is the clothing and outdoor gear company Patagonia. Also based in California, Patagonia may disclose more information about its operations than any company in the country. Included are reports that assess the environmental costs associated with manufacturing, shipping, and selling goods. The process subjects workers and facilities at every step in the supply chain to reviews of their energy use, water use, and environmental impact. It has led to changes in the chemicals and processes used by manufacturers. In one case Patagonia had to find a replacement for a toxic product used to waterproof fabric. In another a bad smell at a factory was traced to a leak that cost more than $1 million to repair. As Patagonia learns about these problems and makes the fixes, customers are welcome to review these reports, and are thus reassured that the company is trustworthy.

To reassure its customers of its transparency, Patagonia created the Footprint Chronicles, a Web site that states the company's mission is to "build the best products and cause no unnecessary harm." A visitor to the Web site clicks on any product and can track its environmental and social impact along its path to the store. As a product crisscrosses the globe, pop-up videos explain each stage of production, from design creation to sewing to distribution, giving statistics for each item's energy consumption, distance traveled, carbon emissions, and waste generated. For instance, Patagonia explains the trade-offs in creating a down vest:

The Good: We use high-quality goose down, an exceptionally efficient insulator. The down comes from humanely raised geese and is minimally processed. The light shell is made of recycled polyester.

The Bad: We had to increase the weight of the shell fabric when we switched to recycled polyester. The zipper is treated with a DWR that contains perfluorooctanoic acid (PFOA), a synthetic chemical that is now persistent in the environment, and the product is not yet recyclable.

Executive Vincent Stanley (no relation to the Giants' Stanley) says this transparency appeals to outdoors-minded customers who may be skeptical about corporations, which they suspect may practice something called *greenwashing*. Akin to whitewashing, greenwashing refers to public relations efforts made to give a firm the patina of ecological responsibility when in fact it remains a significant polluter. By owning up to its true record, Patagonia establishes itself as an honest, trustworthy company.

Stanley, who is Yvon Chouinard's nephew, was Patagonia's first sales manager in 1973. A writer, for the past five years he has managed the editorial department. Transparency provides the discipline Patagonia staff need in order to make substantive changes to their operations and bring themselves closer to their mission of making good products with the least amount of harm to the environment. Honest self-assessments also provide a spur to innovation. "I think what it does for us," he says, "is transparency provides discipline. If you have to say what you're doing and you're not very proud of it, that's something that motivates people internally to change. It also names a problem that might go unnamed because everybody is so busy in the course of work that they deal with the fires. If there's a forest fire building up, you don't see that because you see little brush fires in the course of the day."

Though the Footprint Chronicles have demonstrated that some Patagonia products have negative environmental impacts which are nearly impossible to negate, that presentation of fact rather than message has again helped gain respect among consumers. One key to success in these exchanges, adds Stanley, is plain language. "Our standard for talking to the customer is you want to talk to the customer as though they were a friend or could be a friend."

Friends engage in ongoing conversations—isn't that what relationships are all about?—and they do not expect conditions to remain static. Indeed, as time passes some relationships deepen and grow in trust. Others hit rough patches that require repair. Some fall apart. When they think about relating to consumers through social media like Twitter and Facebook, some of the most forward-thinking entrepreneurs like to imagine trust not as something that can be earned and husbanded (or suddenly lost)—like gold or cash—but rather as a framework in which an ongoing process is conducted.

Trust is a matter of constant interest for Joe Marchese, founder and CEO of SocialVibe, a social media utility that connects people with causes. People choose a charity and a branded sponsor from the SocialVibe Web site, and both are promoted through the user's social media. Based on exposure and influence, participants earn credits toward donations to their cause, and both it and the sponsor generate attention. We sat down with Joe over coffee in Manhattan on a rainy Spring morning. He immediately noted that SocialVibe's credibility relies on the trust of its sponsors to be aligned with the best intentions of the public.

"When I think about trust over the past couple of years, social media has changed the corporate mind-set from 'do no bad' (that would get them in trouble with consumers, lest it be published by the blogging community in the web 1.0 revolution), to companies today doing good things to get people to share them in their social media."

If this movement toward good deeds is aimed at rebuilding trust, it has profound benefits on brand building. The top 10 percent most-trusted brands in BrandAsset Valuator enjoy many competitive advantages:

One of my favorite brands	+381 percent
Feel loyal to the brand	+334 percent
Use regularly	+258 percent
Prefer most	+215 percent
Worth a premium price	+129 percent

At another pioneering media company called Betaworks, CEO and founder John Borthwick told us that under the old rules of trust a firm could conduct itself honorably and reliably for many years and attain a certain status or authority. But then, with a single breach, all of that trust was gone and customers abandoned the relationship. The trouble in this model was that companies set themselves up as institutions, almost like parent figures to consumers, who were correspondingly almost like children. But since institutions are as flawed as any individual person, they inevitably disappoint people in the same way that parents disappoint children. As a result modern companies are showing their human side, while sharing information and communicating constantly.

The new trust model made possible by the immediate and instantaneous flow of information—a type of technology Betaworks helps to develop and promote in what Borthwick calls "the now web"—is much more like a relationship of equals in which everyone knows what is going on all the time. This is what happens when people share news or events, developments, and even mistakes, as they occur. "In the social web, making mistakes is an opportunity, not a crisis," Borthwick says. "Mistakes create an opening for building a relationship."

Betaworks is headquartered in the meatpacking district of Manhattan, where hi-tech start-ups are moving into buildings that once housed butchers and poultry dealers. Located in a high-ceilinged space with bare brick walls and huge windows, it functions as a sort of incubator for ideas that might work in the social media sphere. One of its firms, Twitterfeed, is the largest publisher of posts on Twitter. Chartbeat, another Betaworks company, provides real-time Web analytics in the form of instant reports on visitors to Internet sites and their activities. And fifty million people each day now "crunch" their links down to size using Bit.ly. Another Betaworks enterprise, called ChallengePost, has coined itself "A Marketplace for Challenges." It lets users post problems or browse challenges posted by others to earn money or praise by finding solutions to problems.

All Betaworks activities depend, in one way or another, on the active and continual participation of lots of people in trusting relationships. The online tools they offer are upgraded and improved according to patterns of use and feedback. When something goes wrong, someone in the community notices and company operators get a chance to fix it.

Tony Haile, general manager of Chartbeat and Twitterfeed, told us this problem-report-solution scenario recently played out when a client called GetSatisfaction.com changed the terms of the contract it offers for its services. An influential blogger, Jason Fried of 37 Signals, raised a ruckus, and Chartbeat noticed that lots of people were visiting Get Satisfaction's customer service page and making their service a "trending topic" on Twitter. "Within minutes they clarified the change and initiated a discussion with the blogger and the broader community. By responding immediately to the criticism Get Satisfaction turned the tide. What Get Satisfaction realized before anyone else was that they had the data to transform criticism into new business."

By welcoming customer feedback, criticism, and cooperation, companies developed by Betaworks actually gather information that can make them more successful. This is how these businesses, which get only $100,000 in seed money, try to refine their products quickly and cheaply. Instead of spending time and money testing products or doing studies and surveys, they offer them and invite comments. Tony Haile says, "Authenticity is now about whether your customers can feel your struggles. When they see the process of how a new company tries to go about solving problems, they get a window into their thinking and begin to root for them to succeed." That struggle is a very clear mark of the company's commitment to the service and the community. Failures become talking points, and new developments bubble up from the conversations.

When companies open up their process, they develop more opportunities to deepen relationships. The constant interaction makes it impossible to hide and guarantees trust. To understand this fully, it may help to imagine Betaworks as the great investor Warren Buffet and old-fashioned authority-based commercial relationships as Bernie Madoff. Both generated great returns year after year, but one was a clear box and one was a black box. Black boxes used to be a marketing tool for genius, but the world has recognized that they are actually ways of masking uncalculated risks. Clear boxes let you see the work of a genius. This is the lesson of Betaworks. Trust is generated by transparency and interaction.

"True openness is the only way forward for commerce," Bruce Kogut says. Kogut, who is a professor specializing in ethics at the Columbia Business School and a leading authority on resetting corporate governance, sees the landscape for capitalism as fundamentally changed. Dressed in a brown shirt, Kogut pauses and leans forward for emphasis. "This is a moment of contrition—not just for banks and oil companies, but for all industries. In this new world there is no amount of image making which can help a company whose actions don't align with its words. Trust must be rebuilt from the inside first."

One could look at companies like Betaworks, with a few dozen employees, or Zappos, with a few hundred, and argue that building trust in a direct and personal way only works with small or medium-scale businesses. And many managers at very large companies will likely doubt that Patagonia's friend-to-friend communication style can work for firms with worksites scattered across the globe and customers numbered in the millions.

However, a few very large consumer-oriented companies are proving this theory wrong. (More about them later.) And evidence also points to an emerging consensus on trust among the world's power elite. In January 2010, at the most recent gathering of world leaders in Davos, Switzerland, the most significant take-away concern, according to the *New York Times*, was that trust in governments, corporations, and above all banks has become as elusive as sure footing on the icy streets of the mountain town where the conferees gathered for the World Economic Forum.[5]

In presenting a Davos panel called "Rebuilding Trust in Business," leadership public relations expert Richard W. Edelman announced, "Trust and confidence in business really plunged, particularly in the United States [during the Great Recession]." The drop was matched by declining faith in government, he reported, but his focus was primarily business—where he noted that chief executive officers are considered the least trustworthy source of information about their own industries.

More than half a dozen world leaders—executives, investors, and a labor official—joined Edelman in wringing their hands about trust and speculating about the cause of the decline. However, not one of them brought up the fact that the trust virus first struck more than a decade ago, and that across the United States individuals are not waiting for someone else to fix things. They are already investing their money, time, and energy in trusting relationships that are not dependent on big organizations or influential leaders.

As we read the transcript of its members' remarks, the Davos panel reminds us of the financial experts who say, "By the time the public learns about a good investment, it's already too late to make money on it." Only this time it was the big shots who were behind the man on the street. And they were obviously struggling to catch up. While the roles played by the finance industry, the media, government, and other institutions were well considered, only one speaker—a banker from Turkey named Ferit Sahenk—spoke in terms of the most basic human values, saying, "I want us to get back to the point where we're all in this together." At Zappos, in the subdivisions of Las Vegas, and in countless communities and relationship-oriented workplaces across the country, millions of people have already reached the point Sahenk describes.

Chapter Seven

THE CITIZEN CORPORATION: DEARBORN, MICHIGAN

I n the dark days, Robert Thibodeau felt like all the time, energy, and emotion he had poured into the relationship was going to end up being wasted. The passion he had felt for many years was fading. The trust was almost gone. He was tired of the suspicion and the fighting and worried that the sense of connection might never return. The great irony was, of course, that in his silver-haired middle age Thibodeau had never been more attentive or engaged, and he possessed the wisdom to make things work, if only he could get more support.

In desperation, Thibodeau decided that it was time for him to speak his mind. He chose to do it at a big public gathering where he was surrounded by hundreds of old friends and neighbors. Then in a calm, clear voice he said that everything that was wrong—the broken promises, disappointments, failures, and decline—could be explained by one simple word: *arrogance*.

It took courage, but as so often happens when we finally speak in a blunt and forceful way, Thibodeau was heard. Weeks after Robert Thibodeau spoke his mind at the 2008 International Auto Show, Ford Motor Company's new chief executive officer—an outsider from Boeing named Alan Mulally—began clearing out the bureaucracy that had made the once-great automaker slow, inefficient, and unresponsive. "Twenty-five percent of their field personnel were cut, and I think that told the people [throughout the company] something," recalls Thibodeau. What it told them was that customers and their Ford dealers—the ones who stood behind the cars—were the heart of the business. Anything that failed to serve this relationship was expendable. As Thibodeau explains, "We had to quit drop-kicking customers, and we had to build a relationship [with them]."

Although they sometimes get short shrift from the executives who run the corporations that design, manufacture, and deliver what we drive, the dealership is the point where car companies connect with customers. People who own and work at dealerships represent the brand in the world, where it is judged more and more by the values it represents. In this case, more people ask: Is Ford upholding its responsibilities as a car company and as a part of my community? Does Ford deliver good products? Does Ford listen? Is Ford a good citizen?

Bob Thibodeau Ford is the kind of place you imagine when you think of an established, hometown auto dealer. A modest but crisp-looking white building, the dealership has a glass front topped by the familiar blue oval sign that announces Ford around the world. It occupies a few acres of asphalt on the west side of a four-lane highway in the Detroit suburb of Warren, Michigan.

On the day we visited, half a dozen shiny new cars filled the showroom. At 7:00 AM the service department was already open for customers, but the owner was alone in the general offices. He had arrived early because it's his habit, and because on the way to work he had to swap his own car for a customer's vehicle, which he drove in for some service. This practice—acting as a valet for a valued customer—is something he started doing many years ago to affirm his bond with the people who trust him with their business. He believes these relationships have been the key to his dealership's success. But at times he has feared that even his best efforts to maintain them wouldn't be enough.

Relationships and business suffer, he says, "when I give you such great service, and then after two or three years, you then say to me, 'You know, Bobby, Ford doesn't have the vehicle that I want in the future.'" This happened many, many times, he adds, when Ford "got out of the car business" and focused most of its energies on trucks and sport utility vehicles. (The company also got distracted as it diversified into rentals with Hertz and foreign luxury brands as it purchased Jaguar and Land Rover. The passenger cars that remained in the American line-up were short on quality, style, and technology, recalls Thibodeau. Some, like the original Ford Focus, had so many defects that owners got to know the dealer's mechanics like they were family.

"It was the dealer. And it was the people on the service lane," explains Thibodeau, who kept Ford viable as a car company by fixing the problem-plagued Focus units one at a time for the people who drove them.

Having learned the business from his father, who founded the dealership in the 1960s, Thibodeau didn't have to do any research or make a special effort to be as attentive as he could to the consumer. But big, sprawling companies that maintain layers of management between the folks who make their product and the people who use it often struggle to connect with them. When the vast number of Americans saw their real incomes freeze or decline at the start of the last decade, Ford was not prepared to give them cars that cost less to drive and maintain. As pricey, fuel-hogging SUVs gathered dust on dealer lots, Ford posted a record loss of $12 billion in 2006. It was then that Mulally came aboard and Thibodeau confronted him at the car show.

Ford's troubles were hardly unique—in fact, conditions were probably worse at the two other big American companies, General Motors and Chrysler, which are also based in the Detroit area. In the seven years *before* the Great Recession the region lost more than 200,000 auto-related jobs as foreign competitors took market share. The managers of the Detroit Three, as they are called, failed to meet their main duty to the communities where they lived, which was to build great cars that would keep people employed in their production, distribution, and sales.

As the three companies struggled with similar challenges—old plants, expensive union contracts, sclerotic bureaucracy—Ford moved more quickly and decisively. The firm was still led by a member of its founding family, who felt the crisis very personally. Executive chairman Bill Ford declared, "Bankruptcy is not an option." He began a sweeping realignment: Hertz, Jaguar, and Land Rover were sold. Dozens of nameplates were jettisoned, leaving just ten, and new emphasis was placed on making efficient, reliable cars for the global market. By the end of 2009, roughly 90 percent of the company's cars scored above average for reliability, and one—the Fusion—finished second only to the Toyota Prius hybrid among family sedans.[1]

Better cars brought more people to showrooms like Bob Thibodeau's, but the big boost to the company's reputation came, he said, with something Ford refused to do: accept government aid. When the Great Recession struck, both GM and Chrysler accepted billions of tax dollars under the Troubled Asset Relief Program (TARP), and both declared bankruptcy. Ford, which had already begun a major restructuring of its finances, was well capitalized and able to stand on its own. Ford's self-reliance reminds customers of their own experience with the economic crisis, which hasn't included a federal handout. The Ford story also connects with the DIY zeitgeist. (In BrandAsset Valuator, 62 percent of the population say they are less likely to buy products or use services from a company that takes government bailout money.) In line with this sentiment, the bankruptcies at the other two companies raise concerns about the quality of their cars and whether service will be available in the future.

"Let's face it," says Thibodeau, "Chrysler has been having difficulties for thirty or forty years. I think when the historians take a look at things, they might even suggest that General Motors has been in a downsizing mode for fifty-something years. If you take a look at what General Motors was in the '50s, Frigidaire, locomotives, Detroit Diesel, take a look at that. Have they not been in a slow decline since then? Ford, on the other hand, maybe not."

The difference has been Bill Ford's emotional commitment to the company and its customers, says Thibodeau, and its willingness to change. The entire American auto industry has been struggling to overcome its insularity and become more responsive to both new technologies and new values. In the aftermath of the Great Recession, the banking crisis, and the corporate scandals, the same challenge confronts all major businesses. Customers have become both wary and vigilant about companies and their conduct. Empowered by the Internet, they are quick to criticize but also advise, in a productive way, any company that shows it is willing to listen.

Listening can help a big company make the transition from the old-fashioned process of developing products to sell in the marketplace to a more modern model that is driven by the needs expressed by the public. Many smaller firms, especially those founded in recent years, have figured out ways to do this through relationships. Whether it's Marlow and Sons in Brooklyn or Zappos in Las Vegas, they practice humility and respect and tune their approach through listening. Yes, these smaller organizations were built to operate in this modern way, but big companies can remake themselves to follow these principles too. Lou Gerstner Jr. explained how IBM did it years ago in his landmark book *Who Says Elephants Can't Dance?* Now, after the Great Recession, countless major corporations find themselves in a crisis similar to the one IBM faced twenty years ago.

Bob Thibodeau, who spends every day with customers, sees the problem clearly. Big industries tend to develop unresponsive cultures. The worst are those that revolve around heavy manufacturing—like cars—because they involve people with esoteric skills and special knowledge that might make them feel distant from the person who will ultimately use a car to get to the grocery store. However, it's the driver who will determine whether a car company succeeds. Thibodeau says that the biggest challenge right now for General Motors is probably its impersonal approach to customers and other outsiders. Ford, on the other hand, seems more open both to the people who buy cars and to others who have good ideas for cars. For evidence he points to the "Sync" system that Ford developed with Microsoft, which allows a driver to control communication, entertainment, and information systems by voice command.

Sync helps Ford meet a wide array of customer needs, and addresses concerns about safety that arise when people use their hands to make phone calls or get directions from a satellite system. Just as important, it brands the company as both an innovator and a collaborator. But of course Ford remains a car company, and it will rise or fall on the quality, reliability, and basic appeal of the vehicles that make it onto the floor of Thibodeau's showroom. In 2009, as Ford posted an improbable $2.7 billion profit (after three years of losses totaling $30 billion), Thibodeau was hearing good things about vehicles called the Escape and Fusion and, he adds, the new Taurus—"We can't get enough of [them] right now."

The improvements give Thibodeau hope for the company's future and make him a bit more optimistic about his community of Greater Detroit. A profitable Ford, fulfilling its role as an engaged citizen, will help rebuild the local economy. On a global scale Ford will reduce carbon emissions by delivering more vehicles that run on electricity and alternative fuels like compressed natural gas. But the car that Thibodeau and the entire company are hoping will open a new future for Ford is a gas-sipping subcompact with a name that is almost thirty-five years old.

"This is a competitive, dog-eat-dog industry," says Thibodeau, recalling how the other dogs devoured his business when the original Focus was introduced to negative consumer reviews. ("Fun to drive when it's not in the shop for a recall," reported MSNcars.) However, good fortune can arrive as swiftly as disaster: "It doesn't take but one product to all of a sudden really catapult somebody and put them out in the forefront." The question is, of course, "How do you get to that one product?"

In the case of the Fiesta, Ford has taken a different route from the usual design-test-refine-manufacture method that traditionally produces new cars. For one thing, consider the Fiesta, which as we write is set to debut in the United States for the 2011 model year. Subcompact Fiestas have been sold across Europe since 1976 and were even distributed for a short time (1978–1980) in North America. The new Fiesta "world car" is set to be manufactured in plants around the globe—including a brand new facility in China—and Ford is giving it a big push for the first time in the United States. With over 800,000 Fiestas sold worldwide since the relaunch in November 2008, it's likely to be a success in the United States as well. This car is also the first to be refined by eighty thousand people who had a chance to go for ride and drives and a hundred American "influencers"—drivers selected out of thousands who applied with video pitches—who were given free cars to drive for six months prior to the official release date.

The testers and "Fiesta Agents," as the 100 influencers were known, suggested tweaks in the design that have been integrated into the North American version. One addition is a center console that will provide a comfortable armrest that wasn't built into the hundred cars sent from abroad for the six-month test. Another change made by the public is a special little cup holder, made to secure (you guessed it) a Red Bull can. These refinements weren't major, but they were the direct result of the effort Ford made to share the car with customers before the design was locked in. But it also allowed employees to have direct access to the drivers. Brand managers and communications executives began tweeting—posting comments and questions on Twitter—to communicate with customers as well.

Besides the little improvements, Ford's Fiesta Movement, as it is called, started a hundred lengthy dialogues that blossomed into group conversations as the testers logged more than a million combined miles across North America. Individuals and teams reported on their lives, adventures, and (along the way) their experiences with the car via Twitter, Web video, and blog postings, all aggregated uncensored on www.FiestaMovement.com. With funding provided by Ford, teams of testers held parties, created murals, and cooked up stunts—how many people can you jam into a Fiesta?—that entertained Web fans and drew people to places where they could check out the car.

The Fiesta campaign is the most extensive effort ever made to engage customers in the launch of a new car. In the first few months Ford reported

- More than seven million video viewers

- More than four million Twitter responses

- More than one hundred twenty-five thousand interested new potential customers

- More than three quarters of a million visits to Fiesta photos on Flickr.com

- More than 11,000 people who made reservations to buy the car when it became available

The numbers, although certain to grow substantially before the cars finally arrive at dealer lots, are not astronomical when compared with, say, the viewership for the 2010 Super Bowl (104 million) or the 148 million "hits" garnered by *Charlie Bit My Finger* on YouTube. But consider that the campaign cost Ford very little and that it created, in an instant, a network of tastemakers able to influence the opinions of key consumers—young, media-savvy potential car buyers—as independent agents. These were not, after all, employees of Ford whose livelihoods depended on boosting the car. They were, instead, thoughtful men and women, including more than a few aspiring or practicing artists and actors, who brought their own social networks to bear on behalf of the experiment. Most were eager to get attention for their own activities, so there was mutual gain in the process.

One sure sign of the Fiesta Movement's success is the boom in conversations about the campaign, which are taking all over the Internet. This buzz, which amplified the original effort, has turned out to be especially loud on Web sites devoted to the study of social media. A good example was the back-and-forth posted on Supercollider, a blog run by a London-based advertising executive named Geoffrey Northcott. During a lively discussion about the Ford initiative, posters debated the authenticity of the "move-ment" and the possibility that social networks could get clogged with communications related to product. "You may be my friend," commented one writer, "but if you spam me about Charmin toilet paper for the next three months I will hit the block button faster than you can say 'squeeze.'" Some saw problems in the notion that individuals who received free use of the cars and support for their activities seemed to be sponsored by the company. Others won-dered if as the participants put up their "Hey look at me!" videos they were depriving Ford of the attention it needed.

Northcott himself was intrigued by Ford's willingness to cede control of its message. With a hundred people zipping around in a new kind of car long before it became available to the public, the company was "shifting away from 'control,' which is a very broadcast oriented principle, and towards 'influence,'" he noted in one post. In another he said, "I see this as the cusp of a trend rather than a one-off, and am interested in where this trend is heading, for good and bad."

No one has been more interested in the implications of the Fiesta Movement than the fellow in charge of social media at Ford, a not-quite-forty-year-old named Scott Monty, who left a consult-ing firm called Crayon to join Ford in 2008. A New Englander who rather enjoyed the life he had in Boston, Monty first resisted the idea of joining an old industrial firm that was losing billions of dollars every quarter and was based near struggling Detroit.

"Ford was not on my radar," explained Monty on the day we met him at the firm's famous world headquarters building—also known as the Glass House—in Dearborn. The way he recalls it, when he turned down Ford's initial overture, he wasn't quite ready for a career change. He also wasn't sure the company made cars that were worth talking about. As he explains, "If you've got crappy products and you're doing social media, people are just going to find out about [the bad products] that much more quickly. . . . In that case, you shouldn't be working on your marketing, you should be working on your products."

When he said no to Ford's first approach, Monty expected someone at the company to get upset and say something about how the big, important Ford Motor Company doesn't come calling very often and he should reconsider. Instead, he says, the Ford people calmly accepted his reluctance. This humble response intrigued him so much that he did more research, discovered Alan Mulally's plans for the future, and felt a change of heart. When talks resumed four months later, Monty was more open-minded and let the process go further. At each step he came away impressed by how members of the Ford team were willing to see themselves as not just businesspeople but as citizens who are responsible to every community and every person they contact.

This approach to work matched Monty's own ideas about what gives life meaning beyond the paycheck. "My parents sacrificed a lot and made it possible for me to do anything I wanted," he says. After graduating from high school in a small Connecticut town, where he worked on a tobacco farm in the summers, Monty first considered medicine but then settled on business. He worked initially in health care and then moved into consulting, but he never let go of the idea that no matter what he did he could serve others. "I just wanted to contribute to society in some meaningful way and to be able to do it in a relatively stress-free way and to be happy," says Monty, adding that he believes this goal is really part of human nature and "what everybody wants to do, really."

Monty's belief that work and trade should be about something bigger than making money is a hallmark of the spend shift sweeping the economy. In BrandAsset Valuator, this trend pops up when we ask people to tell us about their favorite companies. Since 2008 most of their top picks are recognized for their strong connection to values, projects, or programs beyond their business activity. Among them:

- Oprah: Media and positive social values

- Johnson & Johnson: Health care and support for the nursing profession

- Fisher Price: Toys and child development

- Wendy's: Hamburgers and child welfare

- Dove: Beauty products and raising the self-esteem of women

- Newman's Own: Food and charity

- Tom's of Maine: Health and beauty products and the environment

The desire for meaning is also quite prevalent in the huge Millennial generation, which has been widely identified with both self-confidence and teamwork and certain communitarian values that make them less likely to promote themselves over others. (See *Millennials Rising* by Neil Howe and William Strauss.) This group, which will eventually dominate the economy, ranks being a good parent, having a successful marriage, and helping others in need far above having a high-paying career.[2] These values mean that they want far more from a job than just a paycheck and, similarly, they expect more from the people they will trust with big-ticket purchases like cars.

Although he's just a little too old to be one of them, Monty understands the Millennials in an instinctive way. As the most diverse generation in history they may also be the most open-minded, and Monty sees in this attitude a real desire for honest communication. "They just want to be heard," says Monty. "That's a great human need overall. People just want to be acknowledged for who they are and the opinions they have. You don't necessarily have to debate them. You don't have to solve a problem, unless they're asking you to specifically do so. They just want to be acknowledged as a human being."

Like Bob Thibodeau, with his careful vigilance over his frustrated Ford Focus drivers, Monty understood that brand equity resides in those who are doing the interacting. His goal became to promote this idea of community across the company. Ford is gaining valuable feedback, which improves collaboration across marketing, R&D, and engineering. Instead of social marketing, you could really describe it as *social as business model* where openness ultimately improves the culture and the cars Ford puts on the road.

In the past, leaders of large American corporations may have preached respect for customers and even pushed employees to practice it, but the vast organizations required to produce, distribute, and sell in the national or global market made this all but impossible. In addition to this problem of bigness, companies also had to deal with the all-too-human desire to hide from problems or responsibility. This problem can be especially powerful in hierarchical organizations or in settings where workers are fearful or insecure. These feelings come to govern interactions both inside and outside the company, making it difficult for consumers to give the kind of honest feedback that can lead to improved quality and service.

At Ford, Scott Monty didn't discover a fear-based culture. "When I was interviewing here . . . I met eight people within five hours. And I was struck that to a person, every single one of them was talented, intelligent, and, most of all, passionate about Ford Motor Company. I had never worked for a large corporation before. I worked for a medium-sized company, but I was like, 'Wow!' over the fact that people can be passionate about the great corporate behemoth."

The passion and dedication Monty felt made him sure that the people who are Ford would do well if they made a deliberate effort to open themselves up to the world via Web-based social media. As he explained to higher-ups, the Internet already brings billions of people into contact with each other and makes it possible for them all to share information. No company could possibly control the flow, which means that it's far better to be a part of it, and to learn to respond in a productive way. Ford's leaders embraced Monty's vision, which meant inviting customers and potential customers to make themselves heard. The Fiesta Movement was part of this strategy, and it required that Ford actually allow people to talk about the car in a way that was "unedited, uncensored, unscripted," adds Monty. "That took a real kind of a suspension of the conservative notion [of managing corporate image] and of fear."

Critics of the Fiesta Movement doubted that young people who had been given free use of a sporty new car would be willing to say anything negative—but in fact, some did. And quite loudly. Paul Stamitiou from Atlanta made it clear he didn't like the styling of the car's hatchback, and he noted in an early post that Ford had scrimped on the rear brakes, equipping the car with old-fashioned drums instead of disk brakes. Stamitiou turned out to be a very demanding techno-critic, and as time passed he had negative things to say about the car's fuel system, its headlights, seats, and even the buttons that controlled the seat warmers. Fortunately for Ford, Stamitiou was also generous in his praise for the elements of the car that he liked.

"Sprinkled throughout the Fiesta are tiny features that make you applaud Ford's attention to detail," he wrote in one blog post. Among the ones he listed were floor mats that lock in place, seat belts that hide themselves when unbuckled, and the aforementioned Red Bull cup holder. Most of all he loved the way the car performed, the surprisingly roomy feel of the interior, and the fuel economy. His bottom-line assessment was, "Easy to drive, park, fill up and live with. Ford got me to rethink small cars."

Although a little more picky than most, Paul Stamitiou offered a capsule version of the range of comments offered by the Fiesta Movement participants. Monty and his bosses at Ford found value in both the praise and the criticisms, which helped establish the site's authenticity. (No one would have taken it seriously if every comment had been positive.) The experience also provided support for Monty's additional efforts at opening Ford to the world. These include a Twitter feed that the team updates on a frequent basis (and is followed by forty thousand people), as well as a number of very active Facebook pages and a series of Ford documents on Scribd. But where Monty seems most effective is as the public voice of Ford across the blogosphere, where he is never shy about responding when people comment about the company. In most cases these encounters are brief. Monty will volunteer to answer a question or settle a debate over an issue related to Ford. But every once in a while an issue will arise that becomes something bigger.

In late 2008 Monty got wind of a San Francisco-based blogger named Stefania Pomponi Butler, writing under the name City Mama, who had some extremely negative things to say about auto companies. (The press was filled with reports on the industry's financial crisis and proposed government intervention.) "She did this anti-U.S. automaker rant that was insane," recalls Monty. "We invited her out to our Chicago auto plant to interact with some of our managers and workers and to talk about quality initiatives and green practices and see what we are doing and who we were. And do you know, she turned around and wrote probably one of the best blog posts I've ever seen."

Titled "How the Women of Ford, an Assembly Plant, and a Guy Named Larry Changed My Life," the post described how Butler's eyes were opened by Ford workers who demonstrated the care and precision they bring to their work.[3] She was impressed by a system that allowed the plant to track down the source of a defect within hours of its being reported and surprised by the effort Ford made to use sustainable materials, like insulation made from soybeans. But she was moved to tears by the humanity of the Ford workers. She wrote:

> It occurred to me that this company was not a heartless, soul-less corporation full of automatons (like so many crash test dummies) churning out crappy cars. This company was made of people. People who cared immensely about the products they were building. People on the line smiled and waved at us. They held up power tools and tires as if to say, "I'm building a damn fine product here. We all are. When are you smug city folk going to take notice? I felt like the worst kind of ignorant, half-clued-in fool.

Although she did marvel at their quality, Stefania Pomponi Butler didn't endorse the cars she saw being assembled, but she affirmed the people of Ford. She did this because a real person— Scott Monty—was receptive to her original complaint about American car companies and was both brave enough and open-hearted enough to contact her and start a conversation. For his part, Monty was able to act only because Ford management had the courage to let him open up the company to the outside world. And they recognized that people were, in the main, reasonable and more than willing to talk.

The next step for Monty will be to involve the entire Ford company—as many employees that care to engage—in a never-ending conversation with customers and potential customers. The idea is to "democratize social media across the organization so that it's not just one department or one individual that holds the power," he says excitedly. "We can deputize anybody who wants to speak about their company. Maybe not in an authoritative way as the official company spokesman, but somebody who can defend and who can educate and who can engage and identify themselves as being from Ford."

If this happens, millions of people will become sources of key information for the people inside the company who need to know about Ford's performance. Sometimes the word from the street will be upsetting, especially if it suggests a defect in a vehicle or, for example, a pollution problem at a factory. But in every case Ford will be better served by a system that invites and speeds communication and human-scale relationships. Ford isn't there yet, but Monty has a mandate to make the company the most socially engaged automaker in the world. "If I do my job well," he jokes, "I'll be out of a job in five years because this will be baked into everything we do." Although Monty's not likely to work his way into unemployment, the campaign to remake the company and improve its standing as an admired citizen is working. In 2009 our BrandAsset Valuator survey found Ford's favorable ratings rose by 13 percent while GM fell by 22 percent and Chrysler dropped by 24 percent.

As Pauline Ores from IBM told us, "In the new world you must be open to being influenced in order to have any influence." Although he might not say it this way, Scott Monty is trying to make all of Ford listen and be influenced by others. This approach recognizes that in the post-recession reality, in which taxpayers have become shareholders (AIG, Citi, GM) and CEOs have become suspects, companies can no longer rely on creating needs in the marketplace and using public relations techniques to build an image. Consumers subject businesses to far more scrutiny, and they have the power to share what they discover with the rest of the world. They value good citizenship in the marketplace—but, as Monty discovered, they are not brutal and unwavering in their judgments. City Mama was open-minded. All it took was for Ford to reach out a hand.

Beth Harte, a social media consultant for many of the largest companies in America, would argue that Scott Monty has succeeded in converting the Ford brand from an object—cars made by a faceless industry—into an interactive human relationship. "People get to know Scott Monty and come to think of him as Ford," she says. "This is possible because social media is different from all other forms of marketing. It's interactive. People don't interact with a print advertisement or a TV commercial, but they expect to be able to interact online, in real time. Allowing customers to give you feedback is always a good thing."

Feedback allows you to change and improve products so they are more useful and, ultimately, more profitable. It reduces the cost of developing new offerings, and it gives you the chance to respond and prove yourself worthy of a customer's confidence. Unfortunately, adds Harte, too many of the people who run large companies are afraid that if they begin a conversation with their customers they will be overwhelmed. "They are still in a sales-oriented mind-set that makes it hard for them to really communicate with people."

Harte divides the history of modern consumer culture into four distinct eras:

- 1800–1900: *Product oriented.* You went to the store, bought some shoes, and wore them.

- 1900–1950: *Sales oriented.* Manufacturers developed products and tried to persuade you to buy them.

- 1950–2000: *Market oriented.* Companies researched needs and tried to meet them.

- 2000–today: *Interactive.* Constant communication and revision to serve the public.

In Harte's view, "Most Fortune 500 companies are still stuck in the sales era." They will struggle to become interactive because it will require much more than embracing a bit of technology. Truly interactive companies must allow the people who engage the public on their behalf to speak freely, respond humanely, and in short "to be really good, friendly people." They must also offer a product or service that is reliably good and friendly, or else customers will soon regard the companies' social media efforts as inauthentic. Harte points to her own cable TV provider—Comcast—as an example of a company that uses the latest methods to connect with people but fails when it comes to service. "Comcast has a huge Twitter presence, but they still have a bad reputation," she says. "They are still too expensive, and they don't resolve problems quickly. Consumers aren't stupid. They see the disconnect between what the companies say and what they do."

Cable companies may have a special problem when it comes to relating to consumers because they are big, they often seem like monopolies in local markets, and they have a long history of poor customer relations. But size, market dominance, and history are not insurmountable problems. Elephants really can dance, as we discovered when we explored Walmart's attempts to go with the flow of social media.

Not surprisingly, the world's biggest retailer (and eighth-biggest company overall) stumbled a bit when it first tried to make itself accessible. "We entered social media as if it was another ad channel," recalls John Anderson, who helped lead Walmart's online efforts until spring 2010. As Anderson noted when we spoke, for years the company did little more online than post information about its stores, inventory, and prices as it reinforced its "save money, live better" mission. Executives understood that their company has had some image problems over the years, including environmental and labor problems at factories that make products for Walmart and controversies over wages and benefits in America. In some communities Walmart's efforts to build new stores have been met by protests from locals who say it competes unfairly with small retailers.

Remarkably, considering the company's size and power, Walmart has responded nimbly to many criticisms. It moved to correct problems at foreign factories and used its huge buying power to push manufacturers to make more eco-friendly products and use greener production methods. Walmart even got into the local foods business, placing large orders for produce grown near its stores with sustainable practices. The idea is to support local farmers, reduce the use of fossil fuels for shipping, and improve the wares available to customers. This program has been such a success that one official of the Environmental Defense Fund recently told the *Atlantic Monthly,* "It's getting harder and harder to hate Walmart." But as successful as they were in some arenas, Walmart's people didn't get the hang of connecting to their customers in social media until they turned the job over to some outsiders. *Eleven* outsiders, to be precise, who came to be called Walmart's Elevenmoms.

Elevenmoms began when Anderson got the job of making Walmart matter in the realm of social media. He made a deep study of the company's dismal online experience and tried to understand what made others more successful. Eventually he concluded that the best way to generate interest and build a trusting community is to stop trying to deliver a message. "This was counterintuitive for marketers who are used to saying to the public, 'Here's the message we want you to receive,'" says Anderson, but he wasn't trying to get attention. He was trying to build relationships. And, as he says, you don't start a relationship by talking about yourself.

Noting that the Great Recession had begun and that everyone Walmart served was feeling the pressure, Anderson went online to search on terms like *frugal* and *bargain.* He found dozens of bloggers, individuals in all parts of the country, offering free advice on how to save money in both mundane and ingenious ways. When he found an especially engaging site, he wrote to the blogger and requested a chat on the phone. "My number came with a 479 [Arkansas] area code, so that at least told them I was probably who I said I was," he recalls.

When the bloggers got over the surprise of hearing directly from someone at Walmart headquarters, they became intrigued by the idea that began to take shape. "Would you be willing,"

Anderson asked them, "to help us create a community of money-saving people?" As he described the idea, Walmart would provide the technical support for a Web site that would host constant conversations about consumer interests, most especially how to get by on less. Contributors would be under no obligation to tout Walmart and, in fact, could critique the company if they wanted to. They could even steer readers toward bargains at other retail outlets including Walgreens, Target, or Kmart.

Melissa Garcia had never actually considered talking to Walmart the way she might talk to a friend. To her it was always "just a really big company" that offered some good deals to shoppers but was actually a bit difficult to deal with when it came to coupons. As someone who had blogged for more than a decade under the name Consumer Queen, Garcia knew more about coupons than just about anyone. She had acquired this expertise as a young mother who wanted to help make ends meet and then began sharing what she learned with an ever-expanding audience of readers who relied on her for information about sales, savings, and tips related mainly to family life. (Garcia also wrote personal notes about her family, including her husband, who has a debilitating spinal disorder.)

Once she understood that Anderson proposed a no-strings-attached offer, Garcia accepted. When ten other women, who also happened to be mothers, also signed up, they quickly agreed on the name "Elevenmoms." Walmart kicked off the project in September 2008 with a YouTube video channel and then a Web site where readers could be linked to videos, articles, and tips. Within two months the site had seen ten thousand dialogues occur among the moms and the readers.

By 2010 the site had added ten more moms (although the name stayed the same), and the offerings included well over a thousand postings and videos. Some were product reviews, as the "moms" agreed to receive and test items sent by manufacturers, but many were personal.

For example, Lori Falcon, who blogged under the name A Cowboy's Wife, put up a video of her son Tyler's first bronco ride and her own "Operation Fatty" campaign to lose weight. (When she announced she had given up soft drinks, she declared, "For a girl who could drink a case a day it was definitely a struggle to cut it off.") She also posts dramatic photos of life on the Texas range— family, flowers, food, and scenic vistas—which she shoots herself. Another of the Elevenmoms, Alyssa Francis, got forty-two responses when she wrote about giving up paper towels in order to save money and the environment.

Consumer Queen Melissa Garcia's site, is more service oriented and offers literally hundreds of deals. When she's too busy to review and post new items, she can count on her mother and husband to pitch in. She also has six volunteers who update the site because they believe in her mission, which is to help families live well on a budget. The work is partly an expression of Garcia's religious values (she calls it her ministry), but she is not an aggressive evangelist. "I'm open and honest," she said, "and people know I'm not being fake behind a Twitter account. I don't preach, but I will say, for example, when I got $1,800 worth of groceries for $20 that God blessed me."

An advertising agency or a public relations office could not create the variety of authentic personalities, values, information, and perspectives that flow through the Elevenmoms site. Walmart's role, as a hands-off facilitator that maintains the community links, reflects well on a company that has suffered with image problems. Inside the corporation, Anderson had to work at persuading his colleagues that it had real value. He told them, "Elevenmoms can act like an outside advisory board; if you use the groups that way, it gives customers a leadership stake in Walmart. The really smart ones understand that this is a listening platform like no other. Sure, we do focus groups—but that's not a conversation. I relate to you differently over time as I get to know you and understand your motivations. Walmart can follow the Elevenmoms and really get to know what customers want."

In spring 2010 Anderson left his position at Walmart but stayed in Bentonville, where the company keeps its headquarters, to start a consulting firm. He hopes his old bosses will take the next step in opening up to the world. This would involve connecting Walmart's people directly to the public via Twitter and other Internet services so they can answer questions or solve problems directly. "We've started a culture of listening," he says with pride. "Walmart is much more engaged. Getting it right is hard, but I think they are committed." Anderson saw proof of this trend when a group of the "moms"—eighteen in all—came to meet the top executive team in Bentonville. "It took the bloggers about three minutes to take over the meeting," he notes. But, more important, the executives let them.

As John Anderson remembers it, Walmart was moved to improve its standing as a good citizen—responsible, engaged, friendly—when previously it suffered pretty low ratings on the scale of kindness in our BrandAsset Valuator surveys. Yet in the past year, Walmart's differentiation is up by 25 percent, and its unapproachable image has declined by the same amount. Perhaps the most telling data comes from Kiersten De West, the founder of the *Shift Report*, who studies social responsibility in corporations. In 2008, only 18 percent of the population viewed Walmart as being socially responsible.[4] But by 2010, it had risen to 45 percent, or a 150 percent increase in two years.

Behemoths—Walmart has almost two million employees and $400 billion in annual sales—don't generally attract a lot of affection, so even when they behave as good citizens they are subject to skepticism. And even when a big company gets everything right, a certain segment of the population will always be critical.

A prime example in the can't-please-everyone category, Microsoft is subject to ferocious and unending criticism from a small but vocal segment of the public who favor its rival Apple's products and style. Certain demanding users, especially those who rely on their computers for filmmaking, art, and complicated design projects, swear by the superiority of Apple products, and the company has stoked their passion by pouring many millions of dollars into advertising that plays on this preference. But while the TV ads make it seem like all the cool kids hate Microsoft, the two companies aren't even close when it comes to the sentiments of the public at large. In our BrandAsset Valuator survey Microsoft always scores high on measures of its reputation, exceeding Apple by a wide margin. Microsoft enjoys a third higher level of trust, leadership, reliability, and social responsibility over Apple. And it is 80 percent stronger than Apple in the public's estimation of being the "best brand." Others have gotten the same result. When the Harris polling organization asked people to rate the sixty "most visible" companies on "Emotional Appeal, Products & Services, Social Responsibility, Vision & Leadership, Workplace Environment, and Financial Performance," Microsoft came out tenth and Apple nineteenth.

How does Microsoft do it? When we looked into the question, we found that despite its size, Microsoft is still widely associated with the single personality of its founder, Bill Gates. No individual is more closely identified with the wonders and benefits of computers and the Internet than Gates. He gives Microsoft a human face and, more important, his philanthropy gives the company a heart. Gates has given away billions of dollars to benefit a host of causes—from fighting malaria to educating poor children—and he has rallied other wealthy people to join him. This pursuit marks Gates and his company as the antithesis of the "greed is good" (to quote Michael Douglas's character in the movie *Wall Street*) attitude that seemed to dominate much of American business and society in the years before the Great Recession.

With Gates leading the way, Microsoft has long been involved in helping solve human problems in its global community. One of its main efforts involved providing local Community Technology Centers—50,000 since 2003—with technology and cash grants so they could serve clients more efficiently and at lower cost. After the recession hit, Microsoft began a program called "Elevate America" that would provide two million people with free training in information technology to help them find jobs in the postindustrial economy. Begun in February 2009, by the time we spoke to the Microsoft executive in charge of the program in spring 2010, Elevate America was running in thirty-three states and serving 800,000 people.

When we talked to Akhtar Badshah, senior director of community affairs, he told us that in its citizen response to the recession in America, Microsoft pursued three main areas of focus: "education, innovation, and jobs and economic opportunity." These targets allow Microsoft to offer more than simple philanthropy, which would be the case if the company chose to get involved in something like food banks. The company possesses valuable experience and expertise in training and developing people and businesses and could be confident it would perform well.

The choice is good for Microsoft because it creates an opportunity for the company to demonstrate its strengths to current and future customers. It also reduces the risk that something could go wrong. Microsoft knows how to train IT workers. It doesn't know how to handle perishable foodstuffs.

Microsoft's program to support basic IT training has been operating worldwide since 2003. "It is focused on the underserved community in order to build their IT skills to gain social and economic empowerment," says Badshah. In other words, the training gives people in less developed countries the skills to work with computers, tap the Internet, and connect with the wider world. Under this model, a craftsperson in rural India might discover a wholesaler in Mumbai who could help sell silverwork to customers in Los Angeles. Although Microsoft might see no direct benefit, the craft worker's success, multiplied millions of times over, would add substantially to the global economy, which must grow if Microsoft is going to continue to expand.

"This program is something that I have managed since 2003," notes Badshah with some pride. "We have over fifty thousand community technology centers that we have supported in 106 countries reaching 170 million people worldwide." Those who want more can pursue higher technical certifications leading to a range of jobs in the formal IT sector. "This training is geared toward individuals who want to become extremely proficient," adds Badshah. "It gives them a leg up."

The key here is that Microsoft uses both its money and its true areas of expertise—Badshah calls them "core competencies"—to maximize the good it can do as a citizen corporation. In this instance, a company can be charitable by redeploying its existing assets and infrastructure into tools for social and economic development. We call this strategy a "virtuous circle," where the pay-it-forward investment is not immediate or measurable in terms of new sales, but the returns are amplified by greater customer and community loyalty and a more friendly environment in which to operate.

As a board member of the Council of Foundations, Badshah has seen a big shift toward this kind of activity as companies seek to do good in areas they know well. Microsoft goes a step further to encourage individuals in the company to apply their own skills and energy and will match the dollars they give up to $12,000 per employee.

Will this type of activism—using expertise as well as cash—bring seemingly aloof corporations into human focus? "It's a little too early to say," argues Badshah. "One thing for sure is that consumers are looking at *Are companies giving back and contributing to society?* far more carefully today than they ever did. And the proliferation of social networking is gaining even more attention. I also believe that consumers are much smarter in recognizing whether there is a deep commitment by a company to bring about change or it is just marketing. I think that distinction is becoming more and more. We want to make sure our investments are not just 'Let's do a few things, get some publicity, and be done with it.' Consumers want to see change, commitment, long-term investment, and that's what we are going to do."

Chapter Eight

INNOVATION NATION: SAN FRANCISCO, CALIFORNIA

B eth Harte, the social marketing expert, believes she saw the future at a Hermes store near her hometown of Philadelphia. During a shopping visit she listened as clerks answered a flurry of calls from loyal customers who wanted to be updated on the scarves in stock. They were each looking for the exact same scarf, which had been purchased by a leading member of a Hermes online community. She had just posted news of her purchase—including a picture—and now everyone wanted it.

"There are three or four online forums dedicated to the bags, the scarves, the jewelry, and so on. Tens of thousands of women belong to these forums," explains Harte. "Some of these people know more about Hermes than the people running the store." More important, the leading members of the Hermes community are more powerful "influencers" than any designer or model who works for the company. "People want to have what the influencer has, and the company needs to be very careful in how it responds."

Imagining the potential for reaching the company's most avid customers, an impulsive Hermes executive might try to get involved with the vast communities of loyalists who gather on sites such as handbagclub.org and My Birkin Blog. No doubt such an executive could craft a strategy for a direct appeal to this community. Some might even attempt an undercover campaign to take over the flow of information. Both approaches would be wrong because either the takeover scheme would be discovered—scandal!—or the mere presence of a corporate voice in the community would drain it of authenticity.

"What would probably happen is that the company would have a person join the community but be required to follow certain rules," says Harte. "For example, if they know jewelry and aren't allowed to go off that topic, they might not respond to something about scarves. How can I form a relationship with the jewelry person if she can't go off topic? Maybe I really like shoes too. If you can't connect with the person by talking about anything other than jewelry, it's not a relationship—it's manipulation, and people can tell."

So what should Hermes do? So far the company has done nothing, and Harte agrees with this approach. "Hermes should let these people interpret the brand themselves because in some cases they know it better than anyone who works for the company. You have to be brave to step back and let this happen. Letting go of control is hard. But in this new environment you don't have much choice if you want to survive."

The new environment, which Harte explores every day as a consultant to top companies, is filled with people who have been bruised and battered by the Great Recession and the scandals in banking, finance, and government. And as every person we met in our journey through the American economy noted, the great spell cast over us by credit schemes and asset bubbles has been broken. Some are responding with anger, but most are more pragmatic. Like all the homeowners who continue to pay their mortgages (even though they are "underwater") and all the entrepreneurs selling homegrown products and services, they are returning to traditional values of responsibility, community, fairness, and value.

By every measure, whether it's the massive BrandAsset Valuator surveys or the sum total of all the stories we discovered, it is clear that a profound shift in how we spend—our money, our time, our trust and confidence—is well under way. In the world of commerce this shift finds people weighing a host of factors before making a purchase. Price is key, but so too is the character of the person or company on the other side of the counter. With every sale we vote with our dollars, and in the aftermath of the Great Recession we're voting for people we know and admire as responsible, generous, and kind. In other words, the good guys.

The spend shift is going to present problems for anyone seen to be seeking special advantages, shirking responsibility, or exploiting vulnerable people or communities. For this reason, General Motors and Chrysler will be at a disadvantage in competing with Ford because they took billions in federal bailout money. Similarly, too-big-to-fail banks can expect more pressure from campaigns that encourage people to move their money to smaller institutions, and food conglomerates will be held accountable for the ingredients in their products by parents who want only wholesome stuff in school lunches and family pantries.

But as tough as the future may seem for companies that were damaged in the run-up to the Great Recession, the opportunities for experimentation have never been more abundant. Rapid advancement in technology, from manufacturing to communications and data handling, has lowered the cost of entry in many businesses. At the same time high rates of unemployment—especially among the young—have increased the number of talented people who are willing to invest their time, hopes, and energy in high-risk enterprises. Finally, American consumers are more open to new ideas than they have been since the 1950s and the dawn of the age of plastic and transistors. Why play it safe with the dominant brands when so many of them have let you down?

In the post-recession era America might be viewed as a kind of "emerging market" where demand is rapidly changing and opportunities abound for those who can respond. In traditional emerging markets, a raw hunger for basic consumer goods feeds the rapid expansion of an economy. Simply put, people suddenly flush with cash will buy almost anything. As the United States moves out of its crisis, the consumer mood offers those who are alert to

the opportunity a chance to tap a growing public desire for a
"values-added" experience in the marketplace. Whether they are
shopping online, at a chain store, or at local farm stand, people
want to feel good about the exchange. They are seeking respect,
fairness, kindness, and quality. The desire for a new and improved
relationship with suppliers, manufacturers, and retailers is so strong
that consumers are willing to abandon old habits and reward the
risk-taking innovators who make the effort.

Not surprisingly, California is a hotbed for innovation and risk
taking. Despite its many problems (most notably a state government in constant fiscal crisis), California remains a leader in
technology and the arts, and it is expected to grow by another
ten million citizens in the next fifteen years. The state also offers
a culture of creative experimentation—maybe it's the influence of
Hollywood—that seems to support the pursuit of dreams. Some,
like the McDonald's hamburger chain, become so real that most
people forget they started in California. Others, like Pets.com,
survive only as amusing memories. (Do you recall the cheeky sock
puppet that starred in all those TV ads?)

Rick Klotz has lived a California success story for most of the
last twenty years. It began when he was still a student at Otis
College of Art and Design and put together a small line of California
"streetwear" to show at a trade exposition. He snagged $250,000
in orders, left school, and quickly turned a collection of T-shirts
and baggy pants inspired by surfers, skateboarders, and hip-hop
artists into a $13 million business. Freshjive, as the company was
called, occupied a far different spot in the fashion world from
Hermes. For one thing, a customer could buy an entire Freshjive
outfit for the price of a single Hermes hanky. The company also
served as an outlet for Klotz's antiestablishment political views. He
put provocative symbols and messages on his T-shirts and used his
profits to publish a radical political journal called the *Propagandist*.

However, Freshjive was still a business, and it was still part of the consumer culture. As Klotz found himself in fierce competition with better-funded rivals like Stussy and Quicksilver, he promoted his brand as if it conferred an identity (albeit one borrowed from celebrities who got the clothes for free) on the people who wore it. An idealist at heart, Klotz was often conflicted about the contradiction inherent in building Freshjive into a worldwide brand while claiming it was an extension of the street scene in Los Angeles. As fashions changed, competition sharpened, and then the recession struck, he was confronted with a choice: shut down or re-imagine the company. He thought about his employees and decided on the harder course.

In 2009 Klotz decided to abandon the Freshjive name. He took the sign off the building and the label off the clothing. He then set about producing an unlabeled line of tailored shirts and pants for young adults. These more structured clothes, including button-down shirts, were made to help the mostly young urban men who once wore Freshjive clothes on the street to succeed in conservative settings like offices and other workplaces. Though distinctive in color and cut, they could not be identified by any logo or symbol. The message in the omission is that Klotz understands we live in a time when materialism is déclassé. It's a "curb your consumerism" statement, he explains. And since he owns the company, the message is personal.

On the day we visited him at his office in the Los Angeles garment district, Klotz was rifling through a collection of old books and photos—many of which he buys in bulk at flea markets—for design inspiration. Elsewhere in the low one-story building a dozen or so employees did the basic work of the "rag trade"—talking to manufacturers, shippers, retail outlets—while also working on a company-sponsored Web magazine called "The World's Got Problems." The site is an outlet for Klotz's confrontational and provocative views on politics, which match his views on business.

"All this stuff—whether I sell it or somebody else sells it—is made in the same factories in China," explains Klotz, talking about his clothes. "The design of the clothing is the real issue. It's what makes what we sell different from what someone else sells." He would rather that customers buy his clothing because they like how it looks and not because they want to flash a label. He is also happy to see people buy fewer items, of all kinds, so they can invest more in their own lives.

"There's baggage that comes with a logo," says Klotz, who explains that he was influenced by Naomi Klein's book *No Logos,* which explored the downside of global branding. By removing his logo, Klotz is showing that he's willing to let go of all the social signaling attached to fashion and let his business stand or fall on quality. In a time when trust is in short supply, he trusts his customers with all the power. They will decide whether his clothes are attractive, functional, and well made based solely on what they see and feel. "That's what it comes down to in this world today, and I'm not scared of it at all. You like it, you buy it. I'm willing to live with that."

With his willingness to trust his customers, Klotz may just be acknowledging a truth that is growing more powerful every day: well-informed consumers are ruling the marketplace. The data to support this trend is collected every day by another California company called GoodGuide, which tracks, tests, and publishes research on the basic "goodness" of products people buy every day. As founder Dara O'Rourke says, the number of people who weigh the environmental, energy, and even political implications before reaching for an item at the grocery store or any other retail outlet has grown steadily for more than a decade. Today, more than half of all the people who respond to BrandAsset Valuator surveys on the topic say that they have avoided a certain company's product because they doubt its goodness. More than two-thirds would rather buy a "green" or "sustainable" product if they have the option.

This trend started more than a decade ago with people O'Rourke calls "deep green" shoppers, who frequent stores like Whole Foods and Trader Joe's. This concern became more widespread as the recession approached and issues like climate change started to worry people more likely to shop at Costco or Safeway. "Now," notes O'Rourke, "it's at Walmart."

The public's concern for the environment can be seen in grocery carts. Almost all categories of consumer goods took a hit during the recession, says O'Rourke, except for organic foods and nontoxic cleaning products, which continued to increase their market share. "We see huge success in 2008 on the launch of GreenWorks by Clorox and 7th Generation [two lines of nontoxic cleaners], which actually grew 50 percent in 2008." The data for O'Rourke's analysis comes from Grocery Manufacturers Association studies. These surveys conclude that consumers have "fewer dollars to spend and they are being more careful in how they spend their dollars in a recession. The number one issue remains avoid bad stuff, find healthy stuff."

With so many people trying to avoid the bad stuff and find the good stuff, O'Rourke saw an opportunity. Since 2007, GoodGuide has reviewed more than sixty-five thousand products and posted findings for consumers. As an independent resource, the Web site has issued some surprising findings. (Did you know that Nestlé's Strawberry Quick has a better environmental score than some organic milk brands?) The site allows visitors to develop lists of favorite products and post them. It also offers an application for iPhones that lets you scan a barcode while you are in a store and get instant information.

As a privately held company, GoodGuide releases no financial statements, and O'Rourke did not say whether he's yet turning a profit. However, the company has grown steadily since its founding—it now has sixteen employees—and "even in the downturn" he had seen steady, uninterrupted growth in traffic at his Web site. We see a continued interest and focus on health; in particular personal health and wellness dominates in all the things we track. "This is a mainstream American thing. No one wants toxic stuff for their kids."

Mainstream America is also becoming comfortable with the rapid exchange of information, especially when it shifts power from the seller to the buyer. As O'Rourke explains it, people have long been aware of the ways that retailers track their behavior with savings cards and other methods that give them information on their habits. Now, individuals have phones that can read bar codes and fetch data via the Internet. With GoodGuide shoppers can get instant, reliable reviews whenever they go out shopping. You can even use special tools on the site to pre-set some personal standards—maybe you want to buy food products from certified organic sources—and it will quickly screen out items that fall short. Using the example of a customer he calls "Ross," O'Rourke cites a hypothetical example:

> Say Ross just walked into a Star Market and we know what Star Market sells, we know what Ross cares about, and we're going to give instant advice on which products in this store meet his values. If he scans a product and we say you know that this is a pretty lousy product, we then tell him, "Here's a better product for you for what you care about."
>
> It could be a health issue—cholesterol issues—or maybe he's opposed to animal testing or whatever. We'll give him instant advice to support a purchase decision right at the moment when he's making the decision.

All of the services that GoodGuide can provide come independent of the manufacturers and retailers, which adds to the company's credibility and the value of its information. However,

O'Rourke has no interest in using his access to consumers to cause problems. GoodGuide will partner with companies that want to offer their own guides. For example, Marks and Spencer, the British retailer, might offer a service that tells customers how much carbon was emitted into the atmosphere to manufacture and ship various items. The idea is to help every player in the economy make improvements to benefit all.

"What we want to be is a platform for consumers making better decisions on what products to buy, retailers making better decisions on what products to stock, and manufacturers making better decisions on what products to build, produce, and how to improve them," says O'Rourke. "We're absolutely interested in working with brands and retailers and getting this information to them in a format that they can use."

The power of information could easily frighten someone who worries about "Big Brother" style bureaucracies or considers the consolidation of so much data—purchase records, motor vehicle records, tax records, and so on—a threat to their privacy. However, the generation that has come of age in the era of the Internet, cell phone cameras, and surveillance systems in every public space doesn't seem to expect nearly as much privacy. They view the constant exchange of information, even rather personal information, as simply a part of the game of life. And it's a game that anyone can play.

With GoodGuide anyone can take advantage of independent product ratings and feel better equipped to face the often dizzying array of choices in the marketplace. (Does anyone really need that many flavors of tea?) With Alice.com, another information-based start-up, individuals can go a step further. They can willingly hand over rather personal information about themselves—like how much toilet paper or deodorant they use—to the companies that make these products and hundreds of other household items. In exchange, Alice.com and the companies keep you supplied, via packages sent free of shipping costs, automatically.

Would you exchange private information about your personal hygiene—or, for that matter, how many trash bags or sponges you use—if Alice.com guaranteed that you would get better prices, never run out, and never have to shop for them again? As it turns out, millions of people would. Among them are lots of mothers who happily trade information for free, reliable deliveries of items like diapers, and senior citizens who can stop worrying about schlepping to the supermarket for supplies in bad weather or when they don't feel like going out. Instead they can count on Alice .com for any of six thousand different products made by 125 manufacturers.

The president and co-founder of Alice, Mark McGuire, spent years developing the idea, only to have it debut at the height of the Great Recession. Although he was concerned that people might not be open to a newcomer, conditions actually worked in his favor. Customers under time pressure, who wanted to reduce their trips to the store, were drawn by the convenience. Cost-sensitive shoppers discovered they could get goods delivered free by Alice at roughly the same price they would pay at a store. And when they stay out of the store, they are less likely to grab an impulse item they never planned to buy.

"They're trying to do things like plan their shopping lists and limit impulse purchases or save as much money as they can by comparing one price of a brand that they typically get to all the other brands they could substitute that for," McGuire says. "Doing that online and through Alice is great. Also, you get automatic coupons with us. There are a lot of retailers, the Walmarts and the Targets of the world, they've done a tremendous job and they're incredibly skilled at getting me in the store to buy a bottle of laundry detergent and walk out with three other things that I didn't think I needed." However, in the new economy, "People are very much focused on their basic essentials and getting rid of those extraneous purchases," adds McGuire. For these folks, "Alice has had perfect timing."

People also don't mind the convenience. Despite tight budgets, "Consumers are still looking to pamper themselves and reward themselves," says McGuire. "Our tag line is *everyone needs an Alice*. It's almost like having a maid or someone that helps out with your house and eliminates a chore. And you can do that in a way that's not wasting money."

For the scores of manufacturers who signed up with McGuire, Alice.com trades its customer data in exchange for best pricing, which gets passed on to the Alice community. But it also solves a problem that major companies have faced as the Internet, digital video recorders, and other technologies have given people the power to delete, bypass, and avoid traditional print and broadcast advertising. With Alice they get one-to-one relationships with customers who tell them everything they need to know about how, where, and when their products are used. Nothing could be more valuable to manufacturers who want to distribute a special offer, roll out a new product, or find a previously unmet need.

Before it was even a year old, Alice.com was so promising that McGuire was able to raise a second round of capital from investors who believe he can succeed. His business model, he says, is like the travel service Orbitz, which arranged to serve as a central booking site for almost all of the world's airlines. Orbitz succeeded by helping them reach customers directly instead of through travel agents who collected commissions from the carriers.

"We set up Alice very much the same way," said McGuire. "All of these big brands are getting killed by these dominant retailers, and they need to find new ways to get to their end customer, but they can't do it alone. As a consumer I'm not going to go to the Nyquil store to buy my Nyquil and the laundry detergent store to get my laundry detergent and pay shipping and get all these boxes. I want to go to one place where I can get all the brands. That's really what created that opportunity for Alice."

As Alice connects individuals in their homes with scores of companies that make and sell specific products, it functions as an "aggregator" of items that are then put in a box and delivered. In the last decade or so the term—*aggregation*—has been more commonly used to describe services that collect and deliver news and entertainment. Services like Huffington Post and The Daily Beast gather snippets from other outlets, mix it with some original content, and offer it tailored to a demographic group that might appeal to an advertiser.

When it comes to television, the dominant aggregator is a company called Hulu, which is definitely not a scrappy start-up. Owned by a deep-pocketed group that includes the media giants Newscorp, the Walt Disney Company, and NBC Universal, Hulu is headquartered in the television capital of the world, Burbank, California. On the surface, the media industry in Burbank seems rich and powerful. American producers still dominate the world market and their products remain a valuable expert commodity. However, TV-land is also besieged by competition from the Internet, videogames, and other new streams of information and entertainment. Profits and jobs are under constant threat, and executives are desperately searching for a solution to the declines in audience.

At first blush the concept behind Hulu, which offers thousands of hours of free TV programming online, seems risky. After all, the service puts control of all the programs in the hands of the viewer instead of a network executive. It doesn't require a subscription payment, like cable or satellite service, and advertising is minimal. As Hulu's chief of technology Eric Feng explains, "What we really try to do is create a single source so that users can go to one place to find the content they love and enjoy watching, and also make access to that content frictionless."

Friction, in Feng's sense of the word, is anything that slows down a viewer's access to *The Office*, *Family Guy*, or any other

Hulu offering. Hulu makes watching television "frictionless" by storing vast amounts of programming and letting visitors watch it whenever they like. "Media is an impulse business. It's not water and food and things that you really have to have every day to survive. And if you don't make it easy for users, they can turn elsewhere for their entertainment needs."

Thanks to a simple search engine users can find what they want quickly, and with high-speed connections the images and sounds flow smoothly. Simple in its design, the site isn't cluttered with excess services. "There were thoughts about doing a lot of social-networking features at Hulu and making it like an application or really investing in widgets and these things," recalls Feng. "We intentionally said no to all those and tried to focus on one thing, which was video delivery. I think that really helped smooth out and really streamline the experience and make it simple and easy for users to understand. So that might be why we've been fortunate to have very much wide appeal and mass appeal. We have one very clear mission at Hulu; when you go to the site, it's very clear, and that's to help you find and enjoy video content."

For consumers, the most remarkable thing about Hulu is that it bypasses the cable and satellite systems most people use to access TV. At a time when everyone seems determined to reduce their fixed overhead costs, no one enjoys paying the monthly bills that come from these intermediaries, especially since they tend to rise every year. Besides, who needs a thousand channels when you only watch five or six programs per week? As Hulu "de-bundles" the programming, TV viewers get to watch the shows they want, skip paying for channels they never use, and endure far fewer commercial interruptions. The site never presents more than six minutes of commercials in an hour, compared with about twenty per hour on regular networks.

For programmers the service delivers a bigger audience, including millions of people who may have been otherwise occupied on the date and time when a TV show was booked into a schedule and sent out across a network. These viewers are valuable to advertisers and, if they get hooked on a series, can make it a long-term success. "We've seen that with a couple of shows here," noted Feng. "One was *It's Always Sunny in Philadelphia*. We actually helped really drive awareness and drive ratings for that show. *Glee* is another example where we helped a new show find an audience. We introduced a lot of people to that show that they may not have found otherwise, and now that they've been introduced to it through Hulu, they're able to enjoy it on television and through their cable subscription." Producers also benefit from Hulu's ability to deliver an entire series, some many years old, to anyone's computer screen.

Beyond determining what they want to watch and when, Hulu users also get the chance to review and comment on programs, take clips to post on their own Web sites, and share as much or as little video as they want with their friends. In essence, the service lets every individual build a personal network, making judgments about thousands of offerings and then announcing those choices to the world. "That type of experience didn't even exist a few years ago, but because of digital distribution, we are now giving consumers unprecedented amounts of control over their content experience and their content choices."

As an innovation, Hulu is a clear success. In December 2009, the tech press announced that the site crossed the 1-billion-monthly-views mark for the first time.[1] However, the company's future depends on profit, and after two years of service Hulu was not yet producing the kind of revenues its owners expect. In March 2010, *Advertising Age*, the bible of the media business, noted a host of financial challenges facing Hulu.[2] First, competitors are rising in the on-demand world.

Second, some programmers who are eager for revenue are pulling popular shows off of Hulu. Third, revenues for the site, while substantial, barely cover the cost of operation.

With pressure for profits coming from Hulu's many owners, the day when the site has to either increase advertising or charge users for what they watch is approaching. Eric Feng hopes that viewer loyalty will make the shift relatively painless, with few people abandoning the experiment because they value what Hulu delivers so much that they won't mind paying a fair price.

For an analogy he points to Starbucks, the chain of coffee and espresso stores that grew from a handful of outlets in 1987 to more than sixteen thousand as of 2010. When the company was founded, Italian-style espresso drinks were not widely available in the United States, and most food service experts believed the American public would resist the strong taste and premium price of these drinks. Starbucks proved them wrong with a high-quality product served in a homey setting that company officials came to describe as "the third place"—a place between home and work where customers felt nurtured and relaxed. Starbucks got hundreds of millions of people into the espresso habit, and one by one they agreed that paying as much as $5 per drink was perfectly fine.

Hulu could become the Starbucks of television, says Feng, a place that "makes it so easy for users to access content that we can really increase consumption. It very much goes back to the Starbucks model, if you will. Who would have thought that people would pay four bucks for a cup of coffee? But when you put that store on every single block and you make it really easy for people to plunk down that four bucks for the coffee, all of a sudden consumption goes through the roof."

If Hulu succeeds the way Feng imagines, it will tap an emerging market for media content that no one else has been able to exploit. The service will do it by the power of aggregation. "By putting everything in one place and making it really easy for users to enjoy that content and perhaps enjoy it by different means—sometimes ad-supported, sometimes paid—by giving users all this choice control I think we'd build a lot of value for consumers out there." The people who make programs and films, especially the ones who have bankrolled Hulu, are betting that Feng's plan will work and that Hulu will become the Starbucks of media, generating billions of dollars that can be poured back into making more programs. This outcome would help save one of America's remaining major exports and thousands of TV production and management jobs in California and elsewhere.

―――――――――

In our search for companies and people who understand the emerging markets of the post-recession economy, we found many that use Web-based technologies to make life a little easier for individuals. Nicolas Felton, for example, explained to us the elegant beauty of Daytum, his system for tracking personal information and then turning it all into fascinating charts, graphs, and reports. The idea was conceived in 2004 out of Felton's own curiosity about how he spent his own time and energy. After collecting data for a year, he published a personal annual report filled with charts and graphs that showed, among other things, playtime versus work time, miles traveled, time spent away from home, and his consumption of everything from music to food and drink.

"While I thought it was just people who knew me who would be interested," he says, "I found out that people wonder the same things about their lives." Indeed, an annual report that sums up all of a person's activities can make order out of experiences that might otherwise seem random and disconnected. Felton made his technology available to the public, and by 2010 more than thirty thousand people were using Daytum to make sense out of the jumble of contacts and experiences that make up their daily lives.

In a time when people present carefully constructed profiles on sites like Facebook in order to make a good impression on others, Daytum offers users the chance to consider themselves in the clear light of numbers. "For me personally the desire for self-knowledge overwhelms any desire to present the best picture of my self," says Felton, "and I think that's true of most people." One year Felton tracked the money he spent on taxis and discovered, to his delight, that he spent far less—about $1,000—than he feared. "This year I'm tracking how many hours I spend in the office," he reveals. "I'm pretty sure it's a surprising and impressive number."

Daytum users, whether they are individuals or businesses, can employ the tools to track themselves privately, or they can then choose to make their information more widely available. Felton, who clearly relishes the insights that come from collecting and analyzing so much information, hopes it can bring people closer together. "For example, if a person in India is using it and tracking their habits, I can compare my habits to theirs and see a one-to-one impact or connection with another person." Companies that use Daytum could discover in its graphs and displays a way to assess their impact on communities. "There is more transparency for companies," he adds, and that transparency could inspire social change.

In following his impulse to help people understand themselves through data, Nicholas Felton found a way to put his personal strengths—design, number-crunching, keen observational skills— to work on behalf of others and make a business of it. Similar idealism can be found at the source of many recession-era start-ups that seek to build community. Two that caught our attention because of their early success were CrisisCommons.org and Kickstarter .com. Both offer people all over the world the opportunity to join with others to do something good.

Kickstarter invites artists and entrepreneurs of all types to make proposals for projects that require funding. They set a target figure, and the site tallies up commitment from individuals who may offer as little as $5 or $10. Funding flows only when the total is reached. Kickstarter makes money by taking a 5 percent commission from donations. The creators get the benefit of no-strings-attached backing. Donors may reap some small reward, like tickets to a benefit concert or a copy of a book, but mostly they get the good feeling that comes with helping others. In many cases Kickstarter provides a central location for friends, neighbors, and others to rally around an artist they know. But founder Perry Chen explains that many of these contributors wind up sticking around to offer help to complete strangers with worthy projects. "Different people come to the party for different reasons, but once they're there, they say 'Hey, this is interesting. Now there is a cool project.'" On the day we spoke, the "cool projects" people could boost included proposals for films, books, and plays. Donors could also chip in to help two women from Peru fly to the United States to show their weaving.

More purposeful even than Kickstarter, CrisisCommons.org promotes what its supporters call "random *hacks* of kindness." Used this way, the word *hack* describes any creative adaptation of a technology or social strategy for the purpose of helping others. For example, when a massive earthquake struck Haiti in early 2010, CrisisCommons convened experts around the world to develop Internet-based tools to translate Creole and English. CrisisCommons volunteers also created a service called "We Have, We Need," which paired organizations with resources to offer with people in Haiti who needed those goods and services.

Over the long term the group's founders hope to create all sorts of relief projects that can be tested in one crisis, refined, and deployed again when the need arises. "At the end of the day there may be systems that are being created, but they're all open sourced and someone will be able to utilize them for the next disaster," says Heather Blanchard. "The Internet is the global communications platform. The structure allows people to self-organize. We're able to give them projects that they can easily train for." If all goes according to the design, CrisisCommons will be the place where a universe of people can express their highest values. "All people around the world want to help people that need help," she says. "Providing a constructive way for people to do that will make all the difference in the future."

For idealists who like the feeling of contributing in a small way to a group effort that can make the world a better place, Internet communities of the sort found at Kickstarter.com and

CrisisCommons.org offer the perfect outlet. Given the low cost of starting these types of organizations, the number and variety of them should blossom in the new economy as activists and entrepreneurs seek to fill every imaginable niche. If they don't exist already, we would expect to one day learn of services that invite people to form helpful communities around everything from wildlife protection to the preservation of old subway cars.

These modest efforts reward people with good feeling, but they may not excite someone who is looking for a more dramatic expression of spend shift values. For this kind of change, change that allows one person to make a very big difference that benefits all of society, you might turn to an aggressive start-up utility company—yes, a for-profit electric utility—called SunRun.

Headquartered on the sixth floor of a century-old office building on Market Street in San Francisco, SunRun was founded by two very serious businesspeople—Ed Fenster and Lynn Jurich—who met at Stanford's business school and had done more than $1 billion worth of deals for various investment companies before turning their attention to the challenge of making solar power work in the American marketplace. The problem, as they saw it, was a matter of finance, not technology. Simply put, residential solar systems cost so much that even with government subsidies few homeowners could afford the cash investment—$25,000 is typical—to get started. If this stumbling block could be removed, demand for residential solar power systems would surge.

For most of its history, consumer interest in solar-generated electricity has come from staunch environmentalists who were willing to pay a high price to make a values statement. However, ever since the 9/11 attacks and the start of the war in Iraq, alternative energy has attracted the attention of a broader cross-section of Americans. Some came to see it as their patriotic duty to do everything they can to lessen U.S. dependence on imported oil. Others, noting the wild fluctuations in the price of both oil and electricity, are eager to get control of their energy costs. Once installed, a solar electric system provides power at a predictable cost, while reducing oil consumption and pollution year after year. However, it could take more than a decade for the savings to equal the upfront investment. How many homeowners can be sure that they would stay put long enough to recoup that money?

Noting that every modern solar electric setup should eventually pay for itself, Jurich and Fenster re-imagined it as an investment that would be literally, and financially, attached to a home and passed from one owner to the next. The initial customer would sign a long-term agreement—eighteen to twenty years—that would set a fixed cost for power. After a down payment of no more than $1,000, SunRun would install and maintain the system for the length of the contract. If the house were sold, the contract would pass to the next owner. (In many cases the value of this agreement would actually be attractive to a new owner, who would be spared rate hikes by local electric utilities.) At the end of the contract term, the current owner of the home could renew it, buy the system outright for a small sum, or have it removed.

As president of SunRun, Jurich often makes the pitch for her service to potential customers and government officials who may regulate electricity or oversee building codes. "We always get the same reaction," she told us over coffee in her office one morning. "This is too good to be true."

The SunRun model may sound too good to be true, but it works because Jurich and her partner were able to leverage their impeccable business credentials to raise more than $100 million in financing to pay for installations. The money came mainly from conservative lenders at U.S. Bank, one of the few institutions that avoided getting caught up in the mortgage crisis that was at the heart of the Great Recession. The bankers recognized that with thousands of homeowners signing long-term agreements, SunRun was actually developing a new type of electric utility with generating capacity spread thinly across the country. Like all utilities, it would enjoy predictable revenues from large numbers of customers.

The difference was that SunRun would never have to buy fuel for power generation, and it would never be affected by environmental regulations.

"We were launched in 2007, and by 2008 we were one of the leading installers of solar systems for the state of California," says Jurich. By the end of 2009 the company was self-sustaining and had moved into Arizona, Colorado, New Jersey, and Massachusetts. Based on hours of sunlight, solar power is workable in at least fifteen states, and Jurich plans to do business in every one of them. And if the business plan is accurate, the company will grow by 200 percent or more for several years to come.

To understand how this kind of growth is possible, it helps to consider the typical SunRun customer—who is neither a granola-crunching young environmentalist nor a survivalist occupying a cabin in the woods. Instead, the company's typical buyer is a middle-aged suburban homeowner who, according to Jurich, "hates the utility companies and all the rate increases and has decided to fix this problem once and for all."

These folks, who still want sufficient power to make sure their beer is cold and their showers run hot, respond to SunRun's message when it emphasizes "how you can save $50,000 over the life on the contract and avoid having your utility bills raised," adds Jurich. "Because of the recession there's been a rush toward getting this type of certainty, this kind of predictability when it comes to costs. In that way, we've been helped by the downturn." Many of SunRun's early adopters have been recent retirees from the military. Having fought in conflicts that were at least partly about oil, they share both a sensitivity to the issue of energy security and a sense of confidence when it comes to unusual new technologies.

Veterans who go solar because they have seen combat in the Middle East may seem to be unexpected allies for someone like Lynn Jurich, who grew up in Seattle and very proudly describes herself as a "real feminist" with a powerful concern for the environment. However, she sees nothing contradictory in this union because both liberal environmentalists and political conservatives see merit in weaning the country off foreign oil. She sees a similar confluence of interests between businesspeople who see profit potential in developing home solar and eco-activists who recognize the contribution capital can make to solving problems. "We're finally seeing environmentalists getting behind something business is doing," explains an amazed Jurich, "and at the same time the titans in finance are less angry at the environmentalists."

The benefits that flow along with the power from a long-term residential solar agreement with a provider like SunRun are profoundly satisfying, according to Steve Northam.

Of all the people we interviewed for *Spend Shift*, Northam is both the most realistic and the most optimistic. After twenty-two years of service in the U.S. Marines, including combat tours in the Middle East, Northam retired knowing one thing for certain: "We cannot depend on the yahoos in some other country, I don't care who they are, for our energy future. You gotta face that fact and figure something else out."

Marines are not shy about solving their own problems, so when he left the corps and settled in Fallbrook, California, Northam devoted plenty of time to the study of energy self-sufficiency. "My electric bill was $300 to $400 per month, and we don't use the air conditioning except for two or three weeks per year," recalls Northam. Conservation helped a little, but Northam was stymied when he looked for a more dramatic solution. Acquiring his own solar power system would require a cash payment of at least $25,000. Such a system would meet nearly all of his home's electricity needs, but every time he sat down with the numbers he had trouble finding enough savings to justify the outlay.

If the Great Recession hadn't struck, Northam might have continued to wait, paying his utility bills and grumbling about it. But when the stock market began its slide and his retirement investments shrank with every passing day, he became ever more determined to find a solution. "We're not passive people by training or inclination," he says of Marines. "Doing nothing is not an option."

A news article about SunRun clued him in to the company's low-cost solar, but Northam decided it wasn't enough. If he was going to make a change, he was going to go big. In a move that shocked his stockbroker—who said he should wait for a market rebound—he cashed out his battered investments and put the cash into money-saving home improvements, including a solar thermal heat system for his pool and a drip irrigation system that would save him thousands of dollars on water. He got rid of his gas-guzzling, V8 muscle car—"even though I loved driving it"—and bought a thrifty Ford Fusion. Finally he signed up with SunRun. The installation required a little extra effort and expense because some trees blocked his roof, but by May of 2009 the panels were up and running.

Altogether, Steve Northam's embrace of innovative technologies and services saves him about $500 per month. This rate of return compares quite favorably with the monthly declines in capital suffered by his holdings in the stock market and should make it possible for him to stay in his home as long as he likes. These financial benefits come to mind first when he talks about the rewards he has reaped from his drive for energy and water efficiency. "I'm a not a tree-hugging, frog-kissing guy," he explains.

However, Northam is a father and a grandfather, and he understands the threat that dependence on oil poses to the environment, the economy, and national security. Northam wants to bequeath clean air, water, and land to his children and grandchildren. He wants them to live in a secure, free country where the cost of meeting their basic needs for food, shelter, and transportation won't deprive them of a dignified quality of life. In these areas of concern, this retired Marine finds common ground with the majority of his fellow citizens, whether they kiss frogs or not. Together they are living out the shift in habits, values, priorities, and investments that began before the Great Recession was ever named and that is already shaping the future.

Coda

The Takeaway:
Los Angeles, California

In Los Angeles the savvy traveler answers his hotel wake-up call, rolls out of bed, switches on the preloaded coffee maker, and taps the keyboard on his laptop computer so it will be fired up when he is finished in the bathroom. When he returns, he spills creamer into a cup of coffee and types "Kogi truck" into a search engine. With two clicks he's got the home page for the best Korean/Mexican barbecue/taco restaurant in the city. The site shows a schedule for Kogi's four rolling kitchens—the trucks are called Azul, Verde, Naranja, and Roja—showing the street corners and parking lots that will get Kogi service. Verde will be at Valleyheart and Lankershim. Bingo!

Across Los Angeles, sleepy locals and visitors alike are making the same connection with Kogi to find out if they can snag lunch, or dinner, or a late-night snack. Those who can be counted among the company's fifty thousand Twitter followers will get instant updates if the truck is stuck in traffic or sells out of $5 kimchi quesadillas. They won't need a tweet to tell them that the line will be long (it always is) or the food will be delicious and fairly priced. (It always is.)

"The social media connect us to the community and let us update them," explains Alice Shin, a member of the Kogi team. "But just like any neighborhood restaurant it's the food and the face-to-face stuff that matters, and we work really hard to make sure that's always good."

Exquisitely tuned to the spend shift mood, Kogi trucks really are the modern equivalent of the neighborhood lunch spot. The operators are outgoing and friendly and they develop easy relationships with their regulars, who form a sort of community. The difference is that the people in this community are joined together by Twitter and a shared passion for the food, not their attachment to a certain neighborhood. Indeed, to spread the love around, the trucks show up at different spots throughout the week and Shin makes sure folks know where to go. This approach is good for business because it widens Kogi's market. It's good for customers because they can wait for the times when the trucks are nearby. And it's good for the environment because one truck burning fuel to reach a location creates a lot less carbon than a hundred cars traveling the freeway to deliver hungry patrons to the same spot.

The Kogi formula is reinforced by the social media connections, which create a kind of intimacy and even insider status for regular customers. The business depends on a constant conversation with its customers, one that makes its operation transparent but also brings a constant, two-way flow of useful information. On the day we hunted down the Naranja truck, we learned the value of being connected—because we missed the tweet that announced "sold out." As we pulled up to the corner, the last lucky customer was walking back to his car with a quesadilla, and a big grin on his face. "Man, you missed it," he smiled. "Better luck next time."

The lucky diner wasn't gloating but teasing, and the moment left us both disappointed and amused. Kogi makes eating a bit of an adventure, and missing with your first shot only makes you eager to try again. When we finally did, we discovered a crowd that was happy to wait in the cool night air and food that lived up to its billing. Chef Roy Choi's Korean tacos were perfectly seasoned with spices from Asia and Mexico and just the right amount of anticipation.

Choi and Kogi exemplify much of what we discovered about how the Great Recession has changed many of us for the better. The enormity of the crisis motivated significant numbers of people to respond with extraordinary creativity, flexibility, and a kind of practical idealism. As long as change is in the air, they seemed to say, we might as well make changes that address our concerns about a host of problems that have been left unattended for too long, including the environment, the moral condition of our institutions, the vitality of our communities, and our personal well-being. There's no turning back.

Because we investigated the post-crisis American experience through the vantage point of consumerism, we were able to measure not just words but actions. Spending habits and preferences guide the work of market experts in much the same way that voting patterns inform a political scientist. Through these diverse interactions we are able to see value shifts that can guide us to where we are going as a society. Harvard professor John Quelch reminds us that we demonstrate our values and our priorities every time we spend money. As Quelch says, "If you want to understand how people really feel, track them day-to-day in the marketplace. And if you want to measure their long-term perspective, study their big investment in items like houses, cars, furnishings, and appliances."

We don't need to wait for another election to understand that a shift in spending is a result of a shift in values. America is moving away from excess and debt-fueled consumption and toward savings and investment. Consumer spending drives more than two-thirds of America's GDP, meaning these spend shifts are changing both our culture and our economy. Consumerism is not going away, but it is changing in ways that will change our society for the better. From the scores of interviews we conducted and thousands of data points we accumulated, we can identify ways that we believe the post-crisis values revolution will change the way we buy, sell, and live.

What follows are new concepts as well as tried-and-true formulas for success. Things like honesty, quality products and services, and building community may seem obvious, but we believe they were forgotten for a while. In a time of mindless consumption, business went astray, losing track of the fundamentals to exploit an irrational consumer that no longer exists. And whereas our leaders encouraged us to "go shopping" after 9/11, this time it's different.

Among these take-aways:

1. We are moving from a credit to a debit society.
2. There are no longer consumers, only customers.
3. Industries are revealed as collections of individuals.
4. Generational divides are disappearing.
5. Human regulation is remaking the marketplace.
6. Generosity is now a business model.
7. Society is shifting from consumption to production.
8. We must think small to solve big.
9. America is an emerging market for values-led innovation.
10. Everything will be all right.

Credit to Debit

We are moving from a credit to a debit society. While consumption will recover, thrift is here to stay. Consumer spending will no longer be able to grow faster than our income as it did during the thirty years leading up to the crisis. Greater savings coupled with less borrowing is resulting in mindful rather than mindless consumption.

As our data has indicated, the prerecession period of over-heated borrowing and spending was not normal, and therefore we should not look at today as the "new normal." The debt and consumer binge was an anomaly. We are now *returning* to traditional values that dominated society and the marketplace in every period but 1990–2007. These values favor common sense, quality over quantity, artisanal and local sourcing, ethical practices, dignity, resiliency, and personal connection. The spend shift is a return to sensibilities that define the American ideal.

It is changing the way we buy.

Today, tighter consumer borrowing standards coupled with more limited access to credit will keep spending in check, resulting in consumers spending money *that's really theirs*. (Earned money is more meaningful, and a little harder to part with.) This means the things we spend money on will take on greater meaning. Savings too will take on greater importance as older Americans seek to repair lost wealth. The home will no longer be the ATM machine for vacations or a surrogate to savings for college and retirement. This is why we'll search for things that offer us value *and* values, such as Ford (which didn't take bailout money and which allows unfettered access to critique its cars), or Berkshares, the community currency of western Massachusetts, which provides both discounts to customers and bonded a community around its local merchants.

It is changing the way we sell.

The companies that succeed will understand the American ideal for a "liquid life." They will help their customers de-leverage by offering simplicity, efficiency, and flexibility to adapt to ever-changing conditions. As opposed to oversized McMansions, Blu Homes builds simpler, modular, and more efficient homes that people can grow into. Hulu allows its users to eliminate fixed costs such as the monthly cable bill. Marketing today means minimizing rather than inviting risk, while giving the consumer greater options in the process.

And it will change the way we live.

Whereas *things* defined the credit age, *meaning* now guides the debit age. We're moving from materialism to what's material. And increasingly it's less about what we carry and more about how we carry ourselves. As we've seen in the data, "what's inside" carries more credence as we place greater value on character, authenticity, and narrative. We are witnessing the return of more simple, efficient, and measured ways of living. We are dismantling ego and artifice, happily disengaging from a consumption arms race. This makes the things we buy more like investments. The lasting lesson from the recession is that in less there is more. That removed from the things we merely want, we find the things we truly need.

Consumers to Customers

There are no longer consumers, only customers. In the post-crisis age, the term *consumer* is a symbol of disrespect and ignorance. It is a demeaning stereotype of a mindless gobbling beast of indifference that ingests an endless abundance of goods and services without regard for consequence. *Consumer* also suggests powerlessness—someone who can be controlled and manipulated for profit.

In this era, marketing is postmodern. The buying public is savvy about marketing, search, and social media, and people will restrain their demand to force business to be about *better* instead of *more*. While overall consumption will be lower, spending will become ever more strategic as people discriminate among categories they value and companies and brands they admire.

With a clearer understanding of their necessities, customers have become *constituencies* who are reshaping companies and their brands to their liking, rewarding those who share their values; who are more ethical, sustainable, and innovate for the greater good. In the old world the consumer was a receptacle. The modern company understands customer value trumps shareholder value. Shareholders want profits today. Customers want proof of tomorrow.

It is changing the way we buy.

More people will practice "Socratic consumption," which means they'll think before they spend. Buying goods and services will take on greater importance, and spending will become more like investing. Recreational shopping will decline as more commerce flows through planned purchases aided by mobile technology and social media. Customers will find strength in numbers by scaling their spending to support their values through smart buying circles like the Carrotmob in Tampa. And with access to real-time information, they can restrain their demand to force quality over quantity from the marketplace, resulting in dynamic pricing models like the ticket schemes used by the San Francisco Giants. Customers will seek to cut out the middleman and deal directly with manufacturers through services like Alice.com. And they can band together to get the lowest prices with technologies like Groupon. Online and bricks-and-mortar shopping will blur into just *shopping*.

It is changing the way we sell.

From merchants to corporations, companies will need to continuously listen, respond, and innovate. Culture and intention will matter as much as product, if not more. Think about Krystle Bone, the customer service representative from Zappos in Las Vegas, or the staff at Andrew Tarlow's Marlow and Daughters in Brooklyn. Customer interest in social responsibility will also create opportunities for lifestyle brands, such as Robin Chase's Zipcar. Here dignity and empathy beat hype and indifference, and the rewards are more loyal customers, who become the brand's marketing platform, such as Torya Blanchard's Good Girls Go to Paris restaurant in Detroit. Customer satisfaction will drive up market share. The most responsive and responsible companies will prosper while all others will struggle against private-label brands or simply fade into oblivion.

And it will change the way we live.

The world of the customer will be much better than the world of the consumer. We will see dramatic improvements in service and quality, at lower prices. We will enjoy greater status and respect in our interactions with businesses and fewer disappointments. We will become brand evangelists for companies, and values-led consumption will simplify brand choice, leaving us time for other pursuits. Indeed, we'll be happier with less choice. Shopping will always be an experience, and buying things will still induce a thrill, but materialism will move to the material—that is, rather than defining our lives, shopping will enhance us as individuals. And the badge that comes from a brand will be more personal and nuanced. Our egos will be fed from displaying our personal values through a brand, rather than conforming to images we used to desperately want others to see. The brands that reflect and champion our values will earn the right to have us as customers. And rather than us joining a brand's world, it will join ours.

Industries to Individuals

Industries are revealed as collections of individuals. In an era where institutional trust is waning, modern commerce will operate on the basis of individualism. The company of the post-crisis age will champion its people as a source of competitive advantage. Employees at many levels will become frontline ambassadors, erasing the distance between the corporation and the customer (and the purchase decision). Think of this change as the rise of the nice guys, who become more effective through sincerity, kindness, and empathy. As customers and businesses move closer together, recruiting and developing a culture to champion the individual will become an essential management strategy for this decade. The human face of the company will become its medium and more important than any marketing campaign. Each individual—each interaction—will define a company's value.

It is changing the way we buy.

Individual recommendations from our peers and from trusted reviewers will play a greater role in our buying choices. We will also allow sellers we trust to act as agents in order to solve problems, offer suggestions, and shape decision making. These collaborations and smarter customer-recognition technology will create opportunities for buyers and sellers to get to know one another and build trust over time, as Pauline Ores from IBM told us. More people will see institutions through the lens of "employee as proprietor," like Miriam Rodriguez at the Dallas Public Library. As Rainy Day, the bus driver, told us, "Individuals and small groups—the minnows and the guppies—need to come up with the innovation and take action."

It is changing the way we sell.

Corporate firewalls will crumble as flatter organizational structures give greater power and latitude to individuals like Scott Monty at Ford, who will interact with the customers and inform product and service offerings. Marketing and sales will be democratized as customer relationships emerge across all levels and divisions in a company and customers work with companies as advisers, like the program John Andrews established at Walmart, with its Elevenmoms.

And like Charles Sorel's Detroit restaurant, Le Petit Zinc, more companies will offer a Montessori approach to corporate training, to emphasize each individual's unique personality and style of expressing the company's mission and values. Astute corporations will follow Zappos' example and recapture control over customer-facing parts of their value chain. There are no longer products. Everything is a service in the post-crisis economy.

And it will change the way we live.

Increasingly we'll buy people and experiences instead of products and services. The companies and brands we support will feel so familiar, they will engender the feeling of a friendship. More of our consumption will be custom-made, as personal attention combined with data capture results in highly individualized marketing that will match our consumption with our own personal characteristics. Products and services will be attuned to our unique nutritional requirements, our skincare type, or the right amount of insurance to match our personal sense of risk.

As commerce moves from mass to micro, for customers and businesses, trust will be the defining aspect in any transaction. This will result in a more civilized, more highly evolved commercial culture where people and institutions treat each other better because they know one another on an individual level. And buying a product that uniquely fits "me" becomes a refuge from the annoying generalizations of our larger culture.

Blurring Generations

Generational divides are disappearing. The shared cultural experience of the Great Recession has ushered in a values-led revolution that is cutting across demography and that has catalyzed other trends that were already at work making generational differences less distinct. Twenty years of Internet experience have given the over-forty crowd greater digital aptitude and faster ability to adapt to new tools and applications. Continued migration into urban areas is dismantling the life-stage sequestering inherent in suburbia. And with a greater number of Boomers and seniors choosing to continue to work, there will be a "lighthouse effect." New ideas, new technologies, and the energy of youth infused with maturity and perspective will help us see further to solve big challenges. Finally, the reappraisal of the money-time-happiness equation will mean less flipping (of houses and other things) and more building, resulting in greater commitment to our businesses, our communities, and each other. All of this means there will be less cultural identification by life stage and more connection through common shared values.

It is changing the way we buy.

Guided by values and beliefs, customers of all ages will be open to useful products and services whether they come from generations gone by (backyard egg production, local pickles) or young newcomers (Brooklyn Industries). Youth-led adoption cycles for new trends and technologies will quickly tip into the broader culture. To get a sense of this trend, consider that 45 percent of Facebook users are older than thirty-five, while half of Hulu's audience is older than forty-five.

It is changing the way we sell.

Marketing by age and life stage will be seen as discriminatory, and some customers (especially Boomers) will reject the natural laws of life-stage paradigms. Pharmaceutical companies, retirement communities, and insurance providers will need to restructure their marketing programs as new sales will come from accentuating prospects' worth rather than remedying their afflictions. Many companies will reconnect by fostering intergenerational mentorship communities, such as the retired engineers who collaborate with amateur electronics enthusiasts through the Adafruit online community. And some of the best new businesses will bring new technology to solve old problems, creating partnerships across generations, much the way RecycleBank bonded Jon Norton and Ron Gonen together in Boston. By their example, commerce will become more inclusive and more empathetic.

And it will change the way we live.

The American educational system has long stressed the need for specialization. But expertise is now just a starting point; the value is in experience. People are discovering that a broader mind-set enables lateral thinking, contextual problem solving, and teamwork. Key to this education is learning from diverse constituencies who are coming together to share skills. Cloud computing will become a form of social behavior as we tap into each other's expertise. And in the process these communities will teach us we're more like each other than we are different. We'll acquire greater understanding of nuance and respect for the other side's point of view. Whether young or old, age will no longer dictate boundaries. And retirement will recede as an option for many, not for financial reasons but because there's too much still to learn and do. Without the pressure to amass wealth and beat the clock, more of us will be seeking more encores rather than departing the stage of life. This may mean twelve jobs instead of one, and pursuing careers that fulfill us rather than sustain us.

A New Kind of Marketplace

Human regulation is remaking the marketplace. We've been done in by complex derivatives and flawed Gaussian formulas used in finance and economics. We have deep mistrust of institutions and even more of the so-called regulators. Now, armed with the realization that there are no safety nets and no authority greater than our own, the post-crisis marketplace will be watched over by the buying public. The emphasis today is on being more human and humane in our transactions with others, and we will set these same standards for business. We will seek simplicity, transparency, and accountability. A company's brand equity will be in continuous flux and will rise and fall on its ability to maintain public trust.

Putting others first will be the best way for companies to address challenges in this new world. Successful managers will practice complete transparency, letting customers see their supply chains, management strategies, and values. Instead of dwelling on their Corporate Social Reputation (an old idea for making firms *look* good) executives will emphasize Corporate Social Intention, which will require them to announce their business and social goals up front. This agenda is both a guide for employees and a pledge to customers.

With faith in government and institutions at low ebb, the best of the values-led companies will become conduits for trust in society. Customers and businesses will move even closer together, blurring the lines of commerce and consumption in the name of social responsibility. The best modern companies will become exchanges for ideas, services, and solutions. These firms will redefine the social requirements of what is truly a "public company," setting the standards for everyone else.

It is changing the way we buy.

As our data suggests, people will continue to read labels more carefully and look for the best deals. They will also use services provided by companies like Betaworks to obtain additional information from the Web. Any shopper with a mobile phone and the GoodGuide will be able to scan a product and access a company's social or environmental record at point-of-purchase. Shoppers will also rely on each other for information, and consult trusted "experts" such as Eric Sturm in Tampa. Like our system of justice, our commercial regulations will be guided, enforced, and rewarded by our peers.

It is changing the way we sell.

As we enter the future, financial leverage will not have the same power as a tool for growth and creating value. Instead, value will be found in relationships that are reinforced by feedback. Companies that respond quickly and sincerely to problems raised by customers will thrive, such as GetSatisfaction's response time to the challenge from 37 Signals. Or Kim Pham in Tampa, who pointed out her energy inefficiencies to customers in her shop, the Kaleisia Tea Lounge. She "saved face" by practicing radical self-effacement. In a modern company, you must shed light on every nook and corner and never fear discovering a problem. After all, every mistake is an opportunity for a correction.

And it will change the way we live.

We saw in Las Vegas how big banks had broken the social contract between customer and financer, and yet eight out of ten people chose to honor the terms of their mortgage. Even under great strain and hardship, people follow their moral code. However, they also want others to show the same commitment. In light of the predatory lending practices, which in part fueled the Great Recession, customers are looking for a new social contract with lenders. Under the new terms, businesses now carry a larger moral burden. If they do not operate with a sense of fairness and in service to their communities, customers will abandon them.

Nevada Federal Credit Union offers a perfect example of how
fairness makes for good business.

Generosity

Generosity is now a business model. Twentieth-century companies
were in the information arbitrage business. They knew more about
their product than customers did, and they used that information
advantage to create profits. Today customers have equal (and
sometimes superior) access to data. The solution for modern companies lies in joining the customers, learning as much about them
as possible, and then acting generously.

Generosity as a business model is *giving to get.* Our data suggests
that kindness and empathy are now dominant discriminators in
commerce and highly prized attributes of the best companies. The
ability of a company to identify with its customers is now a pre-
requisite for any transaction in the post-crisis age. Today, openness, humility, and understanding are critical. And generosity
bonds a company to its community and its stakeholders. Generosity
moves an organization to a greater calling than commerce.

It is changing the way we buy.

As customers, we will all be looking for signs that companies
care about their impact on communities and invest in making
things better. For example, Meetup's creators realized they had to
help develop leaders, or groups would fizzle. With this support
Brianne Swezey bought into the Meetup model and built a six-
hundred-person group in Tampa.

Patagonia reveals its commitments through Footprint
Chronicles, which explain how the manufacturing and delivery of
its products affect the environment. The company is open—
generous with the facts—about the good and the bad, and this
openness invites trust. As Tony Haile from Betaworks told us,
"People want to see your struggles." The key here is to find the
narrative in your enterprise. Today's stakeholders can see through

a glossy cover-up. They crave a true, authentic story. They will be interested in how a company thinks and how it arrives at making decisions.

It is changing the way we sell.

More commerce will be conducted on the basis of a pay-it-forward model, where a sale will no longer be instant—or linear. Selling to your customers will require investing in your customers. One good example is Microsoft's "Elevate America" program, retraining two million people with IT skills. Another good example is Windsong Charters in Tampa, which operates with the Henry Ford–style mantra that everyone should be able to afford a day on the water. Even collaborative competition such as restaurant owners in Detroit helping new start-ups signals a shift in how we define our compensation. As they always have, favors create equity.

Generosity opens up networks, provides access to talent pools, and creates future customers. Ford's Scott Monty posts virtually all of this business thinking on SlideShare. He understands that friends and allies are also future car buyers. In this business model we see that you can no longer manage defensively. In a changing world you have to make decisions that open your business up to the marketplace, rather than thinking about minimizing risks in dealing with the public. The vanguard companies understand that to show your kindness and humanity is now a competitive advantage.

And it will change the way we live.

The rising importance of generosity reflects the fact that the post-crisis era will be defined by inclusion rather than exclusion. Thinking right or left is wrong. Power will come to those who aim to selflessly provide the greatest good for the most people. While much of politics, business, and capitalism itself has missed this point over the past several years, zero-sum wins are nonetheless zero. Leaders have the quality of hearing the masses first. Leaders can feel a movement before others and have the courage to act on it. (Think Ronald Reagan, Barack Obama, Tony Hsieh, and Alan

Mulally.) In a world of shareholders and quarterly profit reporting, generosity as a business model is a counterintuitive concept—but one that resonates with how people feel today.

Consumption to Production

Society is shifting from consumption to production. In the postrecession economy, resourcefulness and self-sufficiency are virtues and excessive consumption is a sign of weakness. Status is no longer determined by what you have but by what you know and what you create.

This cultural shift from *take* to *make* is fueled by the rise in retooling and continuous education. And it is amplified by new technology, which now lowers the barriers to learning and acquiring new skills. As a result, continuous self-improvement is the mantra, and people are geared to learning and wanting encouragement. And in a world with less, surprisingly they're stronger and more capable than they thought.

It is changing the way we buy.

Households will shift between "paid for," "earned," and "free" consumption. "Paid for" consumption follows the traditional cash-for-goods-and-services model. "Earned consumption" includes bartering without money with the help of online services such as Craigslist and rewards for doing the right thing, such as recycling through RecycleBank for discounts. "Free consumption" involves finding value in repairing and restoring what you have and taking advantage of resources like friends, family, neighbors, and even the public library, which are available outside the commercial realm. Moving forward, a greater percentage of our spending will be earned or free, lessening our dependence on creditors and restoring our esteem, pride, and self-confidence.

It is changing the way we sell.

More cooperative models are emerging, like Earthworks and American City Farms in Detroit. Businesses will be built on the encouragement of sustainable customer involvement such as the Kaleisia Tea House in Tampa or CrisisCommons in Brooklyn.

Products will last longer. And since fewer purchases will be new, customer service will be more important. As the customer interest shifts from consumption to creation, more customer inter-action will take the form of teaching, coaching, and inspiring, where often there is not an immediate purchase happening. Teaching and training will need to be amortized as a cost of future sales.

And it will change the way we live.

This is an era of *hyphenated living*. Like the actor-writer-director-producer in Hollywood, we all need a number of talents, skills, and interests so we can respond to opportunity both at work and at home. At work we'll be able to seize opportunities. At home we'll shift from mass consumption of disposable products to the careful selection of quality products and lots of doing it ourselves. As we rediscover the virtues of mending and fixing, our demand for new goods will lessen, creating less waste and more sustainability.

In the post-crisis age, convictions are more important than currency. Our consumption will be attuned to things that we can clearly understand—things whose value we can appreciate. In a world of speculation and bubbles, today it's about real value, like the artists living in $100 houses in Detroit. When you see an asset's true value, you build from there. This is the era of real value creation—of making things, rather than moving paper around.

Think Small

We must think small to solve big. "Never doubt that a small group of thoughtful committed people can change the world; indeed, it is the only thing that ever has."

Margaret Mead's famous phrase has become a maxim for well-meaning citizens bent on creating solutions to the problems of their world. However, in the Industrial Age these agents of change were constrained in their ability to gain rapid distribution of their solutions, so real change took years or even generations.

Industrial logic suggests that trillion-dollar problems must have trillion-dollar solutions, which can only come from big investments in big ideas. But many of the big problems—Detroit's decline, the financial crisis, and loss of trust—can be addressed when we begin to see them as agglomerations of little problems. Individuals and small entrepreneurial companies are innovating to solve problems. Managers at successful companies will find ways to foster similar small-scale risk taking.

It is changing the way we buy.

Americans love the underdog. As people begin to value their consumption more mindfully, the smaller players in any market have a real opportunity to build a congregation, a movement in their favor that cannot be defended by a large-scale competitor. We're buying artisanal food in Brooklyn because we trust the people who are showing how it is produced and handled. We patronize cooperative small businesses like Citybird in Detroit because they use their profits to build up the Midwest region.

Passionate customer groups will also band together to fund the niche offerings that speak directly to their passion points. Think Groupon in reverse. By uniting a pool of demand, customers can fund the existence of a business that they want to patronize. Call it "custopreneur-ism." It's not about a business targeting demand, it's about customers targeting supply. A group of hot-rod enthusiasts fund the creation of a co-op machine shop, or a group of home-schoolers fund a new school.

It is changing the way we sell.

The big leap organizations must make is to simplify and defeat complexity. Daytum takes all your data and organizes it in a way that makes your life understandable to you and to the world. Alice gives you deals for products if you give up information on your shopping habits. Kickstarter has demystified the venture capital process by creating a platform exchange that connects entrepreneurs and investors and ideas with capital in a very open and transparent way. Thinking small also allows for companies to focus on tangible social and economic progress, such as Legacy Books in Dallas, which reminds its customers that its profits flow back into the community.

As more businesses learn to be part of a networked economy and use network logic to understand that a big problem is simply an interconnected series of small problems with solutions that also interconnect, they will uncover solutions to large problems. While there is no doubt that big business is facing challenges to simplify, it is by no means impossible—just look at Walmart, Ford, and Microsoft, who are thriving in the networked economy by adapting their operating, forecasting, and communications units to allow for micro-innovation within their organizations. And trusted aggregators of communities such as Huffington Post, MeetUp, and American City Farms in Detroit are selling individuals as much as their institution.

And it will change the way we live.

This transition in thinking from leverage to community is a by-product of the spend shift, which reveals that scale is no longer a competitive advantage. The economies and efficiencies to keep costs down, along with distribution reach to keep consumption levels up, are less effective today. Large-scale value chains require large customer segments, forcing lowest-common-denominator thinking of "broadly acceptable" rather than "individually inspiring" goods and services. Large-scale businesses are also addicted to their current revenue volumes, creating more incentive to defend a shrinking stream of revenue and less incentive to add meaning and values to their proposition.

Instead of living, working, and thinking big, we'll focus on what UCCA Director of Detroit Sue Mosey calls "really small, credible efforts" that combine imagination and energy to fill a particular need in the community. And as with the army of Davids in Tampa, this is now a network economy that encourages experimentation, accepts failure, and connects the solutions that allow us to think small to solve big.

Values-Led Innovation

America is an emerging market for values-led innovation. As demand falls domestically, America must shift from consumer of quantity to producer of quality. It is on this basis that values-led innovation can reconfigure American business by helping it serve a market that only a few see and really understand. With more than half the U.S. population now aligning their spending with their values, modern businesses that practice in a new way will find an entirely new and vibrant marketplace. By connecting through values, a company can become a category of one. Instead of selling shoes, such businesses are selling empathy and respect. Instead of serving food, they are creating communities of hope. Instead of making cars, they are promising fairness, openness, and shared discourse.

It is changing the way we buy.

Spend shifters will restrict their demand to quality over quantity, forcing business to be about better, instead of more. We will require that companies continuously innovate and make their offerings more relevant to our lives. We will expect more responsive customer service and customized goods. We will reward businesses that are true, accountable, and sustainable, whether it's Etsy who has returned us to the art of craft and community, or Freshjive, a logo-less company that is nonetheless making a brand statement. We won't buy products—we'll buy meaning.

It is changing the way we sell.

Successful companies will have hat-trick business models, where all three parties—the business, the customer, and the environment—win in every transaction. Nexttek, SunRun, and RecycleBank each demonstrate the power of this approach. Instead of creating vicious cycles, where businesses operate apart from sustaining their customers and community, businesses will become central to "virtuous circles." They will thrive because their constituents also thrive.

And it will change the way we live.

The market for values will expand, and it will remake capitalism in the process. We cannot overstate the intensity of the competition required to really succeed in the sobered market on terms that are now clearer—value, quality, clarity, and honesty. Since everything is transparent, what were once initiatives (that is, appendages) such as corporate social responsibility and green programs must now be integral parts of a company's structure. This will lead to relentless improvements in efficiency, culture, and innovation that will propel advances in product quality and improved customer service and relationships with stakeholders.

The mindless consumers who led America into the recession are now emerging as mindful customers. Values are colliding with consumption, making America an emerging market of opportunity for the company that acts with dignity, empathy, and respect. It can become the first major world power to make the transition from Industrial to Industrious, exporting twenty-first-century ideas for global good and for its own prosperity. Given the growing middle classes in Brazil, China, Russia, and India, America can find vital export markets for high-value, high-values American goods, important as emblems of American culture that are more substantial than say, *Baywatch*. The future face of capitalism will be defined by delivering value *and* values.

Everything Will Be All Right

Everything will be all right. The encouraging posters we saw in Detroit that declared "Everything Will Be All Right" reverberated in our minds as we traveled the country, and the message rang true everywhere we went. While pundits and commentators wonder whether the recession will change America, we have breaking news: it's already happening. A gradual yet distinct change is under way. It is not yet visible in Washington, D.C., or on Wall Street. However, it is plain to see in leafy subdivisions in Dallas, on cobblestone streets in Brooklyn, and in the gritty yet hopeful warrens in downtown Detroit.

Just as in previous crisis periods of American history, we are relying on our values to navigate ourselves out of crisis. In sacrificing, reimagining ourselves, and working harder, we have discovered we are stronger and more capable than we thought. The necessity of the recession is becoming the mother of our reinvention—it has rearranged our priorities, awakened our creativity, and reconnected us to the people and things that really matter. The Great Recession has given us an unexpected gift, a renewed source of energy and determination to move forward.

As the era of excess passes, we find in its wake thousands of small, entrepreneurial companies and many big reimagined businesses that are working together with their customers and communities to innovate responsibly. The tools of technology help make this change possible by reducing competitive barriers and creating little difference between professionals and amateurs. This "Pro-Am revolution" is reconfiguring journalism, the arts, and now business. Amateurs bring fresh energy, perspective, and healthy naïveté. With their contributions, the result is a transition from an *industrial* to an *industrious* economy.

We are at an important crossroads in American economic history. For most of us, the worst financial calamity in our lifetime has occurred. People are emerging from this recession forever changed. In every period of adversity, leadership emerges, ingenuity is applied, and prosperity again flourishes. This new era only portends austerity to those who fail to see its opportunities. Those with the right vision will look back at the Great Recession as one of the best things that happened to America.

Suggested Reading

Those interested in reading more about certain aspects of the economy, and the spend shift values, might want to consult sources listed here.

On the Recent Economic Crisis

Michael Lewis, *The Big Short* (New York: Norton, 2010).
Roger Lowenstein, *The End of Wall Street* (New York: Penguin, 2010).
Andrew Ross Sorkin, *Too Big to Fail* (New York: Penguin Viking, 2009).

On Historical Social Values

Robert N. Bellah and others, *Habits of the Heart* (Berkeley: University of California Press, 1985).
Robert D. Putnam, *Bowling Alone* (New York: Simon & Schuster, 2000).
James Reichley, *Religion in American Public Life* (Washington, D.C.: Brookings Institution, 1985).

On Generational Values

Eric Greenberg and Karl Weber, *Generation We* (Emeryville, Calif.: Pachatusan Press, 2008).
Neil Howe and William Straus, *Millennials Rising* (New York: Vintage Books, 2000).

On Human Nature

Richard Florida, *The Great Reset: How New Ways of Living Drive Post-Crash Prosperity* (New York: HarperCollins, 2010).

Dacher Keltner and others, *The Compassionate Instinct* (New York: Norton, 2010).

Alfie Kohn, *The Brighter Side of Human Nature* (New York: Basic Books, 1992).

Frans de Waal, *The Age of Empathy* (New York: Harmony Books, 2009).

On Marketing and Business

Chris Brogan and Julien Smith, *Trust Agents: Using the Web to Build Influence, Improve Reputation and Earn Trust* (Hoboken, N.J.: Wiley, 2009).

Tony Hsieh, *Delivering Happiness* (New York: Hyperion, 2010).

Guy Kawasaki, *Reality Check: The Irreverent Guide to Outsmarting, Outmanaging, and Outmarketing Your Competition* (New York: Portfolio, 2008).

Kevin Keller, *Best Practice Cases in Branding* (Upper Saddle River, N.J.: Prentice Hall, 2007).

Philip Kotler, *Marketing 3.0: From Products to Customers to the Human Spirit* (Hoboken, N.J.: Wiley, 2010).

Charlene Li, *Open Leadership* (San Francisco: Jossey-Bass, 2010).

John A. Quelch and Katherine E. Jocz, *Greater Good: How Good Marketing Makes for Better Democracy* (Boston: Harvard Business Press, 2008).

Acknowledgments

T he authors are in enormous debt to many people who helped make *Spend Shift* possible.

Will Johnson, our business partner and adviser, served as all-around field general, making sure we got the facts we needed and made the connections that brought the *Spend Shift* stories to life. Wise, cheerful, and thoughtful, his voice can be heard throughout this text.

Tyler Fonda is one of the smartest new thinkers in technology and media that we've come across. We have Tyler to thank for our black belt in digital immersion and for uncovering interesting companies for us to pursue.

Kellogg School of Business professor Philip Kotler is the "god-father of marketing," and we were honored with his time and his foreword for our book. Harvard's John Quelch brought us valuable insights and advice into how the consumer is changing. BrandAsset Consulting CEO Ed Lebar—John's coauthor of *The Brand Bubble*—was a generous source of insights. We were also blessed with the guidance of professor Kevin Keller at the Tuck School of Business at Dartmouth, who is a highly respected adviser to companies throughout the world. Columbia Business School professor Natalie Mizik, one the sharpest minds around, shared her expertise in marketing and statistics. We thank them all.

When we needed some expert help in the field, we got assistance from two journalism pros, Amy Choi and Greg Lindsay. We also got guidance and sound observations from two great business writers, Ross Tucker and Ryan Chittum.

At Young & Rubicam we received great support from Peter Stringham and Hamish McLennan, who are champions of the firm's role as a thought leader. Lee Aldridge gave us constant encouragement and backup when we needed it. Christy Liu, Emma Hrustic, and Charlotte Mordin are analytics experts you want in your corner. They helped guide the recession survey work and much of the data presented in this book. Peter-Law Gisiko, Mark Russell, Jason Gaikowski, Mark Rukman, Ashima Dayal, Sean King, Stephen Flemming, Trent Rohner, Michael Sussman, Anuja Palkar, Jackie Leardi, and Jessica Brown were all valuable contributors. Thanks, guys, for your support.

We greatly appreciate the support and patience of Genoveva Llosa, Erin Moy, and Gayle Mak at Jossey-Bass. We thank Hilary Powers for a wonderful edit. We want to thank James Levine from Levine/Greenberg for his constant counsel and Chip Kidd for a fabulous book cover design. And we never go out into the marketplace without Mark Fortier by our side. Thanks to all these amazing professionals.

And most important, we'd like to thank our families, who accepted our periodic inattention to their needs. John's wife, Mary, and their own little "spend shift," Nina (age seven), generously accepted and encouraged this project despite the sacrifices it required of them. Michael's wife, Toni, and his daughters, Amy and Elizabeth, deserve the same appreciation for the same gifts of patience and support. And finally, thanks and love to John's mom, Jan, the retired Indiana University English professor, who is still a pro at editing.

John Gerzema and Michael D'Antonio
New York City
October 2010

Notes

Introduction: Numbers and Their Meaning: Kansas City, Missouri

1. For U.S. GDP, see *World Bank, World Development Indicators*, Washington, D.C.: World Bank, Mar. 1, 2010.

2. There are multiple sources for these observations, but for layoffs see Jeannine Aversa, "Job-Killing Recession Racks Up More Layoff Victims," Associated Press, Jan. 26, 2009; available online: www.huffingtonpost.com/2009/01/26/job-killing-recession-rac_n_161040.html; access date: May 2, 2010. For declining home values see Chris Kissell, "Home Prices Fall in 134 of 152 Metro Areas," Bankrate.com, May 12, 2009; available online: www.bankrate.com/brm/news/mortgages/home-values1.asp; access date: May 2, 2010.

3. Ruth Simon and James R. Hagerty, "One in Four Borrowers Is Underwater," *Wall Street Journal*, Nov. 24, 2009; available online: http://online.wsj.com/article/SB125903489722661849.html; access date: May 2, 2010.

4. See "A Sampled History of Crude Oil Prices at the New York Mercantile Exchange from 2006 to the Present, Including the Most Recent, Week-Ending Close Value," FedPrimeRate.com, n.d.; available online: www.nyse.tv/crude-oil-price-history.htm; access date: May 2, 2010.

5. Louis Uchitelle, "Steep Slide in Economy as Unsold Goods Pile Up," *New York Times*, Jan. 30, 2009; available online: www.nytimes

.com/2009/01/31/business/economy/31econ.html; access date: May 2, 2010.

6. David Brooks, "The Great Unwinding," *New York Times*, June 11, 2009; available online: www.nytimes.com/2009/06/12/opinion/12brooks.html; access date: May 2, 2010.

7. Camille Sweeney, "When Stress Takes a Toll on Your Teeth," *New York Times*, Oct. 7, 2009; available online: www.nytimes.com/2009/10/08/fashion/08SKIN.html; access date: May 2, 2010.

8. Amanda Gardner, "With the Economy Down, Vasectomy Rates Are Up," *U.S. News & World Report*, Mar. 20, 2009; available online: http://health.usnews.com/health-news/family-health/womens-health/articles/2009/03/20/with-the-economy-down-vasectomy-rates-are-up.html; access date: May 2, 2010.

9. "Shark Attacks Decline Worldwide in Midst of Economic Recession," *University of Florida News*, Feb. 19, 2009; available online: http://news.ufl.edu/2009/02/19/shark-attacks/; access date: May 2, 2010.

10. Bill Gross, "Midnight Candles," PIMCO Investment Outlook, Nov. 2009; available online: www.pimco.com/LeftNav/Featured+Market+Commentary/IO/2009/Midnight+Candles+Gross+November.htm; access date: May 2, 2010.

11. "Self Storage: Analyzing the Competitive Landscape—A Market Inventory Study," Self Storage Association, 2006; available online: www.thefreelibrary.com/Two Billion Square Feet of Self Storage Space in U.S.; Self Storage ...-a0142724339; access date: June 7, 2010.

12. Kevin Buchanan, "Square Feet per Person," FortWorthology, Oct. 20, 2008; available online: http://fortworthology.com/2008/10/20/square-feet-per-person/; access date: May 2, 2010.

13. Franciose O'Neill, "Closets Ultimate: Makeovers Set Trend Across North America," Professional Door Dealer, Aug. 29, 2006; available online: www.professionaldoordealer.com/articles/management/68h2914393139324.html; access date June 2, 2010.

14. Martin Crutsinger, "Personal Savings Drops to 73-Year Low," *Washington Post*, Feb. 1, 2007; available online: http://www.washingtonpost.com/wp-dyn/content/article/2007/02/01/AR2007

020100471.html; access date: May 2, 2010. For trending of data back to 1929, see "In Tough Times, Savings Rate on the Rise," National Public Radio, n.d.; available online: www.npr.org/news/graphics/2009/mar/saving-rate/index.html; access date: May 2, 2010.

15. Kevin B. Moore and Michael G. Palumbo, "The Finances of American Households in the Past Three Recessions: Evidence from the Survey of Consumer Finances," Federal Reserve Board, Feb. 2, 2010; available online: www.federalreserve.gov/Pubs/feds/2010/201006/; access date: May 2, 2010.

16. "Q4 Mortgage Equity Extraction Strongly Negative," Calculated Risk Finance and Economics, Mar. 24, 2009; available online: www .calculatedriskblog.com/2009/03/q4-mortgage-equity-extraction-strongly.html; access date: May 2, 2010.

17. Planet Money, "Household Debt vs. GDP," National Public Radio, Feb. 27, 2009; available online: www.npr.org/blogs/money/2009/02/household_debt_vs_gdp.html; access date: May 2, 2010.

18. Carter Dougherty, "Consumer Spending Declines: A Historical Oddity," New York Times, Apr. 14, 2009; available online: http://economix.blogs.nytimes.com/2009/04/14/consumer-spending-declines-a-historical-oddity/; access date: May 2, 2010.

19. Rich Morin and Paul Taylor, "Luxury or Necessity? The Public Makes a U-Turn," Pew Research Center, Apr. 23, 2009; available online: http://pewsocialtrends.org/pubs/733/luxury-necessity-recession-era-reevaluations; access date: May 2, 2010.

20. "New National Poll Shows Library Card Registration Reaches Record High," American Library Association press release, Sept. 23, 2008; available online: www.ala.org/ala/newspresscenter/news/pressreleases2008/September2008/ORSharris.cfm; access date: May 2, 2010. See also Kelley Holland, "Can Volunteers Be a Lifeline for Nonprofit Groups?" New York Times, Jan. 24, 2009; available online: www.nytimes.com/2009/01/25/jobs/25mgmt.html; access date: May 2, 2010.

21. Michael Gerson, "Recession's Hidden Virtues," Washington Post, Feb. 20, 2009; available online: www.washingtonpost.com/wp-dyn/content/article/2009/02/19/AR2009021902577.html; access date: May 2, 2010.

Chapter One. The New American Frontier: Detroit, Michigan

1. Steven Gray, "Luring Buyers on Detroit's 'Lonely Homes' Tour," *Time*, Oct. 13, 2009; available online: www.time.com/time/nation/article/0,8599,1930006,00.html#ixzz017midygn; access date: May 2, 2010.

2. Vince Veneziani, "Detroit's Famous Pontiac Silverdome Sells for Just $583,000," Business Insider, Nov. 17, 2009; available online: www.businessinsider.com/pontiac-silverdome-sells-for-a-paltry-583000-2009-11; access date: May 2, 2010.

3. For Detroit unemployment, see Daniel Okrent, "The Death—and Possible Life—of a Great City," *Time*, Sept. 24, 2009; available online: www.time.com/time/nation/article/0,8599,1925796,00.html #ixzz017nmMjXf; access date: May 2, 2010. For U.S. unemployment see Peter S. Goodman, "U.S. Unemployment Rate Hits 10.2%, Highest in 26 Years," *New York Times*, Nov. 6, 2009.

4. "Detroit: Now a Ghost Town," Time.com, n.d.; available online: www.time.com/time/interactive/0,31813,1925735,00.html; access date: May 2, 2010. The charts of population decline and vacancy rates provide a vivid view of the city's history.

5. Daniel Gross, "Deglobalization: The Surprisingly Steep Decline in World Trade," Slate.com, Dec. 11, 2009; available online: www.slate.com/id/2238188/; access date: May 2, 2010.

6. American Institute of Architects, "A Leaner, Greener Detroit," Oct. 30–Nov. 1, 2008; available online: www.aia.org/aiaucmp/groups/aia/documents/pdf/aiab080216.pdf; access date: May 2, 2010.

7. Brett W. Pelham, "Business Owners Richer in Wellbeing Than Other Job Types," Gallup, Sept. 16, 2009; available online: www.gallup.com/poll/122960/Business-Owners-Richer-Job-Types.aspx; access date: May 2, 2010.

Chapter Two. Don't Fence Me In: Dallas, Texas

1. "New National Poll Shows Library Card Registration Reaches Record High," American Library Association press release, Sept.

23, 2008; available online: www.ala.org/ala/newspresscenter/news/ pressreleases2008/September2008/ORSharris.cfm; access date: May 2, 2010.

2. Julie Bosman, "From Ranks of Jobless, a Flood of Volunteers," *New York Times*, Mar. 15, 2009; available online: www.nytimes .com/2009/03/16/nyregion/16volunteers.htm; access date: May 2, 2010.

3. The NPD Group, Inc., http://www.npd.com/press/releases/ press_091117.html; and Gary Hoffman, "Is 200,000 the New 100,000?" available online: http://autos.aol.com/article/high-mileage-driving/; and http://www.automd.com/About-AutoMD/Press/2-10-2010/; access date: June 15, 2010.

4. Valerie Strauss, "Community Colleges Get Student Influx in Bad Times," *Washington Post*, May 31, 2009; available online: www .washingtonpost.com/wp-dyn/content/article/2009/05/30/ AR2009053001762.html; access date: May 2, 2010.

5. Andrew Goldstein, "Museum Attendance Rises as the Economy Tumbles," Art Newspaper, Dec. 9, 2009; available online: www .theartnewspaper.com/articles/Museum-attendance-rises-as-the-economy-tumbles/19840; access date: May 2, 2010.

6. Mariana Green, "City to North Haven Gardens: No Chicks," *Dallas Morning News*, June 24, 2009; available online: http://eastdallasblog .dallasnews.com/archives/2009/06/city-chickens-flap.html; access date: May 2, 2010.

7. "The Impact of Gardening in America," National Gardening Association, 2009; available online: www.scribd.com/doc/14331718/ 2009-Impact-of-Gardening-in-America; access date: June 7, 2010.

8. For a complete history of the awakenings, see Marshall William Fishwick, *Great Awakenings: Popular Religion and Popular Culture* (New York: Routledge, 1994).

9. For Texas business climate, see Milken Institute Web site, www .milkeninstitute.org/publications/publications.taf?function=detail&I D=38801218&cat=resrep; access date: June 7, 2010.

Chapter Three. The Badge of Awesomeness: Boston, Massachusetts

1. According to creditcards.com, debt peaked at $975 billion in September 2008 and fell to $772 billion at the end of 2009.

2. Robin Sidel, "Debit-Card Use Overtakes Credit," *Wall Street Journal*, May 1, 2009; available online: http://online.wsj.com/article/ SB124104752340070801.html; access date: May 2, 2010.

3. "Quarterly Banking Profile Third Quarter 2009," Federal Deposit Insurance Corporation, *FDIC Quarterly 3*, no. 4 (2009); available online: www2.fdic.gov/qbp/2009sep/qbp.pdf; access date: June 7, 2010.

4. Brigid Schulte, "So Long, Snail Shells," *Washington Post*, July 25, 2009; available online: www.washingtonpost.com/wp-dyn/content/ article/2009/07/24/AR2009072403857.html; access date: May 2, 2010.

5. "The Decline of the Landline," *Economist*, Aug. 13, 2009; available online by subscription: www.economist.com/opinion/displayStory .cfm?story_id=14213965&source=hptextfeature; access date: June 7, 2010.

6. Haya El Nasser, "Housing Bust Halts Growing Suburbs," *USA Today*, Nov. 20, 2009; available online: www.usatoday.com/news/ nation/2009-11-19-suburbs_N.htm; access date: May 2, 2010.

7. Wendy Koch, "Americans Are Moving On Up to Smaller, Smarter Houses," *USA Today*, Mar. 16, 2009; available online: www .usatoday.com/money/economy/housing/2009-03-16-small-homes_N .htm; access date: May 2, 2010.

8. Heather Boerner, "Going Small: Home Downsizing," Good Reading, May 19, 2009; available online: www.cyberhomes.com/content/ news/09-05-19/home-downsizing.aspx; access date: May 2, 2010.

9. "Consumer 'New Frugality' May Be an Enduring Feature of Post-Recession Economy, Finds Booz & Company Survey," Booz & Co. press release, Feb. 24, 2010; available online: www.booz.com/global/ home/press/article/47685488?tid=39964387&pg=all; access date: May 2, 2010.

10. Rich Morin and Paul Taylor, "Luxury or Necessity? The Public Makes a U-Turn," Pew Research Center, Apr. 23, 2009; available online:http://pewsocialtrends.org/pubs/733/luxury-necessity-recession-era-reevaluations; access date: May 2, 2010.

11. Wendy Koch, "Americans Are Moving On Up to Smaller, Smarter Homes," USA Today, Mar. 16, 2009; available online: www.usatoday.com/life/lifestyle/home/2009-03-16-small-homes_N.htm; access date: June 8, 2010.

Chapter Four. An Army of Davids: Tampa, Florida

1. Dana Goldstein, "The New Idealist Social Network," Daily Beast, Mar. 18, 2010; available online: www.thedailybeast.com/blogs-and-stories/2010-03-18/the-new-idealist-social-network/?cid=csi:topnav:givingb; access date: May 2, 2010.

2. Nick Saint, "Groupon and Its Zillions of Imitators Are Trying to Cash in on a New Group Buying Craze," Business Insider, Feb. 23, 2010; available online: www.businessinsider.com/group-coupons-2010-2; access date: May 2, 2010. See also Michael Arrington, "It's Official: Groupon Announces That $1.35 Billion Valuation Round," TechCrunch, Apr. 18, 2010.

Chapter Five. Block Party Capitalism: Brooklyn, New York

1. "Greenberg Millennial Survey: How 'Generation WE' Are Taking Over America and Changing the World," News Blaze, Aug. 25, 2008; available online: http://newsblaze.com/story/2008082505031900025.pnw/topstory.html; access date: May 2, 2010.

2. Mimi Hall and John Fritze, "Health Care: Five Faces of the Uninsured," USA Today, Sept. 22, 2009; available online: www.usatoday.com/money/industries/health/2009-09-22-faces-uninsured_N.htm; access date: May 2, 2010.

3. For one in four trace ancestry to Brooklyn, see Ed Brodow, "Negotiation Boot Camp: How to Resolve Conflict, Satisfy Customers, and Make Better Deals," eNotAlone, 2006; available online: www.enotalone.com/article/20756.html; access date: June 7, 2010.

Chapter Six. The Quality of the Lion: Las Vegas, Nevada

1. Frans de Waal, a biologist affiliated with Emory University, has written quite persuasively about animal cooperation for more than twenty years. See in particular, *The Age of Empathy: Nature's Lessons for a Kinder Society* (New York: Random House, 2009).

2. Michael Maoz, "Trust in Institutions Is Dead," blog post, Jan. 11, 2010; available online: http://blogs.gartner.com/michael_maoz/?s=%22Trust+in+Institutions+is+Dead%22; access date: May 2, 2010.

3. For a graph of Las Vegas housing values, see http://mysite.verizon.net/vzeqrguz/housingbubble/las_vegas.html; access date: May 2, 2010. For lowest price, see Buck Wargo, "New-Home Prices Drop as Number of Sales Rise," *Las Vegas Sun*, Jan. 1, 2010.

4. See Luigi Guiso, Paola Sapienza, and Luigi Zingales, "Walking Away: Moral, Social, and Financial Factors Influence Mortgage Default Decisions," Kellogg Insight, July 2009; available online: http://insight.kellogg.northwestern.edu/index.php/Kellogg/article/walking_away; access date: May 2, 2010.

5. Alison Smale, "Leaders in Davos Admit Drop in Trust," *New York Times*, Jan. 31, 2010; available online: dealbook.blogs.nytimes.com/.../leaders-in-davos-admit-drop-in-trust/; access date: June 8, 2010.

Chapter Seven. The Citizen Corporation: Dearborn, Michigan

1. For reliability figures on Ford cars, see John Neff, "Ford Makes Biggest Gains in *Consumer Reports* Annual Reliability Report, Japanese Still Lead," Autoblog, Oct. 27, 2009; available online: www.autoblog.com/2009/10/27/ford-makes-biggest-gains-in-consumer-reports-annual-relia/; access date: June 7, 2010.

2. "The Millennials: Confident. Connected. Open to Change," Pew Research Center, Feb. 24, 2010; available online: http://pewresearch.org/pubs/1501/%20millennials-new-survey-generational-personality-upbeat-open-new-ideas-technology-bound; access date: May 2, 2010.

3. Stefania Pomponi Butler, "How the Women of Ford, an Assembly Plant, and a Guy Named Larry Changed my Life," City Mama (blog post), Aug. 14, 2009; available online: http://citymama.typepad.com/citymama/2009/08/a-month-ago-bad-kitty-and-i-went-on-a-roadtrip-a-roadtrip-that-we-pitched-to-ford-blogher-was-not-affiliated-in-any-way.html; access date: May 2, 2010.

4. Proprietary data from "The Shift Report," ci, n.d.; available online: http://ci-shift.com/; access date: May 2, 2010. Kiersten De West, founder of CI-Shift.com, prepared this data for us.

Chapter Eight. Innovation Nation: San Francisco, California

1. For Hulu's page views, see Barb Dybwad, "Hulu Set to Pass 1 Billion Streams Per Month, Mashable," Dec. 31, 2009; available online: mashable.com/2009/12/31/hulu-1-billion; access date: June 7, 2010.

2. Michael Learmonth, "Hulu Now No. 2 Online-Video Site, Behind YouTube: Adding Facebook, MySpace Social-Networking Tools," Advertising Age, Mar. 12, 2009.

About the Authors

John Gerzema, chief insights officer of Young & Rubicam, is an internationally known social theorist on consumerism and its impact on business, innovation, and strategy. As a consultant to corporate leaders in many of the world's best-known companies, Gerzema is a pioneer in the use of data to identify social change and to help companies both anticipate and adapt to new consumer interests and demands. In his first best-selling book, *The Brand Bubble*, he presciently identified the beginning of changes in consumer attitudes that preceded the financial crisis and also began the spend shift revolution. It was voted #3 in Amazon's best business books of 2008 and in the best marketing books by *Strategy & Business* for 2009. Gerzema is a pioneer in the use of data to identify social change and to help companies both anticipate and adapt to new consumer interests and demands. He is a much sought-after source for the business press and in-demand public speaker, and his 2009 Technology, Entertainment and Design (TED) lecture—"The Post Crisis Consumer"—has been viewed by tens of thousands of people.

Michael D'Antonio is the author of more than a dozen books on topics ranging from business to science and sports. *Hershey*, his biography of the chocolate king, was named one of *BusinessWeek's*

241

best books of the year, and his book *The State Boys Rebellion* received similar honors from both the *Chicago Tribune* and the *Christian Science Monitor*. While at *Newsday*, D'Antonio won the prestigious Alicia Patterson fellowship for journalists and was a member of a team of reporters who won the Pulitzer Prize. His original story for the film *Crown Heights* earned him the 2004 Humanitas Prize. His work has appeared in the *New York Times Magazine*, *Esquire*, *Discover*, the *Los Angeles Times Magazine*, and many other publications. Michael's most recent book, *A Full Cup*, on Sir Thomas Lipton's extraordinary life and his quest for the America's Cup, has been favorably reviewed by the *Wall Street Journal* and NPR.

Index

BrandAsset Valuator: about, x–xi; brands associated with clarity and sincerity, 126; charting consumer behavior trends, 114–116; companies rated socially responsible, 84; companies recognized for values most appreciated, 167; economic data from, xix–xxix; effect of bailout money on brands, 132, 160; evaluating product's goodness, 187–188; influence marketplace decisions via Internet, 84; international trends in spend shifters, xxii–xxiii; Microsoft's scores in, 179; optimism for entrepreneurship, 12; performance of indestructible spirit firms, 25–26; positive values charted by, xviii; reflecting values revolution, xvii; surveying changing levels of trust, 131, 133; trends in liquid living, 59–61, 209; Walmart's ratings for kindness, 178; watching self-reliance trends, 37–39

Brands: abandoning logos, 186–187; Apple vs. Microsoft, 179; associating with authenticity, 126–127; developing devotion to, 83–84; effect of government bailout money on, 132, 160; enhancing social standing with, 115, 116; evaluating eco-friendliness of, 187–188; focusing on customer's needs, 159–160; future changes for, 211–212; preferences for simpler, 59; trends in agility and simplicity for, 61; trust and building of, 151–152; valuing authenticity over, 114

Brixton Pound, 73

Bronfman, Edgar, ix

Brooklyn Brine, 103–105

Brooklyn Flea, 116–117, 118–119

Brooklyn Industries, 119–123, 214

Brooklyn, New York: building community spirit with Brooklyn Flea, 116–119; developing business to speak directly to customers, 121–123; expressing values on Etsy, 123–126; maintaining feeling of, 112–116, 122–123; pickle production in, 103–107; restaurants creating renaissance in, 107–112; revealing foundation truths in, 116

Brownstoner, 117–118

Burt's Bees, 126

Business: adopting indestructible spirit, 25–26; affecting with conscious consuming, xxvi; avoiding corporate greenwashing, 150; basing on sustainability, 104–105; ceding control of social messages, 165–167; championing local, 49–52; changes based on human values, 216–218; community support for start-up, 15–16; competing with well-funded, 186; connected strongly with values, 167; creating in Great Recession, 10–11; customer forgotten in diversification, 158–159; dealing with public criticism, 178–181; demands for value from, xxx–xxxi; Detroit's entrepreneurial spirit in, 9–13; developing culture within, 136–137; encouraging customer feedback process, 170–173; feeling impact of green shoppers, 188; finding start-up, 5; fostering local, 70–72; full product disclosures by, 149–151; generosity as part of, 218–220; giving to employees to run, 91–92; importance of corporate culture, 168–169; innovating ethics and values of, 5, 8; learning to listen to customer, 161; lending funds based on values, 74; local shops supported by Dallas community, 50–52; losing customer's trust, 131–132, 134; marketing goods with storytelling, 124–125; new ethos for CEOs, 135–136, 138; offering discounted